21st Century Disciples
With A 1st Century Faith

Discipling To Empower And Mobilize Christians For Greater Service

Waldo J. Werning

A Resource Book

Fairway Press
Lima, Ohio

FIRST EDITION
Copyright © 1995
Waldo J. Werning

Scripture quotations are taken from *God's Word* and are used by permission. Copyright 1995 by God's Word to the Nations Bible Society. All rights reserved.

———————————

Library of Congress Catalog Card Number: 95-60869

———————————

ISBN 0-7880-0605-3

Dedicated

to the faithful and caring disciples who walk with me on the Resurrection Road to learn, grow and mature in the Christian faith:

RUTH
— my precious spouse of 50 years who helps me on the Way,

SHARON, DAN, CHARLOTTE, JON, JAMES
— my dear children and their families who seek to confess Christ faithfully with me,

MANY COLLEAGUES, CO-WORKERS, LAY FRIENDS
— so numerous that they will be unnamed, who have edified me to enrich my life and work, especially those who invested in this book.

ALL PRAISE TO GOD WHOSE KINDNESS, POWER AND LOVE HAS MADE IT ALL POSSIBLE!

TABLE OF CONTENTS

III. LIVING WITH MY FAMILY AND FELLOW MEN

IV. LIVING WITH MY RESOURCES   211

V. LIVING IN THE BODY OF CHRIST AND IN THE CHURCH   283

A. The Body Of Christ, The Invisible Church   283

Reviewing And Rethinking — Growing To Maturity

The explosiveness of knowledge and technology in current times requires new evaluations and mature application of Christian doctrine and life. Nothing is more pressing in today's world than being established strongly in the Christian faith and growing spiritually mature to strive for good and against evil.

The same problems which confronted Christians in the first Century still face us in the 21st century: deceiving thoughts and beguiling philosophies, competing saviors, confusing additions to the Gospel, small gods of cultural religion, and insecure Christians who dodge the real issues about the Gospel, unsure of the whole counsel of God. Congregations which began as strong Gospel forces often end up as religious institutions with much quibbling and pretense. Often spiritual, moral and intellectual problems have a damaging grip on the fellowship of believers. Paul's response was always the supreme adequacy of the Christ we have. Christ is all we need, for in Him we find the fullness of God, the wealth of our resources and the hope for a better future.

Misunderstandings constantly arise about the nature of Christianity. Is Christianity a creed, a religious system, a set of doctrinal formulations? Or is it a relationship with a Person, Jesus Christ? Is the church more concerned to make better church members or to grow stronger Christians?

What do we Christians hope to become? What level of spiritual maturity will we accept? What is the standard for our Christian life? Unfortunately, Christians have often settled for a belief in a doctrinal system instead of aiming at a growing relationship with Jesus Christ. Too often members are judged by the church or they evaluate themselves on the basis of adhering to church expectations or doctrinal beliefs as a religious routine. They follow a number of steps for gaining church stature rather than knowing God through faith and communicating with Him through prayer.

The primary Biblical considerations for the Christian faith are relationships: between the Creator and the creature, between the Redeemer and the redeemed, between the Holy Spirit and the Spirit-filled believer. It involves the relationship between each of God's children and between the church and the world. Only in God's Word can we find the understanding of how such relationships can work; only in the Christian church will there be any widespread demonstration that such relationships are possible.

These pages are designed to help us grow as Christians, not merely to become better church members who meet all the requirements to achieve good church grades. We will look at historical questions of Scripture, considering the facts of the texts as the truth of God. We will learn of the Word's power as it encounters our human notions and worldly kingdoms, seeing why the Word is applicable and authoritative. Practically, we will see how Scripture benefits everyday life.

Rooting our faith in the comprehensive purpose and plan of God, we will look at the larger battle involving spiritual forces. This will not be a retreat to a narrow, pietistic church huddle, seeing only several issues important enough about which to get excited. Rather, we will look at a vast range of spiritual issues, not just bits and pieces.

There will be a concern about Christ-like love in action, about clustering and fellowship, about supporting people and helping them to carry one another's load and about the church as God's redeemed and "redeeming" people.

We will see that the transformed life does not come by accident or by chance, but by the renewing power of God. To be formed in Christ and to have Christ formed within us are clearly gifts of God's grace. Our studies of God's Word will continually lead us on paths towards wholeness, maturity, and spiritual formation.

We will make an in-depth study of how we change through growth, knowledge, understanding, attitude, behavior, and relationships. Weakness in one of these areas distorts our Christian life and service. By God's grace it is possible to change various dimensions of life to experience dynamic spiritual growth and gain the hope God offers in the Gospel.

The effective Christian and church will send men and women into the marketplace, to the streets and to the prisons, away from the sacred havens. They may risk their health and reputations to go to the outcasts to speak, pray and work with them. It may mean giving up a motor home or a boat in order to achieve more righteous goals. There is the challenge to take the risk of inviting the unwed mother into our home, not knowing whether she will steal our stereo or TV.

The spiritual growth of God's people is something like an escalator or stairs: not everyone is on the same spiritual level. Various Christians are at different steps in their Christian faith and life. This book is for those who are on the upper stairs, seeking greater maturity of faith in Christ.

Focus Of This Study

God's life, given to us in Christ, is what sets us apart from others. The focus of these pages is to support growth in Christlikeness with an emphasis on the process of personality and character transformation.

We will search for a better understanding of the church, what it is and does, how it edifies, its dynamics of communication and fellowship. Our concern is for both individuality and common fellowship with members and interdependence in our congregations and Christians everywhere. The focus will be not only on knowing, but on being and doing, on receiving God's love and sharing it.

Salvation and our life in Christ are not escape from reality. Faith will not eliminate struggle or pain from our lives and will not give immediate relief at all times. There will be aches, disappointments and struggles that come and go. There will be no heaven on earth. Any hope for lasting joy here and now is counterfeit. We can and should enjoy the riches of a vibrant life and of being Christian and taste God's goodness that gives us inexpressible joy, but we cannot demand that our groaning will end on earth.

This book is not about doctrine and spirituality built upon pretense of any kind, but about reality — the reality of the true God and of real earth people. We cannot love God or people truly if we are consumed with finding perfect satisfaction every day. While this Bible study will bring some relief and offer answers to some enigmas, it deals not with ways to change our circumstances or what's outside, but to change the inside — our spiritual center. It deals with transformation of character that gives us enough taste of God here to make us yearn for experiencing fullness with Him hereafter.

We don't have to avoid subjects that review unpleasant memories or touch tender emotions. We don't have to pretend that things are better than they are. We don't have to rearrange minor facets of our lives, but rather make major changes internally and become truly transformed. Biblical faith will help us face reality, including fears, hurts, and weaknesses which present spiritual challenges that sometimes keep us on edge. We will not ignore the hard issues, critical matters of internal character development and what's happening beneath the surface of our lives.

Growth Objectives

Our growth objectives include knowledge, Bible study skills, attitudes and behavior. We do not present a series of simple Sunday School lessons to inspire, but offer challenging Biblical insights to stretch our minds and spirits far beyond ordinary expectations. This will be a spiritual encounter that will confront us with Biblical truths that should cause us to react as the disciples responded to Jesus at one time: "What he says is hard to accept. Who wants to listen to him anymore?" (Jn. 6:60). When Jesus told them about the coming Ascension and other realities, "Jesus' speech made many of his disciples go back to the lives they had led before they followed Jesus" (Jn. 6:66). When Jesus asked His 12 disciples whether they wanted to leave Him, too, Peter answered, "Lord, to what person could we go? Your words give eternal life. Besides, we believe and know that you are the Holy One of God" (Jn. 6:68-69).

Our desire in Bible study should be to have an open mind, to discipline ourselves and shut out all human and earthly distractions. Objectives for growth begin with an attitude to live within God's will and a behavior pattern which avoids conflict with Christian principles.

We will see that it is all right to be happy and to desire good, and it is acceptable to hurt and to cry. This will occur because of a solid faith rooted in Biblical truths and an exciting faith drawn from a rich relationship with Jesus Christ as He invades every part of our lives. We will go beyond a formal orthodoxy to be drawn by the Holy Spirit into a meaningful life of love in Christ. Then we will want to develop passion in a pursuit of God as we recognize subtle sins, break bad habits and then bear good fruit in our lives.

This message offers an entrance into the reality of Truth — Christ and the Scriptures, which reveal Him together with the Father and the Holy Spirit. We pray that you will get to know Him and yourself much, much better. Listen to Him through His Word. Be prepared to grow and mature. Ask God to give you excitement about your future as you take new steps of faith. Pray that He will make you a 21st Century disciple with a 1st Century faith.

Waldo Werning
Fort Wayne, IN

I.

LIVING WITH GOD

We earthbound creatures become so glued to the things of the earth that we sometimes become too restless when we are asked to set aside time to learn about God, meditate on Him and worship Him. We want to get it over with and "get on with the show." We know all that, we may think. Why spend all that time on this "God stuff"? Just tell us what to do, and stop all the talk.

"Then you will know that I am God" (Ps. 46:10). Can you hear God saying, "Shut up, and listen!"? Can you hear Him pleading, "Be quiet, and take time to get to know Me"? "Surrender yourself to the Lord, and wait patiently for him" (Ps. 37:7).

Meditation on God can start with the five action words in Deuteronomy 10:12-13 which tell us what He asks and how to relate to Him (*fear* the Lord, *walk* in all His ways, *love* Him, *serve* the Lord, *obey* His commands): "Israel, what does the Lord your God want you to do? He wants you to fear him, follow all his directions, love him, and worship him, with all your heart and with all your soul. The Lord wants you to obey his commands and laws that I'm giving you today for your own good."

We will know God only as we stop long enough to see and accept His love: "I love you with an everlasting love. So I will continue to show you my kindness" (Jer. 31:3). "Look at it this way: At the right time, while we were still helpless, Christ died for ungodly people" (Rom. 5:8). "He loves us so much that we are actually called God's dear children" (1 Jn. 3:1). As we know and experience this divine love, our worship of God will be meaningful and realistic.

If our mouths are to shout loudly, "Glory belongs to our God and Father forever! Amen" (Phil. 4:20), we must know that God. To know Him requires time with Him in His message to us, the Bible. "Worship and glory belong forever to the eternal king, the immortal, invisible, and only God. Amen" (1 Tim. 1:17). If we

17

are to have awe and respect for this great God and to adore Him alone, it is imperative that we take time to recognize and understand Him. That's what this chapter is all about.

If at any time we get restless and want to hurry on to the "practical" part, we should be still and know that God wants us to take time to know Him better. Take time to understand Him, relate to Him and speak to Him. If we do not truly know Him and His love, we are not prepared to live for Him or with the other creatures which He created. So don't chafe about all this doctrinal business regarding God, because God is not a doctrine, but our loving Father. Time with our Heavenly Father will enrich our lives immensely. If we apply ourselves to this study, we will never be the same.

The entire Bible provides knowledge and is talk about God, telling how we can know Him, what He is like and who He is. God is a living, speaking and loving God, making Himself known to people in various ways through prophets, evangelists and apostles. The Scriptures give us more than knowledge for the mind; they give grace and faith of the heart which results in a living relationship with Him. This is a personal and intimate contact which affects our lives, for God is a personal, loving, eternally existent and all-knowing Being (1 Tim. 1:17) who is completely beyond any earthly or human dimensions.

Knowing God always involves personal trust and confidence. Confessing His truth and having a personal relationship with Him are aspects of this trust. God is not a god among many, nor does He change or develop.

There is a natural knowledge of God (known from nature) that can be gained from God's creation and His providence, as nature reveals His power, majesty and wisdom. But nature does not reveal His love that saves lost sinners and grants them eternal life (Heb. 3:4). We know God from our consciences (Rom. 2:15) and directly from the Bible (2 Tim. 3:15).

The Nature Of God

God has revealed Himself to us as the source, beginning, purpose, sustainer, power, glory, and end of all things.

Being before all things, being independent, God is not contingent on anything. Everything is derived from Him and dependent on Him. He has roots only in Himself, and everything else springs from Him and has roots in Him. He is eternally self-existent by His own power, which is totally foreign to us because we don't exist by our own power, as we are finite (limited and restricted) and mortal. He is self-sustaining, whereas everything else originates from Him and has no life or sustenance apart from Him. He is able to explain all things, while all creatures made by Him are incapable of explaining themselves or fully understanding their total existence. God alone has the power to sustain human beings. Do we accept this human mental limitation as we try to comprehend God and to fathom and discern His ways with people and His creation?

God's supreme and absolute greatness exceeds all limits, which means that He transcends or is beyond every earthly thing. Thus we talk about God's transcendence (uniqueness), which means to rise or go above everything else earthly. Transcendence describes God's relationship to the world, for He is higher and the absolute power over the world. Neither the world nor any creature has power over Him. Transcendence points to the immeasurable, infinite distance that separates Him from every creature.

We can learn much about God by reading a significant sermon given by Paul on Mars Hill at the Areopagus, a lower hill on the west of the Acropolis, which was the citadel in Athens. Here, where the supreme court met and great ideas were discussed by great thinkers, Paul presented the case for Christianity and spoke about the character and attributes of God. His sermon in Acts 17:18-31 introduced the almighty God to the people of Athens and the world.

Paul preached about the personality, the self-existence, omnipotence and unity of God. He told of the reality, efficiency and universality of divine providence. He spoke of the unity and brotherhood of the human race, as well as the dignity and dependence of man. He revealed the graciousness of God's dealings with the human race, telling of the certainty of judgment, the need for repentance, the reality of a future life and the lordship of Jesus Christ.

Telling also about the absurdity of idols and idol worship, Paul corrected the errors of atheism (the belief that there is no God), pantheism (the theory that everything is God), polytheism (the idea that there are or can be many gods), ritualism (trying to honor God by purely external religious performance), fatalism (maintaining that no intelligence or power presides over the universe and all things come to pass either by chance or necessity), materialism (the notion that material is the power and is eternal), optimism (the delusion that this is the best possible world and sin is a temporary mistake), universalism (the tenet that all will be saved), unitarianism (the belief that Christ was merely an ordinary human being), and annihilism (there is nothing after death).

At a place where orators, historians, playwrights, scholars and the wisest men gathered, Paul presented the doctrine of God in a simple and clear way and preached the resurrection of Christ and of the believers. Paul's discourse can help you gain a fuller understanding of God, who He is, what He is like, and why He does what He does. Read that message now from Acts 17:18-31 and expect to grow in your appreciation of the true God, your heavenly Father.

What Is God Like?

We cannot understand God in human images or concepts. We think of His actions, His dealings with people and His intervention in history. We think of God guiding, loving and comforting His people, and we find Him utterly dependable. Yet we must concern ourselves with who He is and what He is like. The Living God is a personal God whose nature is revealed in many ways. He is not far off. He is here. We pray to Him, and He answers. He has a will and makes decisions. All His actions toward us are personal. His grace, love and goodness, as well as His wrath and judgment, are personal qualities expressed in personal actions (Rom. 2:4; 11:22; Titus 3:4).

The Bible does not tell of the being of God apart from His attributes, inasmuch as God is what He reveals Himself to be. The personal attributes of God are that He is holy, surpassing everything else; He is a Spirit; He is everlasting, unchanging, almighty, knows everything, is loving, glorious, sovereign, omnipresent, just and fair, faithful, good, compassionate, and merciful. He is God, and there is no other.

As we think about the character of God, we first acknowledge His holiness, which means that He is perfect and totally divided from us sinful human beings. He is so far above and beyond us that He seems almost totally foreign to us. Only God is holy in Himself (Ps. 77:13; 1 Sam 2:2).

God's holiness (Is. 6:3; Ex. 15:11) is so central to Biblical teaching that it is said of God, "Holy is His name." We pray in the first petition of the Lord's Prayer, "Hallowed be Your name." His name is holy because He is holy. His holy character has much to say about people's relationships, government, finances, romance and athletics — everything with which we are involved — because He is the one that established us in life and in business.

God's holiness separates Him from all that is not God. Holiness denotes God's purity, radiance, absolute moral perfection in every way and His absolute otherness. Holiness means God's absolute perfect nature, that only He can do what He does. His absolute majesty is a show of His holiness. In the New Testament the glory of God is always associated with Christ, either in His birth, activities, transfiguration, death, resurrection, or ascension. God is absolute purity and righteousness — the direct opposite of sin.

God describes His own characteristics: He is a Spirit (Jn. 4:24). He is everlasting (Ps. 90:2), without beginning and without end. He is unchanging (Ps. 102:27). He is almighty (Gen. 17:1; Lk. 1:37) and omnipotent, which embraces the whole spectrum of God's attributes and actions. God has the power to do anything He wills to do. His power embraces His justice, wrath over sin, control of all things, benevolence, love and saving grace, and even His eternity. God is limited only by the limits He sets upon Himself. Being all-powerful, God can frighten us because of our sins; but His love assures us that He is our merciful God in Christ Jesus, able and willing to save us and care for us in every way.

21

God knows everything; He is all-knowing, omniscient (Jn. 21:17; Ps. 139:1-4). He is the architect of the universe. God has a perfect knowledge of His creatures and His people. He knows perfectly our weaknesses, our needs and the secrets of our hearts (Ps. 44:21). He knows the good He has for us. No desire for peace or forgiveness and no groaning is hidden from Him (Ps. 38:9). This is a great comfort to those who trust in Him (Ps. 103:14; Mt. 6:32). Even though we cannot see that far or that high, God sees us and has His own plan for each of us. We are not social security numbers among billions of people to God. We can see only little bits, but He sees all.

God is everywhere at the same time, all-encompassing, omnipresent (Jer. 23:24). He is ever-present at any moment in time. There is no place we can hide from Him. He penetrates every aspect of our life in His majestic holiness. This is not some vague "everywhereness," but a dynamic, gracious, real presence of our God in His own being from Person to person, as a vine giving life to branches (Jn. 15:1) or a head related to the body (Eph. 5:23). For example, the Holy Spirit dwells in all believers in Christ, not merely figuratively through His gifts, but actually in believers (1 Cor. 3:16-17). God dwells in believers in a mystical union with all the fullness of His wisdom, holiness, power and other gifts (Eph. 3:18).

God does not only love, but He **is love** (1 Jn. 4:8), absolute love. That love shows itself in that He satisfied His justice by providing the payment for sin in the death of His Son, Jesus Christ, the "Lamb of God." God has lovingly judged sin in the sacrifice of His Son and so offers mankind complete pardon from the guilt of sin.

God is just and fair in all things (Deut. 32:4). He is the moral judge of the universe and will judge the world according to His justice. Even though we may not understand His ways all the time, He is good. Or, as Robert Schuller says, "Life's not fair, but God is good."

God is faithful (2 Tim. 2:13). He is true to Himself, His Word, His promises, and to us. We are as safe as the promises of God. God is good and compassionate (Ps. 145:9).

In an ordered universe in which there is authority and submission to authority, God is the Ultimate Authority (Rom. 13:1; 1 Pet. 3:22). To ignore Him as such is to invite disharmony, conflict and catastrophe into our lives. God has the right and the power to do what He wants (Dan. 4:35). We admit this every time we pray the Lord's Prayer in the concluding phrases (Mt. 6:13).

As God delegated authority to others, there are a number of authority and submission relationships that involve people: man is to submit to God (Jas 4:7); man is to have authority over the earth (Gen. 1:28); the husband is to be the spiritual head of the wife (Eph. 5:22-23); children are to obey parents (Eph. 6:1); people are to submit themselves to those who govern them (1 Pet. 2:13-14); Christians are to heed the guidance of spiritual leaders (Heb. 13:17). All of these are under God's authority and umbrella, as Jesus set the example (Heb. 5:7-9). All earthly authorities are limited to God's order and are within divine limits.

God is unchanging, and His character is always the same. His revealed name is more than a label, for it is a revelation of what He is always, eternally. His truths do not change even though human ideas may be unstable. His ways do not change, nor do His purposes. His Son does not change, for He is the same yesterday, today, and forever (Heb. 13:8). "A changeless Christ for a changing world" is strong consolation to all of God's people.

God Of Justice — God Of Love

No single analogy can explain God or His dealings with us in the world. The prevailing analogy of Justice is the model of the law court. It explains something of the nature of sin and salvation that no other model can illustrate.

There is a purity behind God's anger, too intense to ignore evil. He cannot pretend that wrong is not there. His justice is too true to let sin go unchecked and unpunished. At the same time, His love is too honorable, just, pure, lovely, gracious and absolute for Him to ignore what corrupts and destroys. God can never tolerate or overlook sin. God's wrath has none of the sinful associations that are attached to human wrath.

23

God cares about people and their sin. In His holiness, all sin must have punishment. He will not overlook the evidence because that is against His own nature. God's verdict rests on justice, not on the lowering of His standards. The ultimate question requires an understanding of how God can be merciful without compromising His justice. How does a holy God declare His holy justice and still express His holy love? Sinful man has failed the holy requirements of God, and so God deals justly in punishing the unjust. All people are sinners through Adam and Eve, and there is no merit in them that will calm the anger of God. With the Reformer, we must see the connection between the justice of God and the statement that "The person who has God's approval will live because of faith" (Rom. 1:17). Thus the justice and love of God includes that righteousness by which through grace and sheer mercy God justifies us through faith. God's Law, which we will study later, makes demands that can only be met by the love of God. By His love, God is both just and the justifier. The burden of guilt is lifted and the torment of conscience is ended by pure grace.

God's justice is satisfied as He exercises His love toward individual sinners by giving His Son to be their Savior. By the Holy Spirit, He brings believers to know and enjoy Him in a covenant relationship. Everything that happens is ultimately designed to express God's love in order to save us sinners from our own mistakes and for the furthering of God's good purpose for us. When God sees that we may destroy ourselves through our obstinate actions, He speaks the Law to correct us or redirect us through corrective action. But it is an expression of His love in order to gain or keep us. The true story of our lives will one day prove to be divine love and mercy from first to last.

It is important to understand clearly God's wrath and judgment, for the very idea is naturally offensive to us. It seems barbaric and seems to belong to the age when people believed in retribution. These are not just Old Testament ideas which Christ made obsolete or which are outdated by modern culture. The facts of absolute right and wrong, justice and guilt are not canceled in the person of the compassionate Son of God, nor is divine wrath; rather,

He paid for forgiveness of all wrong. Indeed, Christ taught it most clearly as He told His hearers what happened to Sodom and what will happen on the Last Day to those who reject God and His will.

The glory of the Gospel is that God made a way to justify us, which He bases on the perfect obedience of Christ and a perfect sacrifice for the guilt of sin. It is impossible for us to deserve grace, for grace is totally undeserved; only justice can be deserved. People should be careful in asking for justice, because they might get it. There's a confusion between justice and mercy. When God's justice comes, we are offended because we think God owes us perpetual mercy.

The essential nature of God is love — all-embracing, unmerited, conquering, merciful, chastening, everlasting, jealous love. He has given Himself unreservedly for us. God does not withdraw His love from His people when their lives are not what they should be, or when we sin. That is why we can have total confidence in our relationship with Him, knowing that above all He wants us to be saved, to live under Him in this kingdom, and to live with Him eternally.

God's love sent Jesus, His own Son, as a substitute for sinners, taking the guilt of us who could not pay the penalty for our sins. He died, the righteous for the unrighteous. Christ's death removes God's wrath against us and places it upon Christ. God's love is supreme as Christ gives us the victory. Christ's death satisfies God's pure demands.

God Is Gracious

The God of justice — God of love is the God of grace. God's grace is His unmerited mercy seen in His forgiveness of our sins and His goodness to us in our daily lives. It is divine compassion which results from His unconditional and indescribable love freely given. It is the guarantee of His eternal Kingdom.

The key word to describe the relationship between God and people is **grace**, in which our loving God is always the giver, and we are always the undeserving receivers. Many people believe that they can exercise some kind of power over their gods, but no one can manipulate the True God in either creation or salvation. His grace is the basis for the summons to be obedient to Him. God did not rescue Israel from bondage and various slaveries because of any good or virtue in the people, for the good was all in God. He did not act because they were strong or lovable, but the power and love was in Him. He did not give Israel the land of Canaan because of the righteousness of the people, for they had none. Even when Israel responded to God's continuing kindness with repeated sins, God showed grace by forgiving and rehabilitating them.

The entire Bible reveals the relationship between God's action for us and our action for Him, beginning with what He has done for us, and then what He expects of us. God's grace always initiates all of our action. Grace does not give us a rule to keep but gives us God with the strength to serve Him.

God The Justifier

Sin created the gulf between us and God, and our efforts cannot bridge it. The Cross is the bridge. Faith worked by the Holy Spirit causes us to see the bridge and walk over it.

The word "justified" is borrowed from the court of law. A justified person has no legal charges against him. He is righteous in the eyes of the law. That is what is so remarkable about our sinful condition resulting in being justified by grace through faith in Jesus Christ. Justification is the foundation upon which our right relationship with God is built, totally a gift from God.

We cannot do anything to be justified for Christ does it all, which rules out works. Through faith God reckons righteousness to believers. Remove the doctrine of justification from the church, and the church has nothing to offer. The buildings stand and the traditions remain and some people will come, but there is nothing left to give salvation and rehabilitation. Without faith, a company of believers degenerates into a religious club. Justification through Jesus stands totally against formalistic religion and idle ceremonies.

The first consequence of being justified is to have peace

with God (Rom. 5:1). This is not a state of mind, but a restored relationship, not just general peace, but peace **with God**. Peace with God is based on the fact that "So those who are believers in Christ Jesus can no longer be condemned" (Rom. 8:1). In Christ there will be no rejection in our earthly life or at the day of judgment by God. No one can bring charges against us, because Jesus has taken our own charges upon Himself.

Sin separates us from God, but repentance and forgiveness in Christ are God's means to bring us together with Him again. A sense of separation and alienation plagues too many Christians and prevents them from knowing and loving God as they ought. Anyone who believes that he is an independent being, separated and apart from God, will be overcome and beaten by troubles, hardships, misery, grief and distress. He will never experience the abundant life which is meant to be ours in Christ. "What will separate us from the love Christ has for us?" (Rom. 8:35).

Our need is to affirm the God of "no condemnation, no separation," of whom Paul said, "I am convinced that nothing can ever separate us from God's love which Christ Jesus our Lord shows us. We can't be separated by death or life, by angels or rulers, by anything in the present or anything in the future, by forces or powers in the world above or in the world below, or by anything else in creation" (Rom. 8:38-39). Paul was so distressed about those who have refused this love of God which justifies all mankind that he was willing to be separated from God if thereby his own race of people would be saved (Rom. 9:3-4).

The direct result of being justified by faith is that we have access to God (Rom. 5:2). To have access means that we can be in His presence without any cost. This is not a religious club to which only paid-up members have admission. Justification means that Christ has signed us into His Father's presence. Our names are written in God's family register in heaven (Lk. 10:20).

God also gives a certainty and assurance to those He justifies. Doubt is not a luxury which we can harbor, for with Paul we know whom we have believed (Rom. 8:39). God cannot deny Himself by going back on His own verdict, which is based on the perfect work of His Son and assured fully in His Word.

Justification also stabilizes us when we falter or fall. Not recognizing this, unbelievers run away from God when they are caught in their sins. God's justification draws us Christians back when we sin.

Who Is God?

The Bible teaches that there is only one God (Deut. 6:4), and in that one God are three Persons: Father, Son, and Holy Spirit (Mt. 28:19; 2 Cor. 13:14). Our feeble and fallible minds find it difficult to understand how there can be one God in Whom there are three Persons, and how each Person can be fully God. Each Person is distinct from the other two Persons. Evidence of the personal nature of the Father, Son and the Holy Spirit is provided in Jesus' discourses in John 14-16, where He urges His disciples to believe in the Father and in Him. He also tells of the Father sending the Comforter, the Holy Spirit. He is not speaking about activities or attributes or relationships or symbols, but about the mystery of three living Persons in one Godhead. The doctrine of God as the Trinity is so firmly based in Scripture that it is the fundamental article of the Christian faith. He is God almighty, Who has creation power, salvation power, and sanctifying power. The Christian Church of all ages confesses this Triune God in the Apostles' Creed (and strongly in the Athanasian Creed), in its three articles of faith.

Paul focuses on the Trinity and gives praise to the Three-In-One in a Gospel explosion in Ephesians 1, which tells of God's plan of salvation for lost humanity: God the Father planned it (1:3-6); Jesus Christ executed God's plan (1:7-12); the Holy Spirit guaranteed that the plan would be ultimately completed (1:13-14). Each one of those sections shows the reason why God did it: that we might be saved to the praise of His glory.

The Apostles' Creed, written about 160 A.D., did not add to the Bible but summarized the teachings of the Bible. The Nicene Creed, written in 325 A.D. at the church council of Nicea, emphasizes Jesus as true God. The Athanasian Creed, written in 450 A.D., is a detailed statement and confession of the Trinity.

28

The Father — The Creator And Provider

The Apostles' Creed opens with the declaration, "I believe in God" and then defines the Person and work of the First Person of the Trinity with "the Father almighty, maker of heaven and earth." His creating and providing power includes: He made us and gave us our various abilities and all we need to sustain ourselves; He preserves us, defends us against all danger, and guards and protects us against all evil (Gen. 9:3; Mt. 6:25-34; Ps. 36:6-7; Ps. 91:9-10).

The Gospel of John, showing the relationship between the Son, Jesus, and the Heavenly Father, has given indication of the Father's nature and work: The Father has authority to command (Jn. 6:38; 17:4); the Father has love and affection (Jn. 5:20; 15:19); the Father provides fellowship (Jn. 8:29; 16:32). The Father is the cause of all that exists whether of matter or spirit, and He together with the Son and Holy Spirit made man to bear His image. He relates to us as Father, forever indicating His good will toward humanity.

The children of God are ruled, loved and cared for by the Heavenly Father in and through Jesus Christ their Lord. Being adopted as sons and daughters is the highest privilege that the Gospel offers. Our entire Christian life has to be understood in terms of our adoption as children of God. The Sermon on the Mount is instruction for the children of a family, God's family. In that Sermon, Jesus teaches us to pray, "Our Father..." (Mt. 6:9). God's adoption of us shows us the greatness of His grace and the joy of the Christian hope.

The Father's grace (unmerited love) will abound toward us, and He gives hope for receiving every good thing (Rom. 8:32). Our lives in this world are under God's loving control (Rom. 8:28). As we look at the attributes of the Father, He proves to be our strength (Ps. 18:1), our rock (Deut. 32:3-4), our refuge (Ps. 59:16), and our rescuer (Ps. 34:7).

He is the God Who says: "The Lord Almighty says, 'I will be your Father, and you will be My sons and daughters'" (2 Cor. 6:18). Some are willing for God to be the God of heaven but not the God on earth, because they want to direct their own lives and personal affairs, keeping God far off. Those who do not trust in God's almighty ability nor allow Him to guide their lives and be the bountiful Supplier of all their needs will face the wrath of this gracious but just God. God alone conceived, designed and ordered all of life, the entire universe and its individual components.

The interrelationship of the Father with His family is the very core of the Christian faith. Christianity is the way of the Father with His family. He cannot be understood by looking at earthly fathers. Christianity is not a world philosophy or wisdom but a divine-human relationship. It is not even a theology or science of God but rather the union of God and His children.

When people truly want to understand God, themselves or the universe in relation to themselves, they must inquire about origins and ask the question, "Why creation?...Why and how did God create?" The reason for the earth and all it contains is man, for it was designed to support man physically (Ps. 115:17). But what is the reason for man? God. The reason for this is that God wanted sons and daughters to love Him and to care for His creation. God's heart yearns for loving children.

God created everything visible and invisible (Col. 1:16). Created means to "make out of nothing." He spoke the Word, and it was there (Gen. 1:3) — instantaneously. By faith we believe that God created perfectly the world and everything in it (Ex. 20:11; Gen. 1:31; Heb. 11:3). God formed man in a special way from the dust of the ground and gave him the breath of life, making him in His own image (Gen. 1:26-27; 2:27). God also made the woman in a special way (Gen. 2:18, 21-24). Man was made in the image of God, which means that Adam and Eve saw the reflection of God's holiness in themselves.

God did not give up His control of His creation in any way, for He is also a provider and preserver (Heb. 1:3; Ps. 36:6; 145:15-16). God preserves by natural means and by miracles, and He protects by keeping evil away and making evil serve our good. God created holy angels and sends them to protect us (Ps. 91: 10-11; Heb. 1:14).

Do we establish our positions as loving children of God on earth on the opinions of men or on the Word of God? Human theories about God and creation must constantly be revised and updated. People should not be quick to scoff at or to rearrange the first three chapters of Genesis and other portions of Scripture which answer the question, "Why creation?...What is God's plan for the earth and man?"

God's Miraculous Creation

Our world is filled with many marvelous things which God created. Some are big things: the entire universe with the sun, moon, solar system packed with planets and stars, and earth's mountain ranges. Some are little things: a tiny warbler bird flying 20,000 feet high in a prevailing wind on a course for several days and 2,400 miles in migration. Still others are efficient and ingenious things: the human body with its miraculous complexity and unity, gulls that desalt seawater, eels that emit electricity, octopuses that travel by jet propulsion, bats that use sonar, using the laws of nature.

Everything was accomplished with intelligent direction and supernatural intervention. The eye, like many other parts of the body, gives evidence of intricate design. Charles Darwin obviously acknowledged this: "To suppose that the eye...could have been formed by (evolution), I freely confess, seems absurd in the highest degree." [1]

As we look at God's record of Creation both in His Word and in nature, we Christians affirm first that as God is absolute, so there is such a thing as absolute truth which can be absolutely known. It is not a matter of whether we are dogmatic or not, but a matter of which dogma (human or divine) is the true dogma with which to be dogmatized. It is a question of following divine bias or human bias. The issue is one either of accepting impossible chance for our origin and survival or trust that the God of the Bible is responsible for life and its origins according to His report. This is not a matter of science versus religion, but religion versus religion. Both Christianity and evolution are beliefs about origins and existence and are, therefore, religions.

One can only observe what exists in the present, for there was no earthly scientist there to observe or report about the first life being formed. Evolution is a belief about the past based upon human speculations by people who were not there and dare to try to explain how all the evidence of the present originated. Evolution pictures in the books and reconstructions in museums are human stories of human preconceived bias. That is all they can ever be. The correct use of science finds that the only way one could ever be sure of arriving at the right conclusion about origins or anything else depends upon one's knowing everything there is to know. In origins a person never can know if he has reached the point where he has all the evidence. That means that we cannot be scientifically sure about anything concerning ancient origins.

Christians accept God's record in Genesis by faith. Biblical creation has as its source the One Who claims that He was the only One there, and He moved men by His Spirit to write His words so that we would have an adequate basis for understanding all we need to know about creation, beginnings and God's purposes. A creationist's view consists basically of a threefold view of history: a perfect creation, corrupted by sin, and restored by Jesus Christ.

In six days God created everything from nothing, and each part was designed to work with all the others in perfect harmony (Gen. 1). All was "very good." We, however, no longer live in the world God originally created, because Adam and Eve placed their desires above God's Word (Gen. 3). This brought death and struggle into the world as God cursed the creation because of sin. People became so violent and corrupt at one time that God destroyed the world by a flood and gave it a fresh start with Noah. Trillions of dead things buried turbulently in rock layers remind us of God's judgment on sin. In God's time, Christ came to redeem and restore as He conquered death through His death and resurrection.

Truly the Bible is the Word of One Who knows everything there is to know. Thus we judge human theories on the basis

32

of God's Word, not on man's word, no matter how brilliant man may be. It is arrogant for people to begin with man's word and then with that word judge what the Bible records or how it is to be interpreted. Scientists make new discoveries and their theories change, forming a changing attitude toward Biblical truth continually.

Without an absolute God, we are left with nothing as established truth. Both creation and evolution are belief systems, and neither of them can be proven scientifically. It is a question as to whom we choose to believe: fallible man with his theories or the infallible God with His infallible record. People may have the same facts, but they find different interpretations of these same facts.

The real issue is that there are two religions in conflict: one human and one divine, one speculation and one the record of the Creator. If the record of the Bible is continually subject to reinterpretation based on what men believe they have discovered, then we are left with man's unproven hypothesis and flights of fancy standing before the face of the one true God.

Christians and non-Christians alike need to hear God's incisive talk with Job in Job 38-42, beginning with 38:4, "Where were you when I laid the foundation of the earth? Tell me if you have such insights." Listen to the stern lecture, sometimes seemingly sarcastic, toward men who dared to tell God that He does not know how to control life and the world or report His creating activity, suggesting that God should follow the counsel of men. God advises men to stop the idle talk, "Who is this that belittles my advice with words that do not show any knowledge about it?" (38:2)

Hear the darts of truth and questions about man's puny knowledge and wisdom of the world: "Who determined its dimensions? Certainly you know! Who stretched a measuring line over it? On what were its footings sunk? Who laid its cornerstone?...Who shut the sea behind gates?...When I said, 'You may come this far but no farther. Here your proud waves will stop'? Have you ever given orders to the morning? Or assigned a place for the dawn?...Have you even considered how wide the earth is? Tell me, if you know all of this. What is the way to the place where light lives? Where is the home of darkness that you may lead it to its territory, so that you may know the path to its home? You must know because you were born then and have lived such a long time!" (38:5-6, 8, 11-12, 18-19, 21)

See what He writes about the weather, "Have you been to the warehouses where snow is stored or seen the warehouses for hail that I have stored up for the time of trouble . . .Which is the way to the place where light is scattered and the east wind is spread across the earth?. . .Does the rain have a father? . . . From whose womb came the ice? . . .Can you bring out the constellations at the right time or guide Ursa Major with its cubs? Do you know the laws of the sky or make them rule the earth?...Can you send lightning flashes so that they may go and say to you, 'Here we are'? Who put wisdom in the heart or gave understanding to the mind?...Who provides food for the crow when its young ones cry to God and wander around in need of food?" (38:22-24, 28-29, 32-33, 35-36, 41).

Listen to God's account of animals and birds, "Do you know the time when the mountain goats give birth? Do you watch the does when they are in labor?...Who lets the wild donkey go free? Who unties the ropes of the wild donkey? I gave it the desert to live in and the salt flats as its dwelling place...Will the wild ox agree to serve you?...Does your understanding make a bird of prey fly and spread it wings toward the south? Is it by your order that the eagle flies high and makes its nest on the heights?" (39:1, 5-6, 9, 26-27)

When origins are determined, we are involved with Job in this dialogue, "The Lord responded to Job: 'Will the person who finds fault with the Almighty correct him? Will the person who argues with God answer him?' Job answered the Lord, 'I'm so insignificant. How can I answer you? I will put my hand over my mouth'" (40:1-4). Even after Job shuts his mouth, the Creator continues His lecture to the creature, "Brace yourself like a man! I will ask you, and you will teach me. Would you undo my justice? Would you condemn me so that you can be righteous? Do you have power like God's? Can you thunder with a voice like his?

34

Then dress yourself in majesty and dignity. Clothe yourself in splendor and glory. Unleash your outbursts of anger. Look at all who are arrogant, and put them down. Look at all who are arrogant, and humble them. . .Hide them completely in the dust and cover their faces in the hidden place. Then even I will praise you because your right hand can save you" (40:7-11, 13-14).

See how God describes his creation of the elephant in Job 40:13-24! Note the challenge about pulling in the leviathan (possibly a hippopotamus, large crocodile or some large extinct animal), as God asks whether we can make a pet out of him like a bird or put him on a leash for our girls (Job 41:1-10).

Human theories and guesses are as nothing in the light of God's Word. Let Christians stand with Job, "I know that you can do everything and that your plans are unstoppable. You said, 'Who is this that belittles my advice without having any knowledge about it?' Yes, I have stated things I didn't understand, things too mysterious for me to know. . . I had heard about you with my own ears, but now I have seen you with my own eyes. That is why I take back what I said, and I sit in dust and ashes to show that I am sorry" (Job 42:1-6).

Whatever we believe about our origins affects our whole world view, including the purpose and the meaning of life. We can see from Job that evolution is a religion which leads people to try to justify writing their own rules and to rebel against God. Christians accept God's record because they accept a God to Whom they are answerable, and the only One who offers grace. Scientists continually change their answers and offer no grace.

We are dealing with a spiritual question, and the evidence is clear to those who live in faith, "From the creation of the world, God's invisible qualities, his eternal power and divine nature, have been clearly observed in what he made. As a result, people have no excuse" (Rom. 1:20). No Christian should be found standing with a pagan philosophy of origins, because "They are deliberately ignoring one fact: Because of God's word, heaven and earth existed a long time ago. The earth appeared out of water and was kept alive by water" (2 Pet. 3:5).

Those who try to reinterpret Genesis to fit evolutionary

theories should read Job, New Testament passages, and Isaiah: "'To whom, then, can you compare me? Who is my equal?' asks the Holy One. Look at the sky and see. Who created these things? Who brings out the stars one by one? He calls them all by name. Because of the greatness of his might and the strength of his power, not one of them is missing" (Is. 40:25-26).

We can be certain of the Creation account because Christ was there. God reports through John that **Christ the Word** was present: "In the beginning the Word already existed. The Word was with God, and the Word was God. He was already with God in the beginning. Everything came into existence through him. Not one thing that exists was made without him. He was the source of life, and that life was the light for humanity" (Jn. 1:1-4). Christ is shown to be the Lord of all creation (Col. 1:16).

The Biblical doctrine of origins is foundational to all other doctrines of Scripture, and the Gospel is integrated completely with it so that the tearing away of either the Gospel or creation tears away at God Himself and of Christ. If we tear away the fabric of beginnings, we destroy the truth of our own existence. Genesis provides the basic account of life and the universe, the origin of man, of government, of sex, of marriage, of culture, of work, of nations, of death, of the Chosen people, of sin, of the Savior, of the solar system, of diet and clothes. The meaning of all things today is dependent on their origin. Evolution is a sinful and rebellious departure from divine truth, for it is an attack on the existence of God and His nature.

Ultimately, evolution is a blind faith, man's subjective opinion. Christianity, on the other hand, is an objective faith, as our object is the Father-Creator and Jesus Christ the Savior, Who reveals Himself in His Word. This is set in proper perspective in Hebrews 11: "No one can please God without faith. Whoever goes to God must believe that God exists and that he rewards those who seek him. Faith led Noah to listen when God warned him about the things in the future that he could not see. He obeyed God and built a ship to save his family...Faith convinces us that God created the world through his word. This means what can be seen was made by something that could not be seen" (6-7, 3). All real evidence points toward a miraculous and instant creation of a completed "young earth" and of a mature Adam.

The two religions of creation and evolution present two conflicting world views, one supernatural and one natural, one of grace and one of law. The first centers on the Triune God as the Maker, Ruler, Judge and Savior to Whom we are responsible for our thoughts, words, and deeds. All our actions are to be oriented toward Him and His purposes in creation. The second world view centers on depraved man as the measure of all meaning in life with the cosmos and nature as the ultimate reality. The first view is reality which reflects the physical, psychological and spiritual complexity of all people. The other is such an impossible chance that equals the fairy tale which transforms a frog into a prince, removing all rational thought in determining origins and working systems of all living beings.

The issue is between operating with the worldview of Jesus or of modern sinful man, of the Bible or of culture. Whichever man selects becomes his reality into which he fits his values and decisions. His worldview functions as eyeglasses through which he views people and the world. A worldview includes assumptions about God, reality, knowledge, morality and man. The Biblical worldview and the naturalist evolution worldview present an unreconcilable conflict. They are two maps in total conflict, as the contrasts of two gates (Mt. 7:13-14), two builders (Lk. 6:46-49), two masters (Mt. 6:24), and two tables (1 Cor. 10:20-21) show. The price is too high to barter Biblical facts in order to gain hoped for acceptance from the academic community, thereby trivializing the Gospel. When we accept the God who presides in a universe of law and order, we are freed from a precarious universe of chance which operates by the whims of a capricious deity. We are dealing with the source of human life, not of natural forces.

The contrast is between the God of grace who is operative in creation as revealed in the Gospel and the god of legalism as revealed in the universe which came from chance that depends upon the brutality of a world without God. The latter, evolution, springs from the heart of Satan: "You'll be like God"

(Gen. 3:5). The devil unravels creation by confusing minds with the theory of evolution.

Ken Ham in *The Lie Evolution* tells,

> *"Evolution also destroys the teaching of the New Heavens and the New Earth. Evolution necessarily implies that before Adam there was struggle, cruelty and brutality, animals eating animals, and death. Is the world going to be restored to that? If you believe in evolution, you must deny a universal paradise before Adam (because you believe that there was death and struggle millions of years before Adam), and also at the end of time (because the Bible teaches the world will be restored to what it used to be). Thus, evolution not only strikes at the heart and the foundation, but at the hope of Christianity as well.*
>
> *"Christians who do believe in evolution must accept that evolution is still going on. This is because of the death and struggle we see in the world around us and the mutations (mistakes in the genes) that are occurring are used by evolutionists to try to prove that evolution is possible...Christians who accept evolution must agree, therefore, that evolution is occurring today in every area, including man. However, God has said in His Word that when He created everything He finished His work of creation and pronounced it 'good' (Gen. 1:31-2:3). This is completely contrary to what evolutionists are telling us. Theistic evolutionists cannot say that God once used evolution and now does not. To say that evolution is not occurring today is to destroy evolutionary theory, as you have no basis for saying that it ever happened in the past."* [2]

The issue of origins is primarily a spiritual one, and it should not be surprising that unregenerate man will not come to a correct conclusion regarding the world's supernatural origin: "A person who isn't spiritual doesn't accept the teachings of God's

Spirit. He thinks they're nonsense. He can't understand them because a person must be spiritual to evaluate them" (1 Cor. 2:14).

The doctrine of creation describes a relationship more than a process. Sin-blinded minds cannot understand that there are no blind forces worth noting in nature. Even unprejudiced reason should be able to understand that life originated from an intelligence capable of creating complexities like the honeybee, and are not originated from a miracle-working amoeba and creator-slime which ultimately grew into all the complex creatures on earth.

Thus we see that evolution (whether theistic or not) destroys the essential doctrines about God and the Gospel itself. This results from ignorance or unbelief, as John tells us that Christ "was in the world, and the world came into existence through him. Yet, the world didn't recognize him" (1:10). Evolutionists certainly deny this Christ when they deny Him as Creator.

The great myth of the world is evolution. Until sin entered the world, there was no death for Adam and Eve or for other creatures. "So sin came into the world through one person, and death came through sin. Death spread to everyone, because everyone sinned" (Rom. 5:12). Before the Fall, only plants were eaten, not animals (Gen. 1:29-30). There was no bloodshed before Adam sinned, for everything was perfect and death was not a part of any animal existence. The Bible teaches that creation was finished, that God had finished His work of making things on the sixth day of creation. There are about 165 passages in Genesis that are either directly quoted or clearly referred to in the New Testament. The Bible reveals that Adam was no primitive savage, nor the ancestor of one. He gave names to all the livestock, birds and beasts (Gen. 2:20). Adam had a language, which he utilized. Genesis 5:1 already speaks about a written account. They had musical instruments and worked with brass and iron (Gen. 4:21-22).

Fossil records are no comfort to evolutionists. There is no evidence that very simple life forms gradually appear, or simple forms gradually change into complex ones, or that there are beginnings of new body features such as limbs, bones and/or organs.

The fossils are missing in all the important places; for example, fish show up in the fossil record seemingly from nowhere, mysteriously fully formed. The fossil record registers a creation pattern of complex life forms suddenly appearing, complex life forms multiplying in biological families (though allowing for variety), no transitional "links" between different kinds, and no partial body features, all parts complete.

How could partially developed organisms reproduce offspring before necessary and essential, fully functioning, highly complex, male-female reproductive systems themselves had already fully evolved instantaneously? We know today as fact that no creature can survive being partially formed, or that life cannot be evolved from non-life by chance chemical evolution. Nor does the fossil record convincingly document a single transition from one species to another, as each major form or kind of plant or animal has a separate and distinct history from all the other forms or kinds. These are life realities simply representing natural and logical observations and reasoning.

It is irrational how some Christians deify evolutionary science as they believe scientists who say that evolution is a fact. Is the earth really without a Creator-Designer? Or is evolution a great fraud? Some have given a reverence to evolutionary science that dethrones God or that makes mockery of God's Word. Yet the same ones who enthrone naturalism at the same time ignore the history of fossil frauds. The critical point is whether Christians know their divine identity in this struggle and recognize the self-revealing God of the Scriptures who is also the Savior of sinful man.

The naturalism of evolution produces no rational basis for order in life or society. It provides no purpose to living, as life remains an accident. It gives no real value, as nothing has objective or lasting value. It is a total antithesis of the God who creates us with purpose, value and order in a world of laws and order.

While man physically fits the general description of a mammal, no greater mistake could be made than to consider man merely an animal at any point of history. Man is unique and differs from all animals in many properties, beginning with his brain, which is more complicated than anything else in the universe. Form remains remarkably constant within any given line of descent: elephants remain elephants, mice remain mice, and fruit trees remain fruit trees generation after generation. The differences in man's moral and spiritual values, which stem from qualities like love, justice, wisdom, power, and mercy, all reveal him made in the image and likeness of God the Creator (Gen. 1:26).

The flight of a rocket into orbit requires adherence to laws of motion and gravity. Such laws require a lawmaker. The earth orbits the sun and consistently makes a complete rotation on its axis every 24 hours, providing regular periods of light and darkness, and its tilt allows for necessary seasonal changes. The atmosphere shields the earth from harmful radiation and from meteors. Water is an extraordinary substance. There are 70 separate chemical reactions involved in photosynthesis, a truly miraculous event in plants. All these are things which only creation can explain.

The Bible knows nothing of a right relationship with God that does not include a right understanding of and a right relationship with creation and the Creator. Ignorance toward the created world is sad. Creation was a divinely planned, orderly, organized process.

The Person And Work Of Jesus Christ

The second Person of the Triune God, Jesus Christ, at one time in history took into Himself human nature or form, fully and wholly man, but without sin (Lk. 1:35). He was conceived by the Holy Spirit and born of the Virgin Mary (Mt. 1:18-25), lived, suffered, died and was resurrected, and ascended into heaven, where He sits at the right hand of the throne of God now. He always has been, and always will be, true God. Jesus Christ is one Person of the Godhead in Whom there is a union of two natures — the divine and the human clearly outlined in Colossians 2:9, "In Him, that is, in His body, lives all the fullness of the Deity."

Jesus declared Himself as divine and claimed the authority to forgive sins; He recognized Himself as the Author of eternal life and the Judge of all men. Christ's compassion for sinners and the needy is a clue to His deity. He came to earth to lay down His life for others that they might be restored and brought back to life. To accomplish this, Jesus Christ became for some measurable time the rejected One, the Person who bore the wrath of God against the sin of the whole human race. As the Lamb of God, He became the slaughtered sacrifice as a payment for human sin.

The barrier between God and man, caused by sin, must be destroyed. How can sinful human beings regain God's favor and get rid of their guilt? God alone can do it, so He expressed His love in the only way that man can be saved: "God sent his son into the world, not to condemn the world, but to save the world" (Mt. 3:17). This momentous event was planned by the Triune God and announced thousands of years prior to Christ's arrival. His coming in human flesh changed the course of human history: "A virgin will become pregnant and give birth to a son, and she will name him Immanuel" (Is. 7:14).

The mission of Jesus Christ on earth was to remove the barrier that separated us from God through His death on the cross: "They receive God's approval freely by an act of his kindness through the price Christ Jesus paid to set us free from sin" (Rom. 3:24). His cross was not the end, for three days after His death He became alive: "He was placed in a tomb. He was brought back to life on the third day as the Scriptures predicted" (1 Cor. 15:4). For 40 days after His resurrection, Jesus was seen by many people on numerous occasions (Acts 1:3). Then He gave final instructions to His followers and was taken up into heaven where He rules at the right hand of God (Acts 1:8-11). He was the representative for the human race, doing what we could not do, as he suffered that which we deserved for our sin. The fruits of His work to save all humanity are freely offered to us and received through faith (Eph. 2:8-9).

The Bible shows Jesus' life to be one of active obedience and passive obedience. In active obedience, Jesus lived the life of an obedient Servant, a life totally dedicated to doing the will of His Heavenly Father (2 Cor. 5:21; Gal. 4:5-6). Jesus' crucifixion was not an accident that He and His Father and the Holy

Spirit had to accept. It was God's eternal plan of love for the salvation of mankind. We dare not romanticize the conditions of His coming. He was God become man to dwell among us. He came into a very messy situation from His birth to His death to help us overcome our difficulties, frustrations and misunderstandings.

In His passive obedience, Jesus surrendered His life into death on the cross, and so took into His own body the punishment that all sinners deserve for their sins (Jn. 3:8; 2 Tim. 2:10; Rom. 5:19). Jesus could have refused death, but in love He allowed it to happen in order to carry out His mission for all mankind. Jesus was not a victim when He was crucified. In obedience to His Heavenly Father, He controlled the course of events so that He as the Son of God willingly sacrificed His very life for our salvation (Jn. 10:17-18).

The Bible also shows Jesus' condition of humiliation and exaltation. In His state of humiliation, even though He never ceased to be God nor became anything less than God, He did not always or fully use the power and the other divine qualities which He had as God. Though He always possessed these attributes, He humbled Himself (Phil. 2:4-11). In His exaltation, we see the ascended Lord (Acts 1:1-9) using His divine powers and abilities that had always been His as God (Mt. 28:19-20). His steps into exaltation were that He descended into hell, rose again from the dead, ascended into heaven, sits at the right hand of God the Father Almighty, and from there He shall come to judge the living and the dead. He is both true God-true man, present everywhere to comfort and reassure us (Heb. 2:14-18; Eph. 1:19-23).

The Bible also speaks about three aspects of Christ's work: prophet, priest and king. Christ's work had a strongly prophetic character by proclaiming the will of His Heavenly Father (Jn. 17:8). Jesus was the priest or "Go-between" between His Heavenly Father and sinful humanity, as He offered Himself in sacrifice as the "Lamb of God who takes away the sin of the world" (Jn. 1:29-36). As the High Priest, Christ represented the whole world before the Father and sacrificed **Himself** for the sins of all (Heb. 7:26-27). As king, Jesus rules the entire universe in the kingdom of power (Eph. 1:20-21), and rules His Church in the kingdom of Grace (Eph. 1:22), and rules heaven and the world to come in the kingdom of glory (Col. 1:15-20). As King, Christ won the victory over sin, death, and the devil so that He might rule in the hearts of believers by His Word. Now He is the "...Lord of both the living and the dead" (Rom 14:9). His realm is the whole earth. He has all authority and establishes order, giving direction as Lord of all.

It is truly comforting to know that the visible Son showed us the Invisible Father (Jn. 1:18; 2 Cor. 4:4; Heb. 1:3). We can understand what our invisible God is like by noting the manner in which Jesus on earth dealt with people in need (Mt. 8:1-4), how boldly He confronted the devil and the demons (Mk. 1:25; Jn. 18:4-8), and how He showed love and patience to many people and was ready to sacrifice Himself (Mk. 10:32-34). As Jesus treated people during His time on earth, so the Father treats us now. Every authority and power in the universe is under the rule of Christ, for God "has put everything under the control of Christ. He has made Christ the head of everything for the good of the church" (Eph. 1:22). He overcame Satan, death, the heavenly powers, the power of sin, and the Law. Everything is under His authority (Phil. 2:9-11).

The Gospel of Matthew shows Christ to be divine royalty, as His lineage is traced to a sovereign (David) and to a sacrifice (the son of Abraham). This Gospel stressed what Jesus taught. Mark reveals His ministry and work, showing Him to be a servant. Luke traces His ancestry to the first man, Adam, and shows that He came to save the lost. John strongly stresses His deity. Acts shows that evangelization is all about Christ. The Epistles interpret and apply the redemptive work of Christ to the life of Christians in the Church: justification, sanctification, consolation, emancipation, unification, exaltation, completion, expectation, faithfulness, steadfastness in Christ and glorification. There are also exhortations to maturity, wisdom, submission, servanthood, communion and continuation in Christ.

No force has been able to overcome the absolute power of Christ's cross. Its influence is greater than that of any organization, university or government. Before He was nailed to the cross, Jesus foretold the power and the love of His cross for the good of men: "When I have been lifted up from the earth, I will draw all people toward me" (Jn. 12:32). A Christianity robbed of the lifting of the cross has lost its radical nature and power. What the sun is to the solar system, what the needle is to the compass, what the heart is to the body — that the cross is to everyone who wants to find any hope for salvation and for positive direction in life.

Christianity is shown to rest not upon earthly principles, philosophy or ethics, but upon the facts of the Incarnation and the Resurrection, the fact of the Eternal Word truly becoming flesh and dwelling among us, that we may behold His glory, "full of kindness and truth" (Jn. 1:14).

When John wrote of Jesus as the Son of God, he wrote in such a way as to show Jesus as the Son Who was a personal Deity. When John referred to Jesus as the Word, people who knew the Old Testament knew it to be God's creative utterance, His power in action fulfilling His purpose. Therefore, it is a significant teaching in John 1:1-14 that Jesus is the Word: "In the beginning the Word already existed...The Word was with God...The Word was God...Everything came into existence through Him...He was the source of Life...that life was the light of humanity..." Here we see His personality, deity, incarnation, revelation and creating and animating power.

Ephesians 1:7-10 places the work of Christ into sharp focus: God chose us in Christ before He actually created the world. We were adopted as God's children through Jesus Christ. His glorious grace was freely given us in Christ. Jesus Christ is the Person through Whom we receive God's spiritual blessings.

Paul's words flow gloriously in Ephesians and Colossians about the many riches which God has in His heavenly storehouse for us because of Christ Jesus. There are sweeping crescendos to show that everything prayed for on our behalf is available, and to lead us to accept the Incarnation (Christ became flesh) as the ultimate revelation of God.

The disciples proclaimed Jesus as Lord (2 Cor. 4:5). Jesus is Lord because of His relationship to the universe and His authority over nature (Mk. 4:35-41). Jesus controlled the fierce forces of nature by the sound of His voice, as the wind and the sea recognized the command of its Lord (Mt. 8:27). In the power of Christ men met something more frightening than they faced in nature, for they were in the presence of the Holy One.

As we consider Christ's authority and power, we learn that He knew His identity and commission as the Son sent from the Father (Jn. 17:2). He knew He could exercise this authority (Mt. 8:5-9), that He was recognized to be authoritative (Mt. 7:29), that He had all authority in heaven and on earth (Mt. 28:18), and that He would eventually hand back His authority and power to God (1 Cor. 15:24-28).

Jesus was not just one of the earthly saints or the greatest saint and spirit on earth. Salvation is not in doctrines about Christ, but in the Person of Christ. He is not part of an arid intellectual formula to gain some kind of heavenly bliss, He is the Living Christ, Who is Savior and Lord, with Whom we have a living relationship by faith. Christ does not merely add something to the sum total of the world's knowledge of religion, but He is the center of all truth and life.

God's plan of completed salvation is based on the perfect sacrifice of His Son, Jesus Christ, by which He declares us sinners holy, just, righteous and worthy of eternal life only because the Father, by an act of grace, looks at Christ's substitutionary death. Thus He considers and makes the believer justified, perfect with a right standing before His Throne. The incomprehensible love of God reaches down to take the worst sinners who by faith receive Jesus as Savior by the Spirit. He adopts them as His sons and daughters to be heirs of heaven's riches. Salvation is freely given to the repentant believer by God's act of grace.

Can you imagine a Sovereign ruling the world from several planks stained with blood? Jesus' cross is His throne, which is the rallying point for all His earthly subjects. The shadow of His throne stretches across the globe through the centuries: "In the cross of Christ I glory, towering o'er the wrecks of time." The Cross, which led to the grave, also led to the open tomb and the

Ascension Mount. Christianity is the only religion that sends good news from the cemetery. Jesus lives and rules!

Let every knee be bowed and every tongue confess that Jesus Christ is Lord, to the glory of God the Father! (Phil. 2:10-11)

The Third Person Of The Godhead — The Holy Spirit

Christ gave a promise of the coming of the Holy Spirit Who would teach and guide believers in all Truth (Jn. 14:26; 16:13). The third Person of the Godhead is the Holy Spirit, Whose chief work is to enlighten our minds (1 Cor. 2:14; 1 Pet. 2:9-11) and sanctify or give strength for holy living (1 Cor. 6:11; 2 Cor. 13:14; 2 Thes. 2:13). The work of the Holy Spirit is called regeneration and sanctification. He uses the Word as the means to invite and empower us personally to receive God's gift of salvation and sanctification (1 Pet. 1:23; Rom. 10:17). The Holy Spirit uses baptism for regeneration (Jn. 3:6; Tit. 3:5).

Think of all the things the Holy Spirit does for us. He enables us to respond in faith to God's love and guarantees our eternal inheritance (Eph. 1:13-14). Romans 10:14-17 teaches us that the Holy Spirit gives us the Word of God. He enlightens, persuades and empowers us to accept the Word and gives us faith to trust in Christ for salvation. The Scriptures teach us the things that Christ wants us to do as His disciples, gives us strength to continue to believe and do these things which Christ entrusted to us, enables us to persevere in the Christian faith and life and gives us eternal life.

The Holy Spirit ignites Truth in our hearts (Jn. 14:26). He gives an understanding of prophecy (Lk. 18:31-34), of the plan of God (Jn. 2:18-22), and of the promise of the Father (Acts 11:15-17). The Holy Spirit inspires witnessing (Jn. 15:26-27) and gives the words of witness (Acts 4:5-14), and words of wisdom (Acts 6:9-10). The Holy Spirit illuminates the future (Jn. 16:13) by giving insights for the church's needs (Rev. 2:1-3, 22) for the coming glory (Rev. 19:1-9; 21:1-7).

It is the Holy Spirit's task to lead us into all Truth and into a pure relationship with Christ, reproducing His holy nature

47

in us (2 Thes. 2:13-14). He leads on the path of correction to convict the world of sin (Jn. 15:8-11), to chasten in order to purify the Church (Heb. 12:6-16), and to cleanse believers (1 Cor. 6:9-11). He places us on the path of holiness to lead us to spiritual maturity (Eph. 4:10-16), and to spiritual fruitfulness (Gal. 5:22-25). We have protection on our path through the spiritual weapons: the Word of God (Eph. 6:17), and the whole armor of God (Eph. 6:10-17). The Holy Spirit teaches us to worship the Son of God by singing in unison with the whole Church (Eph.5:18-20; Col. 3:16). He also leads us to sing even in unfavorable circumstances (Acts 16:25), and to sing in unending praise (Rev. 5:9-10; 15:3-4).

The Holy Spirit equips us for service by giving us gifts (1 Cor. 12:4-12) and by providing proper motivation for our service and ministry (1 Cor. 13:1-13). He energizes us for work and gives us power to witness (Acts 4:33) by producing a fellowship, a community of caring (Acts 4:32 ff) and a fellowship for praying (Acts 4:23-31). He directs mission activity (Acts 10:19-20; 13:1-4) and defeats Satan's schemes (Acts 5:1-11).

The Holy Spirit teaches us to wait patiently for the glory of God under the most severe circumstances such as death (Acts 7:54-60), privation (Acts 4:32-37) and prison (Acts 12:1-17). The Holy Spirit abolishes inequalities among people on the basis of sexual (Acts 2:17-18; Gal. 3:28), racial, national or cultural differences (Acts 2:5; 10:34; 11:12, 7). A new people of God has been and is being created as all-inclusive by the Spirit (Eph. 2:15, 19, 21-22).

The Holy Spirit is intimately involved in our moral lives (Rom. 14:15; 15:16) to overcome the works of the flesh or sinful nature (Romans 7 and 8) and to produce ethical behavior (Gal. 5:22-25). He gives Himself to the Church to be its life and witnessing power (Acts 1:8). He bestows the love of God and makes real the Lordship of Jesus Christ in believers so that both His gifts of words and service may achieve the common good to build and advance the Church.

By the Word of Law and Gospel, the Holy Spirit guides, strengthens, comforts and empowers the will of believers to reject sin and wrong.

Satan Distorts The Picture Of God

The fiercest enemy of every human being, from the Garden of Eden to the present time, is the devil, author of all evil. He is the motivator of man's immorality, dishonesty, murders, individual problems and wars. He writes the script under limitations set by God for human sorrows, sickness and death itself. He competes against God for influencing us and directing our lives.

There are two supernatural powers at work in the world: that of the Holy Spirit by the Gospel and the Word of God, and that of Satan who opposes God. From Genesis to Revelation the work of Satan can be traced as deceiver of the whole earth, beginning with when the results of the deception in Eden are unveiled. The subtle form of the devil's method of lying in Eden was to work upon an innocent creature's highest and purest desires, and cloak his purpose of ruin under the guise of seeking to lead the human being nearer to God. He used false promises of "good" to bring about evil by suggesting evil to bring about supposed "good." Eve was blinded to her personal responsibility to God and was deceived (1 Tim. 2:14). The devil's true objective is to get a child of God to disobey God. He gives a distorted view of God.

The Word of God tells of the reality of supernatural powers under Satan's control with his multitudes of helpers called demons or evil spirits (Lk. 10:17, 20). Satan is presented as Lucifer, the first and most glorious creature of God, who subsequently sinned (Is. 14:12-13; 28:11-19). He was created by God as an angel of light, but he rebelled against God. In his rebellion, Lucifer drew a multitude of angels with him and became "Satan," a Hebrew word meaning opposer or adversary (Rev. 12:9).

Having lost the war in Heaven, Satan was thrown down to the earth with all his army (Rev. 12:7-12; Lk. 10:12). Thereafter, he constantly mobilized and deployed all the forces that his evil commanded, ruling over the kingdom of darkness organized in opposition to God (Mt. 12:26). This opposition centers on man and God's purpose for man upon earth (Gen. 3:1-15). The devil desires to destroy what God is doing.

Satan is not a medieval goblin or modern spook, not a sort of scapegoat on whom we can conveniently place our hang-ups. He is a personal spiritual being with personal pronouns applied to him by Christ, and by the demons to themselves (Lk. 8:27-30). Demons may assume personal names such as Legion (Lk. 8:30). They use intelligent speech (Lk. 4:33-35, 41; 8:28-30). They recognize the identity of Christ (Mk. 1:23-24) and of Paul (Acts 16:16-17). When they appear, they may emerge as though they are angels of light (2 Cor. 11:14) or as hideous and fearsome beings (Rev. 9:7-10, 17; 16:13-16).

Satan pretends to be what he is not, as he deceitfully presents himself as light instead of darkness (2 Cor. 11:14). He shows no mercy or compassion and is as ruthless as a lion (1 Pet. 5:8). He is the evil prince of this world (Jn. 12:31), knows how to use his power and will make his own rules for every occasion. He quotes and misquotes Scripture, using it in part when it suits him and never hesitating to take it out of context, as he did with Jesus. Jesus called Satan a liar and the father of lies (Jn. 8:44).

The devil hinders the advance of the Gospel, as he blinds the minds of people (2 Cor. 4:4) and so opposes Christ's mighty mission to win mankind, as Paul experienced (1 Thes. 2:18). Skillful and diabolical in undermining the children of God, the devil has an infinite variety of methods and means to accomplish his evil designs (Job 2:4; 2 Cor. 11:14; Eph. 6:11). Rarely attacking Christians frontally or bombarding them with gross power, he uses subtlety and practices gradualism instead (2 Cor. 11:3).

Describing the spiritual wickedness in heavenly places, Ephesians 6:4 tells that the satanic forces are divided into principalities, powers, world rulers and wicked spirits. This supernatural world of spiritual beings or evil persons have intelligent power of planning (Mt. 12:44-45) and strategy (Eph. 6:11).

When the Word gets out, Satan seeks to squelch it, and if it reaches the hearers or readers, he brings out the weapons in his arsenal to keep them from believing. He tries to confuse minds about divine truth. Jesus made this clear in one of His parables in which He compared the preacher of the Word to a sower who distributes seed. "Some people are like seeds that were planted along the road. They hear the word, but then the devil comes. He takes the word away from them so that they don't believe and become saved" (Lk. 8:12).

So effective is Satan's disguise that he can acquire almost total rule over a Christian's life while the victim does not suspect the identity of his evil tempter. The nature of his disguise usually is the mask of self. Behind most of our thoughts and actions is the Evil One, but because of his camouflage, we do not suspect his presence. It is difficult for us to believe that someone else has the power to engineer our behavior without violating our free will. The devil knows how to play with our weaknesses and our vanity, so we need to be aware of the chinks in our spiritual armor. He works for self-deception of the individual.

Satan got into trouble by saying, "I'll be like the Most High" (Is. 14:13-14). The chief characteristic of Satan is his complete selfishness and preoccupation with himself.

Satan and his evil angels seek to control individuals (Eph. 2:1-2), political governments (Dan. 10:13, 20) and the whole world's philosophy and course of history (Jn. 12:31; 2 Thes. 2:8-10). The demoniac of the Gerasenes was governed by thousands of unclean spirits, and no one was able to bind them (Mk. 5:1-4). Their powers are used in terribly wicked ways. They are always opposing God's purposes and oppressing humanity. They oppose especially believers in Christ, as they wage direct warfare with believers. They plant doubt about God's truths. They tempt to specific sins such as hypocrisy, deception, adultery, worldly-mindedness, dependence upon human wisdom and strength, pride in spiritual matters and doubts.

The devil and his evil ones seek to weaken the Church of Jesus Christ through false teachers (1 Tim. 4:1-5). They promote erroneous doctrine, denying that Christ is the God-man (1 Jn. 4:1-4) and lead people to bad lifestyles (Col. 2:18-23). They promote division in the church. They take advantage of unresolved anger and turn it into bitterness. They lead Christians into compromising situations and discourage them in their spiritual battles.

The devil not only has a program of total evil, but he is also a skilled technician in planning his work. He works through pride, temptation, lust, drunkenness, violence, materialism, drugs, abuse, false prophets, worldliness, depression, anger, selfishness and false intellectualism.

The story of Job is about the devil's corruption against God's goodness, in which Job moved from victim to victor. We see the striking comparison between God's supreme love and the poverty of Satan to which he reduces people by his complete evil. The account of Job shows us the perfection of God and the wickedness of the devil, that God is all good and that the devil is all bad.

All of Satan's ways are counterfeit and his promises are lies. His design is to distort the name and work of God, of Christ's kingdom and of godliness. He seeks to cheat God of His glory.

We must thank God that the activities of Satan and the demons are controlled and often overruled by God. Their powers are curbed. Their doom is sealed, although they are not totally impotent, as we see in Scripture. Despite the great power of Satan and his warriors, believers may confidently rest in the love and care of their loving Father and Savior. Satan and his hosts were defeated at the cross. God guarantees that He will never leave us or forsake us. Neither can the devil or any demon separate us from the love of Christ (Col. 2:15; Heb. 13:5).

The devils believe and tremble (Jas. 2:19). They are no match for the Savior, their Judge. Christ limits them and will finally cast them into the lake of fire for eternal punishment. We may confidently rely upon Christ in the midst of the devil's war against us to protect our salvation, to guide our lives in victory and to keep us on the path of righteousness and obedience to His Word. Christians need not fear the devil or demons, for Jesus gave authority to His disciples to withstand the power of the enemy (Lk. 10:19). The power to overcome evil is found in the Gospel that liberates captives and disarms the powers of evil.

Holy Ministering Angels

God has given us His helpers, the holy angels, to minister to us and to contradict the devil and his tricks. These ministering angels serve all believers in their calling and work (Ps. 91:11-12) and at death (Lk. 16:22).

Angels worship before the throne of God and serve Him obediently (Ps. 148:2; Heb. 1:6). They celebrate before the throne of God when sinners repent (Lk. 15:10). Luke 16:22 tells about the angels escorting the soul of a believer to heaven. Acts 12:43 tells about angels who are commissioned to execute divine judgment upon Herod.

We have great comfort in the fact that God has sent us holy angels as guardians. Whatever our need, problem or challenge, these ministering angels will help bring God's good for us. "He will put his angels in charge of you to protect you in all your ways" (Ps. 91:11). "What are all the angels? They are spirits sent to serve those who are going to receive salvation" (Heb. 1:14). Knowing this, Christians will take advantage of the protective force God has given them, praying daily that God's holy angels will care for them.

Know And Confess The True God

More important than knowing **about** God, is to know Him and to live with and for Him. Talking about God is totally different than living with God.

God wants us to confess Him before people. "If you declare that Jesus is Lord, and believe that God brought him back to life, you will be saved" (Rom. 10:9). "God lives in those who declare that Jesus is the Son of God, and they live in God" (1 Jn. 4:15). That is a living relationship between God and man, where both are truly alive.

Confessing Christ openly is very profitable: "So I will acknowledge in front of my Father in heaven that person who acknowledges me in front of others" (Mt. 10:32). Peter made a remarkable confession which revealed his relation with God: "You are the Messiah, the Son of the living God!" (Mt. 16:16).

The consequence of refusing to acknowledge Jesus is terrible: "But I will tell my Father in heaven that I don't know the person who tells others that he doesn't know me" (Mt. 10:33).

Instead, we must confess with Martha, "Yes, Lord, I believe that you are the Messiah, the Son of God, the one who was expected to come into the world" (Jn. 11:27).

For all of God's grace we are to thank and praise God with all our life. Praising and rejoicing in the Lord result from His love which we have experienced.

A Living Covenant With The Living God

God acted on behalf of His people and proclaimed a relationship with His people in a Covenant. The word 'covenant' occurs quite often in the Biblical narrative, even with references to covenants being made with people. For example, God commits Himself to individuals in an irrevocable permanent promise that could not be canceled with Abraham (Gen. 12:1-3), Noah (Gen. 9:16) or David (2 Sam. 7; Is. 55:3). They were unconditional.

God made this kind of covenant with Israel at Mt. Sinai, where He took the initiative, as He always does. He reminded His people of His goodness and mercy toward them and summoned them to respond with obedience. Their service to Him could be seen by their serving others. Failure to keep the covenant would spell disaster. The Sinai Covenant was one of human obligation and contained stipulations or commandments that were revocable. Disobedience on Israel's part could cause God to declare the covenant "null and void."

As New Testament Christians, our salvation was made possible by the covenant of the shedding of Christ's blood. Without blood there is no covenant with God (Lev. 17:11). In the Old Testament bloodshed was only symbolic of the blood that would be shed by Christ to bring peace with God. Hebrews 13:20 calls it, "blood of an eternal promise." On that basis God promised, "I will never abandon you or leave you...May this God of peace prepare you to do every good thing he wants. May he work in us through Jesus Christ to do what is pleasing to Him." (Heb. 13:5, 21). What God promised in the Old Testament about the New Covenant (Jer. 31:31), He inaugurated in the life and death of Jesus Christ (Mt. 26:28; Heb. 8:8; 12:24).

Based on God's promise and His irrevocable covenant, we are not building the church, but He is building it. It is His Church. We rejoice in the covenant in Christ that made us members of His Church. God made us His covenant people in our baptism, and we are continually assured of it in the Gospel and Holy Communion.

God Reveals Himself And Communicates To Us

God has definite means of communicating His saving truth to people, and His **Means of Grace** is His Word. God has chosen this way to convey His truth and grace to people.

He does not use a celestial public address system, nor speak this truth through nature; He has chosen His Word and Sacraments to convey the truth. Through these means, He forgives and changes sinful people. The Bible conveys this message through written words, and the Sacraments convey the divine promise through "visible words."

It is not only the Incarnate Word (Christ) and the written Word (Bible), but also the demonstrated Word (Christian life), the proclaimed Word (sermon), the celebrated Word (worship) and the visible Word (Sacraments) that carry the message of salvation as a means of grace by God to people. This is how God communicates with us.

Communicating Through The Written Word

God utilizes the Bible to reveal Himself, drawing back the curtains that separate Himself and humanity. He reveals the truth about His relationship to creation in general and to people in particular. He reveals what He has done for mankind and what He wants people to believe about Him and do for Him. For living the Christian life, God tells by Law and Gospel the principles which are to direct and determine our thoughts, words and deeds.

We learn Who God is, how He acts, why He acts the way He does and what His plans and purposes are for all of history and for our lives. His written Word (as the Sacraments) is His presence among us. The Bible is God's letter to the human race, telling people that He is love and that He has devised a plan to help people overcome injustice, suffering and eternal death.

How do we know God? He has given us His Word to reveal Himself and to communicate to us. But how can we know what is authentic? How can we trust it?

"Your words are truth" (Jn. 17:17). "...No prophecy ever originated from humans. Instead, it was given by the Holy Spirit as humans spoke under God's direction" (2 Pet. 1:21). "When you received God's word from us, you realized it wasn't the word of humans. Instead, you accepted it for what it really is — the word of God" (1 Thes. 2:13). "God spoke through the prophets in the Old Testament and the apostles in the New Testament" (2 Pet. 3:2).

What makes the Bible so radical among all other writings? Someone has said, "It cannot be tested for truth, for it is the test of lesser truths. No light can be thrown on it, for its own Light blinds the investigators. It ends all religious speculations and demolishes all man-made religious ceremonies and sacrifices." The presence of God is not remote and distant, but the very life of God is evident in the world through the Gospel. The True God is not yet to be discovered, for He is here!

The words are God's Words, not man's (1 Cor. 2:13). The entire content is inspired or God-breathed (2 Tim. 3:16). While it was not dictation, all the words of the Bible are God's Word because the Holy Spirit taught human writers not only the thoughts but even the words they wrote (verbal inspiration).

God's word must be accepted by faith. "...Whoever goes to God must believe that God exists and that he rewards those who seek him" (Heb. 11:6). The fruit of this faith by God's grace is an enduring experience with God.

What do we mean when we say that the Bible is the written Word of God? The Bible is a revelation from God in which He reveals things which He knows and which we are incapable of learning apart from His communication with us. The entire message is an inspired, faithful and infallible record of what God intended us to know about Himself, about what He has done for our salvation, the world in which we live, our spiritual allies and adversaries and our fellow men.

Can there be such a faithful record of God's revelation? We have seen from God's Word the process that He used to convey

His message. Inspired by God means that truth is communicated only by true words.

How can we be certain of the Word when we have only copies and not the original manuscripts? Significantly, the accuracy of the Bible copies have increased during the past century rather than decreased. There had previously been many more unanswered questions than today, and we are moving in the direction of resolving textual and critical problems instead of multiplying them through new manuscripts that have been discovered. It has confirmed rather than diminished the accuracy and authority of the Bible. Certainly errors of inaccurate transcription have entered the copies, but we know that copyists are human while God Who gave the original manuscript is divine. We trust God's Word about the trustworthiness of the initial transcription by the prophets and the apostles which they received from God. The Holy Spirit enlightened their minds.

Nowhere do the Scriptures allow us to believe in the inspiration of copyists or translators or interpreters, but the Scriptures teach the inspiration of God in the original copies (called autographs). Each one spoke not by dictation, but as he was moved by the Holy Spirit. It is stated in human speech with human beings as writers, yet the product is pure, perfect and infallible.

The Holy Spirit Himself refuses to allow the existence of anything false or fallible or merely human in the Scriptures, as God originally gave them to His penmen. The Bible also forbids a theory of human reason or insistence on allowing man to be the ultimate judge of God's revelation. We dare not submit the mysteries of God to the judgment of our reason or try to raise and advance our reason to the level of divine truth. The Bible's own testimony is sufficient to indicate its highest claims.

Therefore we do not approach God's Word to contradict it by human reason. Faith is the basis for approaching the task of interpretation, whereby we derive meaning from the written Word of God. Not all approaches of interpretation are equally valid; if any approach places reason above faith, we will easily be led to misinterpretation. Interpretation must first be literal, taking the words and statements in their normally understood meaning, including picture language where it is obviously intended, not seeking to read into it some hidden or mystical concept.

Interpretation also involves cultural understanding of the history of the day in which the author wrote. We should not strip the terms down to match a human world view and culture but rather view the text in the historical setting of the original writers and readers. Interpretation must be submitted to evaluation from pertinent evidence in the Bible's context. No human opinions or extra-Biblical sources can invalidate the truth of the Scriptures. We dare not read into God's Word what we want the message to be, but rather read the text as accurately as possible to determine the author's intent. Words, grammar, context and cross references are major considerations.

The Word of God is a very powerful instrument that has tremendous effect on life: "God's word is living and active. It is sharper than any two-edged sword and cuts as deep as the place where soul and spirit meet, the place where joints and marrow meet. God's word judges a person's thoughts and intentions" (Heb.4:12). The Bible should not leave a single part of our life untouched, for it can lift us, scare us, crush us and take us apart before it puts us back together. Most of all, its message of Gospel will save us and bring us into the merciful presence of our Father in heaven. It pulsates with life. Facts about true geography and true history may be interesting, but the true nature of the Bible is the message of grace, of Law and Gospel, of judgment and love.

God's Word not only refers to another time, another life and another world. Its relevance is not only for death, but also for this life. While the Word does look beyond this world, it also looks deeply into this world, rescuing us from its traps and pitfalls. It enlightens our minds so that we avoid spending our emotional energies on trivialities while remaining apathetic about the serious tragedies that afflict the human family. Darkness and obscurity find their solution in a search for God which can be satisfied only in the Word.

God's Word alone will provide the values and power for us to make proper decisions in moral conflict, personal problems, human relationships and responsibilities. By the Holy Spirit, the

Word will convict us with the realization that God really exists, that He really cares, and that His love requires a response. By grace we as believers accept the external Word of God because the Holy Spirit has spoken an internal word of confirmation in our heart and mind.

God's Word is food for the soul (Job 23:12). It is a light in darkness (Ps. 119:105). It is a powerful influence (Jer. 23:29). It purifies the life (Jn. 15:3). It is a saving power (Rom. 1:16).

Daniel March wrote,

> *"The Bible is the oldest and the newest of books. It surveys the whole field of time, and it looks farthest into the infinite depths of eternity. It lends the most vivid and absorbing interest to the scenes and events of the past, and it keeps us in the most active sympathy with the time in which we live. It gives us the most reliable record of what has been, and it affords us our only means of knowing what is yet to be. It is so conservative as to make it a solemn duty to study and revere the past, and it is so progressive as to be in advance of the most enlightened age. It is strict enough to denounce the very shadow and semblance of sin, and it is liberal enough to save the chiefest of sinners. It is full of God, and must therefore be read with a pure heart or its true glory will not be seen. It is full of man, and must therefore always be interesting and instructive to all who would know themselves."*

Summary Of God's Message In The Old And New Testaments

The Bible is divided into the Old Testament (before Christ) and the New Testament (after Christ). The Old Testament is the history of God's people, the Children of Israel, and it contains various prophetic promises of a coming Savior, who was Jesus Christ. The New Testament gives an account of the earthly life, suffering, death and resurrection of Jesus Christ, together with an account of the Church of Jesus Christ.

Overview Of The Old Testament

I. The Five Books of Moses

1. *Genesis* is the book of origins, providing an account of the origin of the universe, the human race. It records the early history of God's Chosen People, which includes the promise of a Savior.

2. *Exodus* records the bondage, deliverance and beginnings of Israel on the way to Canaan under Moses' leadership.

3. *Leviticus* is the book of laws concerning morals, cleanliness, food, and sacrifices to have access to God.

4. *Numbers* tells of Israel's pilgrimage in the 40 years' wandering in the wilderness.

5. *Deuteronomy* is a repetition of the laws given shortly before Israel entered Canaan.

II. The Twelve Historical Books

1. *Joshua* is a record of the conquest of Canaan under Joshua, and of the division of the land among the 12 tribes.

2. *Judges* is a history of the six times Israel was conquered, and of the various deliverances through 15 judges.

3. *Ruth* conveys the beautiful story of Ruth, from whom David and Jesus Christ descended.

4 & 5. *1 and 2 Samuel* are the history of Samuel, revealing the early years of the monarchy in Israel under the rule of Saul and David.

6 & 7. *1 and 2 Kings* are the early history of the kingdom of Israel and of the divided kingdom, and the appearance of two godly characters: Elijah and Elisha.

8 & 9. *1 and 2 Chronicles* are a record of the reigns of David, Solomon and the kings of Judah up to the time of the Captivity.

10. *Ezra* is a record of the return of the Jews from Captivity and of the rebuilding of the temple.

11. *Nehemiah* is an account of the rebuilding of the walls of Jerusalem and the re-establishing of the sacred ordinances.

12. *Esther* is a story of Queen Esther's deliverance of the Jews from the plot of Hamaan, and the establishment of the Feast called Purim.

III. The Five Poetic Books

1. *Job* tells of the problem of affliction, the patience of Job in the face of the maliciousness of the devil, the vanity of human thought, the need for divine wisdom and the final deliverance of the sufferer.

2. *Psalms* is a collection of 150 spiritual songs, poems and prayers used through the centuries by Jews and by the church for worship and devotions, many of them written by David.

3. *Proverbs* is a collection of moral and religious rules and discourses on wisdom, temperance, justice and many other topics.

4. *Ecclesiastes* presents reflections on the futility of life, together with our duties and obligations to God.

5. *Song of Songs* is a religious poem which symbolizes the mutual love of Christ and the church.

IV. The Seventeen Prophetic Books

THE FIVE MAJOR PROPHETS

1. *Isaiah*, the great prophet of redemption, is a book rich in messianic prophecies, mingled with misfortunes and griefs pronounced on sinful nations.

2. *Jeremiah*, the weeping prophet, lived from the time of Josiah to the Captivity, having the main theme of backsliding, bondage and restoration of the Jews.

3. *Lamentations* is a series of sad cries by Jeremiah, bewailing the afflictions of Israel.

4. *Ezekiel* is a book of striking metaphors which vividly portray the sad condition of God's people, and the way to gain future exultation and glory.

5. *Daniel* is a book of personal biography and prophetic visions concerning events in both secular and sacred history.

THE TWELVE MINOR PROPHETS

1. *Hosea* is filled with striking metaphors describing the sins of the people showing the apostasy of Israel, which is characterized as spiritual adultery.

2. *Joel* urges national repentance and its blessed result, calling it "the day of the Lord," showing that a time of divine judgment may be transformed into a season of blessing.

3. *Amos*, the herdsman prophet, a courageous reformer, denounces selfishness and sin through a series of visions.

4. *Obadiah* tells of the doom of Edom and final deliverance of Israel.

5. *Jonah*, the "reluctant missionary," learned the lesson of obedience and the depth of divine mercy through his bitter experience.

6. *Micah* presents a dark picture of the moral condition of Israel and Judah, but foretells the establishment of a messianic kingdom in which righteousness will prevail.

7. *Nahum* reveals the destruction of Nineveh and the promise of deliverance of Judah from Assyria.

8. *Habbakuk*, written in the Babylonian period, presents the mysteries of divine providence as to why a just God can allow a wicked nation to oppress Israel.

9. *Zephaniah*, with its somber tone and threatenings, relates a vision of the future glory of Israel.

10. *Haggai* scolded the people for slackness in building the second temple, but promised a return of God's glory when the building was completed.

11. *Zechariah* helped arouse the Jews to rebuild the temple, sharing a series of eight visions and telling of the ultimate triumph of God's kingdom.

12. *Malachi* is a graphic picture of the closing history of the Old Testament, showing the necessity of reform before the coming of the Messiah.

Overview Of The New Testament

I. The Four Biographical Books — the Gospels

1. *Matthew*, one of the 12 Apostles, stressing the Kingdom of Christ, shows Jesus to be the kingly Messiah of Jewish prophecy.

2. *Mark* emphasizes the supernatural power of Christ and His acts over nature, disease, and demons exorcised for the good of man.

3. *Luke*, "the beloved physician," presents the most complete biography of Jesus. It portrays Him as the Son of Man, full of compassion for sinners, poor people and women.

4. *John*, "the beloved disciple," reveals Jesus as the Son of God and records His deeper teachings.

II. One Historical Book

The Acts of the Apostles with Luke as author is a sequel to the Gospel of Luke with the theme being the origin and growth of the Early Church, from the Ascension of Christ to the imprisonment of Paul in Rome.

III. The Thirteen Letters of Paul

1. *Romans* (to Rome) is first a masterful exposition of Law and Gospel to show the need for and the nature of the plan of salvation, and offers exhortations related to spiritual, social and civic duties.

2. *1 Corinthians* (to Corinth) tells of the cleansing of the church from various evils, together with doctrinal instructions.

3. *2 Corinthians* characterizes an apostolic ministry and the vindication of Paul's apostleship.

4. *Galatians* is a defense of Paul's apostolic authority and of the doctrine of justification by faith, with warnings against false teachers and reverting to Judaism.

5. *Ephesians* is an exposition of the glorious plan of salvation, emphasizing that all barriers between Jews and Gentiles are broken down.

6. *Philippians* is a love letter to that church which reveals Paul's intense devotion to Christ, his joyful experience in prison, and his deep concern that the church should be steadfast in sound doctrine.

7. *Colossians* tells of the transcendent glory of Christ as the Head of the Church, calling for abandoning all worldly philosophy and sin.

8. *1 Thessalonians* is composed of apostolic commendations, reminiscences, counsels and exhortations. A special emphasis is given to comforting, and hope of the final coming of Christ.

9. *2 Thessalonians*, a sequel to the first, is written to enlighten the church concerning the doctrine of Christ's second coming and to warn believers about unrest and social disorders.

10. *1 Timothy* provides counsel to the young pastor concerning his conduct and ministerial work.

11. *2 Timothy*, written shortly before Paul's death, gives instructions and counsel to his "true son in the faith."

12. *Titus* gives counsel and exhortation to a trusted friend who is pastor in a difficult place, emphasizing especially the doctrine of good works.

13. *Philemon* is written to a man of that name, beseeching him to receive and forgive Onesimus, a runaway slave.

IV. The Eight General Letters

1. *Hebrews* tells of the transcendent glory of Christ and of the blessings of the new dispensation, compared with those of the Old Testament.

2. *James* is addressed to Jewish converts and emphasizes practical faith, which manifests itself in good works as contrasted with mere profession.

3. *1 Peter*, written by Peter to encourage saints scattered throughout Asia Minor, tells of the privilege of believers, following the example of Christ, to have victory in the midst of trials and to live holy lives in an unholy world.

4. *2 Peter* is a warning against false teachers and scoffers.

5. *1 John* is a deep spiritual message from the Apostle John to different classes of believers in the church, laying great stress on the believer's privilege of spiritual knowledge, the duty of fellowship and brotherly love.

6. *2 John* is a brief message on divine truth and worldly error, warning against heresy and false teachers.

7. *3 John* contains character sketches of certain persons in the church.

8.   *Jude* provides historic examples of apostasy and divine judgments, with warnings against immoral teachers.

V. *One Prophetic Book*

Revelation, written by the Apostle John, is a series of prophetic visions dealing with events in religious history. It portrays a great moral conflict between divine and satanic powers, ending in the victory of the Lamb.

Law And Gospel

The two main teachings or doctrines of the Bible are Law and Gospel. The Law tells us what to do (Ex. 34:11; Lev. 19:2), and what we are not to do (Deut. 5:11). It informs us that we have sinned (Rom. 3:20), and that we are condemned because of our sin (Deut. 27:26). It teaches us that we are all sinners who deserve God's punishment of death and damnation. The Law acts as a mirror to show our sins, as a curb to discourage sinful action, and as a guide to show us the will of God for our lives.

The Gospel shows God's love for us and what He has done and continues to do for us. While the Law shows us our sins, the Gospel shows us our Savior. The Law tells us what to do and what not to do; the Gospel tells what God has done and still does for our salvation and for strength for Christian living. While the Law and Gospel are to be used with all people, the Law is to be presented especially to unrepentant sinners; the Gospel is to be presented especially to sinners who are troubled because of their sins.

The Law as a mirror may reveal a dirty face, but it cannot wash it. The Law serves to reveal to man his shortcomings, but it lacks the power to change him and make him whole. Only the Gospel absolves and cleanses and empowers. Two great principles are operative: the Law of God and the grace of God.

Compare the Law and Gospel in the way they affect and influence us:

Law	Gospel
Bad News	Good News
Lost	Found
Destroys	Heals
Self-righteous	Christ-righteous
Works on behavior	Works on the heart that directs behavior
Makes people sad, mad, bad	Makes people glad
Condemned by God's justice	Saved by God's grace
Freezes the heart	Thaws the heart
Weight is on man	Weight is on God
Puts a man on his own (do something)	Puts a man in Christ (faith)
Obedience to commands	Faith in promises
Multiplies sin	Erases sin
Keeps in slavery	Makes us free

Believers do not gain assurance of justification from seeking to keep the Law, but from embracing God's mercy in Christ. Because of Christ's sacrifice, the Law does not lose its force against the Christian because the commands are an inferior or faulty form of ethical demand, but because its requirements have been fully met for the Christian by Christ. The Law is still an expression of the will of God in the sense of being a guide. The Law is not discarded by Christ but is seen from a new perspective: under grace it becomes a guide as the "standards of the Spirit, who gives life through Christ Jesus..." (Rom. 8:2) Our response to God's love is to seek to be obedient to the Law.

The Law signifies the command of God, while the Gospel refers to the promise of God. While the Law condemns and accuses, the Gospel saves and heals. The Gospel sets us free from the curse of the Law.

The Gospel contradicts all required ceremonies, rituals legalistic and moralistic demands. The Gospel does away with external requirements for salvation, but not the demands of the Law. Jesus said that He had come not to abolish the Law and the

Prophets but to fulfill them (Mt. 5:15). The imperatives of the Gospel deepen rather than relax the demands of the Law. Grace in which promise and command are united supersede the Law that promotes sin and death because of our incapability or unwillingness to obey the dictates of God. Thus we do not overthrow the Law, but by our faith uphold the Law (Rom. 3:31). Our righteousness does not come by the Law, but by the grace of God.

When we are self-satisfied or arrogant, we need to hear the Law as the word of judgment and condemnation. When we are in agony because of our sin, we need to hear the promise of mercy given in the Gospel, which then sends us back to the Law as a guide for righteous living. When we are tempted to take the law into our own hands, we need to hear the threat of the higher Law that holds us accountable before God. The Ten Commandments are a moral form or code of the Law of God.

Only the Gospel of Christ's love for us gives us the power and motivation to perform the Law, even though only partially. We are justified by faith, but for doing good works (Eph. 2:8-10). The Gospel sets us free to obey God. It also releases us from moralism which says, "Here is a rule, keep it." For grace says, "Here is God, be like Him!"

The Law and Gospel form an inseparable but at the same time paradoxical unity. Both have their source in Divine Revelation, but they appear to stand in conflict against each other. This tension is resolved in Jesus Christ, which cannot be understood by reason but only grasped by faith.

The Gospel apart from the Law becomes cheap grace, and the Law apart from the Gospel results in work righteousness. The unity of Law-Gospel is seen as the Law drives us to the Gospel, and the Gospel through forgiveness points the Christian to the Law for guidance for life. The Law points us to the Gospel that we may be justified, while the Gospel sends us to the Law to inquire what our duty is.

Apart from the Gospel, the Law gives a misunderstanding rather than a true picture of the Christian hope. The Law by itself can arouse feelings of unworthiness, but it cannot lead us to confess that we are sinners or know that we are loved by God. It can remind us of our guilt but only with the Gospel can the Law convict us of our sins. Not until we know Jesus Christ are we really confronted with the full significance of the Law. When we discover that it was our sins that sent Jesus to the cross, then the Gospel moves us to repentance and faith. True repentance does not result from a fear of God's wrath, but from a Gospel awareness of God's love and forgiveness in Christ.

Shaped By His Word (Information-Spiritual Formation)

It is important to discover the relevance of Biblical doctrine to everyday life, its challenges and its problems. No Biblical subject is too deep or complicated to study in clear and creative formulations for the purpose of helping to grow in knowledge, grace, faith and Christian living. The Bible is more than a credo. It is a life-changing message: "...You will be able to determine what is best..." (Phil. 1:9-10). Biblical knowledge provides benefits toward reality in faith, brings values for our decisions, gives stability during testing and temptation, equips us to handle the truth correctly and to detect and correct error, and gives us confidence for our daily lives.

Those who study the Bible for purely intellectual reasons or for being able to debate Biblical truths need to be reminded of 1 Corinthians 3:18, "Don't deceive yourselves. If any of you think you are wise in the ways of this world, you should give up that wisdom in order to become really wise." The Bible is not only able to make us wise unto personal salvation, but also leads us to spiritual maturity and fruitful service.

Mere information and head knowledge about the Bible are totally insufficient. Spiritual formation, the inner development of character in a believer, is a major concern of Bible study. Spiritual formation is the process of being conformed to the image of Christ. This is not an option, something for Christian enthusiasts or a pursuit for the pious only.

Spiritual formation is moving from knowing to being to doing. It involves informing the mind and forming the life. Information also involves being "in formation." One of the vital dynamics of a Christian is to be formed spiritually in every action, in every response made, in every relationship experienced, in every thought held and in every emotion lived.

Spiritual formation means that our minds will be renewed by the Holy Spirit and conformed to the Spirit of Christ: "...change the way you think...every person must make his own decision...However, we have the mind of Christ" (Rom. 12:2; 14:5; 1 Cor. 2:16). This means that we reflect more Christ-like characteristics in our personalities, actions and everyday relationships. We increasingly recognize the power and presence of Christ in our lives and in our tasks.

Christ wants to develop us to our full potentials. Are we willing to be developed by God in accordance with His working through His Word to shape us according to His plan? As we study His Word, we should pray that we will adopt Biblical values, accept the challenges of the times in which we live, and fit our unique gifts and personal development into a productive pattern of life.

There are five points of reception in a person that God uses to communicate with people:

1. The Mind. God can illuminate our minds through His Word to see Him and to grasp the meaning of our lives more clearly.

2. The Will. God can touch our wills (hearts) by inspiring us with new hopes and giving us the willingness and the strength needed to serve despite our weakness.

3. The Emotions. God can reach us through our emotions or feelings by His precious Gospel and the gentle touch of His loving care and power.

4. The Imagination. We can receive the impulse of God's grace in our imaginations. Though this can easily be misdirected, by grace through knowledge of the Word we can gain a visual imagination of God's love for us.

5. The Memory. The memory is another channel of human reception as God stimulates our stored memory to recall previous experiences of His love and to prevent us from repeating previous mistakes.

Spiritual formation means that we are objects of nurturing in God's Word as we are recipients of His love and mercy, willingly opening ourselves to learning His truth and His way by the guidance of the Holy Spirit. Instead of being the subjects who control the objects of the world, we are the objects of the loving purposes of God Who seeks to guide us toward maturity. We are not the controllers who bring about the desired results in our lives, but we allow the Spirit to act in our lives to bring about God's purposes. Thus our aim is not to be gratified for self-centered ends, but rather we desire to yield to the will of God. Instead of being our own production manager, we are God's workmanship maturing in faith for good works (Eph. 2:10). Indeed, we become God's resource distributors.

God communicates with us not only for information but also for spiritual formation. We go beyond asking, "Where did all this start?" and go on to face the question, "To what is this leading?" Our focus is not just on the last or next 24 hours, but rather on the last 24 centuries and the next 24 years. This study is not just a splattering of religious facts; it is a pause and a concentration on each one of us as inheritors of a world history dating back to the Creation that will continue until the day of Christ's coming. Our minds center on the activity of God all over the world from the beginning until the end as it relates to our individual lives.

The God of Abraham, Isaac, Jacob, Sarah, Ruth, Rebekkah, Matthew, Mark, Luke, Mary, Martha and Priscilla is the God of history. Now we are part of God's story to work out His plan at this point of time.

As our Bibles are opened and read, God communicates to us. We must approach the Bible with the spirit of Psalm 119:18: "Uncover my eyes so that I may see the miraculous things in your teachings." We need to realize that God will open our mind: "However, the helper, the Holy Spirit, whom the Father will send in my name, will teach you everything. He will remind you of everything that I have ever told you" (Jn. 14:26). "Now, we didn't receive the spirit that belongs to the world. Instead, we received the Spirit who comes from God so that we could know the things which God has freely given us" (1 Cor. 2:12). Reading and studying the Bible consistently and systematically allows God to direct us into all truth.

Baptism And Its Eternal Benefits

God shows us His love and miraculous power through baptism. Tragically, Christianity has become divided on the benefits of baptism which is commanded by God. The basic question is, "How does God deal with man?" The **initiative** of action is always God's. He calls and man is to respond. He offers and man is to receive. He commands and man is to obey.

Jesus commanded baptism in Matthew 28:19, "So wherever you go, make disciples of all nations: Baptize them in the name of the Father, and of the Son, and of the Holy Spirit."

The differences in understanding baptism have sprung from a misunderstanding of how God works in the life of a sinful human being. Does God work apart from His stated means? Does man have a part in performing God's saving work? This is the **basic question**: "Is baptism God's action toward man (Gospel) or man's response to God (Law)?" The Scriptures show clearly that baptism is initiated as God's action, not man's action. Baptism is the **beginning** of God's action of grace and love in a person's life, not the end. Baptism is **pure Gospel** — God's loving action toward undeserving and helpless sinful human beings. The human part is to respond.

Baptism is a real event of God's mercy, power and presence, **ordained by God**, not by man. It is not first an act of believing man, but an **act of God** (grace). It is more than a response and an act of obedience of man (Law). It is not merely a **symbol** or **representation** of some spiritual power, but it **is** God's power in the **washing of regeneration** which joins a person with Christ and into God's family. Baptism is God's means of uniting us with Him and to each other.

The Bible Tells Of The Benefits Of Baptism

How do we know that baptism is not ordinary water only, but is properly understood in God's command and used together with God's Word, rather than merely a symbolic act? What is the real purpose of baptism? Why does everyone need baptism? Are special blessings connected with baptism?

The Bible's teaching regarding the need, nature and benefits of baptism include:

1. All people have inherited sin and are sinful by birth, stand guilty before God, and are condemned eternally if they do not receive God's means to remove that guilt. "Indeed, I was born guilty. I was a sinner when my mother conceived me" (Ps. 51:5). "So sin came into the world through one person, and death came through sin. Death spread to everyone, because everyone sinned" (Rom. 5:12). Once slaves to sin (Rom. 6:6), now instruments of righteousness (Rom. 6:13).

2. Our baptism washes us clean and makes us holy before God, a washing of regeneration. Through our baptism we are saved, declared not guilty and receive the full benefits of all Christ did for us as a free gift of God. "...But you have been washed and made holy, and you have received God's approval in the name of the Lord Jesus Christ and in the Spirit of our God" (1 Cor. 6:11). "...Washing it using water along with spoken words" (Eph. 5:23). "...Noah...eight in all were saved by water. Baptism, which is like that water, now saves you. Baptism doesn't save by removing dirt from the body. Rather, baptism is a request to God for a clear conscience. It saves you through Jesus Christ, who came back from death to life. (1 Pet. 3:20-21). "...he saved us through the washing in which the Holy Spirit gives us new birth and renewal..." (Titus 3:5).

3. Through our baptism we have participated in the burial of Christ. Our old inherited life of slavery to sin is dead and buried; we died with Christ and no longer need to fear death, for we have actually passed from death to life spiritually. This is an actual participation in an historical event of Christ's death. Our old man is put down and we are now dead to sin's power; sin no longer has dominion over us. "This happened when you were placed in the tomb with Christ through baptism. In baptism you were also brought back to life with Christ through faith in the power of God, who brought him back to life. You were once dead because of your failures and your uncircumcised corrupt nature. But God made you alive with Christ when he forgave all our failures" (Col. 2:12-13). "If we have died with Christ, we believe that we will

also live with him...So consider yourselves dead to sin's power but living for God in the power Christ Jesus gives you...as people who have come back from death and are now alive..." (Rom. 6:9, 11, 13). "... all of us who were baptized into Christ Jesus were baptized into his death" (Rom. 6:3).

4. Through our baptism we have participated in the resurrection of Christ and have been raised from spiritual death to a new life totally by God's power. "...all of us who were baptized into Christ Jesus...As Christ was brought back from death to life by the glorious power of the Father, so we, too, should live a new kind of life. If we've become united with him in a death like his, certainly we will also be united with him when we come back to life as he did" (Rom. 6:3, 4-5).

5. At our baptism we received Christ Himself as a garment or a covering. This garment identifies us as children of God, heirs of God's promises and eternal life. We were adopted into God's family and became part of Christ's body, the one holy church through baptism. "By one Spirit we were all baptized into one body..." (1 Cor. 12:13). "Clearly, all of you who were baptized in Christ's name have clothed yourselves with Christ" (Gal. 3:27). "... so that we would be adopted as his children" (4:5). "...as Christ loved the church and gave his life for it. He did this to make the church holy by cleansing it, washing it using water along with spoken words" (Eph. 5:25-26).

6. Because of our baptism and indwelling of the Holy Spirit, we have power over the devil and our sinful flesh. At our baptism we receive the Holy Spirit, not in part, but in full measure, and no further baptism is required or is beneficial. "...We, who have the Spirit as the first of God's gifts..." (Rom. 8:23). "But you have been washed and made holy...in the name of the Lord Jesus Christ and in the Spirit of our God" (1 Cor. 6:11). "By one Spirit we were all baptized into one body..." (1 Cor. 12:13). "He saved us through the washing in which the Holy Spirit gives us new birth and renewal" (Titus 3:5).

7. Our baptism causes us to live our life now under God's grace rather than under the law. "Certainly, sin shouldn't have power over you because you're not controlled by laws, but by God's favor" (Rom. 6:14).

8. Because of our baptism we can and should be instruments of God, sanctified, useful to Him in serving others and telling others how they can have a right relationship with God. "Never offer any part of your body to sin's power. No part of your body should ever be used to do any ungodly thing. Instead, offer yourselves to God as people who have come back from death and are now alive. Offer all the parts of your body to God. Use them to do everything that God approves of" (Rom. 6:13).

The heart of baptism is the Word of promise, and only faith can receive such a promise. Such faith is the gift of the Holy Spirit. It is a miracle of grace.

How Much Water Is Required?

The Word of God is the power and the water is the symbol in baptism. Those who insist that immersion is the only right way to baptize say that "Romans 6:4 is a **literal burial** in water." However, they do violence to that verse because they cut a phrase in half and are not obedient to the sense of the full verse. That Scripture says that "when we were baptized into His death, we were buried with Him..." They do not bury them in the water until they are dead. To say that the word "death" is figurative or spiritual, and the word "buried" is literal or physical, makes the text ludicrous and nonsensical. This is a spiritual burial for which Christ uses visible means — water. The power is in the Word, not in the water. The water is the instrument, while the spoken Word performs the miracle of regeneration.

Others may say that when John baptized Jesus He went down into the water. But how deep? Ankle deep, knee deep, neck deep? Who knows and how can personal views be proven? Let the water be the symbol and the baptism be the reality, not vice versa. The word "baptize" means to wash (which can also be immersion), as can be seen in Mark 7:3-4, There it talks about a ceremonial washing of hands, and washing after going to the market place, and washing of cups, pitchers and kettles and other household goods.

74

Who Should Be Baptized? Everyone? Infants Too?

God's grace through baptism is the **only revealed biblical answer for children**. The Bible shows that baptism supplies the **only way children can become or be members** of the body of Christ, or else their guilt remains before God. If they are not baptized, they are not part of the body of Christ (1 Cor. 12:13). Those who deny baptism to children must call into question the means of grace, baptism for all people (Jn. 3:5-6). If it is not valid for babies, how is it valid for other people? The same logic must cancel it out for everyone. There is no other act for regeneration which God proposes for children.

Children are sinful by nature and must be born again to be saved and have the assurance of eternal life (1 Pet. 3:2; Lk. 12:15-17; Jn. 3:5-6). The entire Biblical doctrine of baptism is the basis for infant baptism. Baptism is the act to transmit the guarantee of the child's redemption. It is not an empty ritual, but a promise of the Gospel. **The Bible does not leave to the arbitrary decision of individuals or churches** whether this sacred act which Christ commissioned is valid for children (Mt. 28:19). Baptism is the recognition of the doctrine of sin and grace for **all** people, children and adults. Baptism is the way God assigns adults and children to Christ and gives them the Holy Spirit and makes them members of His Church. Baptism provides God's power to children in this unique and special way.

Infants are to be baptized because they are a part of "all peoples everywhere." Baptism is the only means God has given us by which infants can be born again. Children also need to receive the Kingdom of God by water and the Spirit, and the Holy Spirit does this through baptism which works faith in them.

Colossians 2:11-12 reminds us that circumcision performed on Israelite boys in the Old Testament has a similarity to baptism, but baptism is the circumcision of the heart. Babies in Israel did not make the decision to be circumcised, nor were they really conscious of what was happening. The parents acted on the command and promise of God. In this act they were adopted into the family of God, and although they were not conscious of this adoption, it was still a reality.

All people are born dead in sin, but how do they become spiritually alive? The Bible shows that they become alive only through baptism. Babies do not have spiritual life until baptized. It is obvious that baptism is an act in which God is acting upon man, not man merely trying to react to God. Only God can give spiritual birth, wash away sin and give saving faith, which is His loving will for persons of any age.

Normal procedure for baptism for adults was that they accepted the Word first: "Those who accepted what Peter said were baptized. That day about 3000 people were added to the group" (Acts 2:41). There are examples of children being brought by their parents (Acts 16:15, 33).

The validity or importance of infant baptism does not rest on church practices but on biblical imperatives. The demand of proof rests upon those who deny baptism to infants. **Where is the exception stated in the Bible**? God indicates that in Holy Communion there are to be exceptions (they are to be able to "examine themselves"), but no such restrictions are stated in baptism. The belief clause is not restrictive to allow baptism to follow faith when all the texts are considered.

The church father Origen (185-254 A.D.) wrote: "The Church receives from the apostles the injunction to give baptism even to infants..." **The interpretation of "adults only" baptism was introduced later and apparently always remained a minority position or opposition viewpoint**. The Universal Church never elevated "adults only" baptism to a doctrine of the church. There has been no time in history when infant baptism has not been practiced, having begun at Christ's time. "Adults only" baptism was introduced along the way as an opposition view, a minority view introduced with arguments by reason, not clear Scripture.

When Jesus says that adults are to receive the kingdom as little children, by what Scripture should we disqualify children from that Kingdom which they enter by the baptismal grace to which Jesus invites them? Man's questions or doubts are human argumentations and can never outweigh Christ's Great Commission to baptize all nations (including infants). God's Word nowhere makes a distinction between adults and children for receiving His grace,

He even adds in Acts 2:39 that the **baptism promise is also "to your children."**

If not in baptism, **when and how do children become regenerate (saved)**? If they are automatically saved until the age of 12, **how do they become unregenerate (unsaved) at that time**? The human pious opinion repeals God's justice and limits His love on the basis of human reason, thus violating His Word which we studied in the previous 8 Biblical points. What a terrible thing of God to dump sin and guilt on children at a humanly suggested "age of accountability" if He had held it back allegedly until that time (which is only a human notion).

What is the Biblical basis for an "age of accountability"? Infant innocence does not fit the facts of life or the fits of anger in the life of a one year old, or of the plain statements of the Bible. Children do not become sinners by sinning, but they **sin** because they are **sinners**. They rebel against their parents because they are sinners. Therefore, they are in need of grace through baptism as seen in John 3:5-6, "No one can enter the kingdom of God without being born of water and the Spirit. Flesh and blood give birth to flesh and blood, but the Spirit gives birth to things that are spiritual."

How are infants saved since they have original sin? As baptism is a miracle in adults, so it is in infants. Romans 5:1, 12 and 8:1 show that the human being is justified by faith. Baptism is the only means God has revealed to work faith in a child. Because the baby cannot yet verbally express that faith, does not disprove God's Word. Most five-year-olds can express faith in Christ, so why discriminate against them by those who deny baptism to children until the arbitrary age of 12? John 3:5-6 records that Jesus said that He was telling the truth that no one (children were not an exception) can enter the kingdom of God unless he is born of water and of the Spirit. He continued, "...but the Spirit gives birth to things that are spiritual."

No one would debate that a baby's entrance into the world is by physical birth, and no one dare contradict Jesus here when He says that entrance into the spiritual world is by water and the Spirit (baptism). When Jesus told about the wind blowing wherever it pleases and that you can hear it but not see it, the same is true of baptism, as much a mystery but just as much a reality.

Some even go so far as to say that it is a sin to baptize children. If baptism of children is a sin, why does the Bible not warn against it? Is it a transgression of the law? No law is violated. Failure to baptize is not only contrary to the Great Commission but also to other clear words of God. Baptism declares, signifies and seals what God has done, does and will do for me, not what I do for Him. It is primarily a seal of God's work, a regenerating work of the Holy Spirit, not a decision of faith on the part of man to receive a blessing. That is why God never dictates the amount of water required or the age of the person who is a candidate for baptism.

Baptism spiritually means everything that water means physically: cleansing and health. Baptism is the external evidence of God's presence among His people. We are not saved by baptism but by grace through faith, which is mediated by baptism. Baptism is God's method to dispense that grace. Without that grace, no person, not even a baby, can stand before the Judgment Seat of God justified and declared righteous.

Let baptism be a daily reminder of the dying to our sins and arising to holy service to God. Our baptism gives us a daily dying and resurrection. There are no shortcuts or substitutes for this daily dying. Baptism is a power to salvation, and also to sanctification.

Thank God that baptism is His action, not man's. If it were man's, we would forever have to doubt the efficacy of our baptism. God leaves no doubt that He has acted for **all** creatures, so that all are to be brought to baptism. This does not mean that one who has been baptized cannot fall away from God. Some who are baptized can and do lose their faith, for "whoever does not believe will be condemned" (Mk. 16:16).

Our baptism reminds us that day by day our new nature is to arise as from the dead to live in righteousness and purity by God's grace. Our baptism gives us this desire and power because the blessings that Christ gives here strengthen us and lead us to want to thank Him with our whole life. Truly, God communicates to the Christian in baptism.

The Lord's Supper

God also communicates with believers through the Lord's Supper. He offers us great gifts in this communion with Him.

Immediately before His betrayal on Maundy Thursday, Jesus met with His disciples in an upper room in Jerusalem to celebrate the Passover meal (Lk. 22:19-20; 1 Cor. 11:23-25). He replaced that meal with a new and better Meal, which He commanded the disciples to celebrate often in remembrance of Him. This is called the Lord's Supper. Other names are Holy Communion, the Lord's Table, the Sacrament of the Altar and Eucharist.

Jesus is present both as the Giver and the Gift in, with and under the bread and wine (Mk. 14:22, 24). Since He stated that the bread and wine are His Body and Blood, we speak of this presence as the **Real Presence**.

It is a spiritual meal in which Paul says that whoever eats the bread and drinks the wine in an unworthy manner will be guilty of sinning against the body and blood of Jesus (1 Cor. 11:26-28). In a natural way we receive bread and wine and with these elements by a miracle we receive His Body and Blood. Even though the bread and wine are not changed into Jesus' body and blood, by faith we know by the Scriptures that in, with and under the bread and wine, we receive the true body and blood of Christ. Paul tells us that we participate in the body and blood of Christ when we receive the bread and wine (1 Cor. 10:16). The bread and wine are supernatural bearers of Christ's body and blood.

The benefits of Holy Communion are forgiveness of sins and assurance of eternal life (Mt. 26:26-28). There is a power in it because God's Word of promise is connected with it. Through His Word in Holy Communion, Jesus strengthens our faith as we trust His promise and make the blessings of this sacrament our own. We are to do this often.

We prepare ourselves to receive Holy Communion in a worthy way by examining ourselves beforehand (1 Cor. 11:28). This is very important because we are warned that we can eat and drink unworthily and be guilty of sinning against the body and blood of the Lord, thus bringing judgment on ourselves (1 Cor.

11:27, 29). Proper preparation requires us to go in faith and to have hearts that believe and desire the forgiveness of sins. We are careful about whom we invite to receive Holy Communion because we do not want those who commune to bring God's judgment on themselves by receiving it in an unworthy manner.

The Lord's Supper is instituted as God's action prompting man's response. With the promise of forgiveness of sins, the Lord's Supper is more than a mere memorial which we conduct. It is rather a continuing occasion for Christ to share His grace effectively with believers.

Living With God Through Worship

A Christian's relationship with God embraces the entire life. There is much more to Christianity than the habit of going to church for an hour on Sunday for worship. Some people unfortunately equate Christianity with merely "going to church."

Christians are baptized into the family of God which gathers together regularly for worship. God commands His people to worship (Ps. 100). This worship carries a blessing for God's people, for it leads them to think about, listen to and talk to God.

Worship, whether formal or informal, is a major obligation of God's people. It is an adoration of God, a confession of our sins, and praising Him for His mercy and forgiveness. It is a celebration of God's supreme worth, as His "worthiness" is extolled. Worship means to give worth to someone. Thus we come to God with a sense of His holiness and awesomeness — His worth.

Worship is directed at One who is the source of our lives. Worship results from knowing God, His mercy and love. We worship God because of Who He is and what He has done for us, and because of the relationship we have with Him. Right worship is founded upon a right relationship with God. Our worship expresses the fact that we belong to God fully and without reservation (Rom. 12:1).

If one does not have a strong conviction for worship, the solution is not to work up feelings of love, gratitude and awe toward God to gain a certain spiritual or emotional condition. Rather we should engage in a deeper Bible study and understanding of Who God is and what He has done for us in Christ. Our worship of God flows from these realities.

We need to take the focus off ourselves and place it on God. Furthermore, we should not focus exclusively on weekly church services or an isolated religious act performed once a week, but build worship into every part of our life day by day. Rich intake of God's Word will make worship an informal daily experience rather than only a formal weekly affair. Reverence for and worship of God comes from an intimate knowledge and relationship with Him.

Some expressions of worship in the Bible are vocal expressions of singing with one voice (2 Chron. 5:15), singing antiphonally (Ex. 15:21), singing with the Spirit (Eph. 5:19), shouting (Ps. 47:1) and silence (Ps. 46:10). There is physical expression of reverence and adoration in kneeling (Ps. 95:6), bowing down (Ps. 95:6), raising hands (Ps. 63:4), and standing (Ps. 134:1). There is instrumental expression through harps, lyres and the cymbals (1 Chron. 25:1), musical instruments such as trumpets (2 Chron.7:6), and stringed instruments and flutes (Ps. 150). There are liturgical expressions such as the Psalms, the Gloria in Excelsis (Lk. 2:14), the Magnificat (Lk. 1:46-55), the Benedictus (Lk. 1:6-78), and the Nunc Dimittis (Lk. 2:29-32). There is sacramental expression through the Lord's Supper (1 Cor. 11:17-34).

True worship must always be directed towards the Living God. It is not a performance in order to display the talents of pastors, of singers or of anyone else. The focus must be on fellowship with God.

Worship allows for a time of confession where assurance is given of forgiveness of sins. It is a time of silence or quiet, where we withdraw from the business of life to center attention on God. Some silent meditation balances out constant talking and noise. Joyous thanksgiving and praise also has a vital place in worship.

As God confronts us meaningfully in worship, we will be moved to rejoice and to repent. This is not a private affair, for God deals with His people in togetherness. When God's people come together for worship, they are not to keep Jesus encased inside them with contents undisclosed or so protective that our minds and hearts cannot be penetrated by the powerful Word. Being open to all that God has to offer, and awaiting the strengthening of our relationship with Him, we open our ears and raise our voices in confession, submission, supplication and praise to God. It isn't that we go to get something out of worship, but that we go to participate in worship. We do not come spiritually hard of hearing, dumb or empty-handed. Our hearts and hands are ready for sacrifice.

Beginning with the prayer, "Come, Holy Spirit," the well-planned worship is not only Biblical, but practical and usable. The service should allow the worshipers to behold God's glory and to express praise and joy.

The church service is especially for God, and we are there to give Him pleasure. How much do we value our relationship to Him: 15 minutes, one hour, two hours? How often? Only formal worship in church? What about informal worship daily?

Healthy worship is a product of healthy belief and healthy learning. The Word in our hearts will express itself in worship on our lips. A living God should receive lively praise from His people. Worship, both public and private, should be so meaningful that we regret that it is over and are always ready to come back for more.

When we stop focusing on ourselves but look to God and see all the good things that He has done, our mouths and lives will express praise and thanksgiving (Ps. 106:1). We are thankful for the gift of Christ (2 Cor. 9:15) and for Christ's power and His kingdom (Rev. 11:17).

Communication With God Through Prayer

As God speaks to us in His Word, we speak to Him through prayer. Intimacy with God is experienced through prayer, speaking to Him whose Word we have read to guide the events of our daily lives. Prayer is the breath of life that through the Word sustains the Christian life. It is not only our acknowledgment of our dependence on God, but the confession that our hope is in God, above all earthly satisfactions, and that our destiny lies only in the will of God, not in our own personal ambitions.

To say God is Lord implies our communion and fellowship with Him. Jesus showed by example and also taught His disciples to pray, commanding prayer and attaching the promise of an answer. Prayer was a dramatic part of Christ's life.

Do you long for a more satisfying prayer life? A vigorous prayer life begins with retreating from the arduous demands of daily work to a quiet retreat, then asking Jesus: "Lord, teach us to pray" (Lk. 11:1). It was Jesus' prayer life, His communion with His Father, that the disciples longed to experience. Under His tutoring, Jesus taught them to pray. As He taught them the Lord's Prayer, He warned them that they were not to pray like the hypocrites, who reserved their praying for public occasions, nor like the heathen who loaded their prayers with empty and meaningless phrases. (Mt. 6:5, 7)

As God communicates with us through His Word, so we communicate with Him through prayer.

Communication Between God And Man

↙ GOD ↘

WORD   PRAYER

↘ MAN ↗

If we do not have a dialogue with our Heavenly Father, we are having a monologue with ourselves, which makes us idols. Thus our prayers must express our sincere intimate relationship with God. We do not pray in order to change the will of God but to ask God for strength.

Prayer is a personal communion or person-to-person relationship with God. We are to pray to God for our own sake, for He does not need our prayers. We need God, and we need to pray to Him, as prayer is fellowship with Him. It reminds us that the focus of our lives must not be on ourselves, but God Himself.

How To Pray

The Bible teaches us how to pray. We are to pray in Jesus' name, not as a matter of form but in recognition that there is spiritual power in Jesus' name (Jn. 14:13-14; 16:23, 26). He is the High Priest, who "always lives to pray for them" (Heb. 7:25).

We are to ask simply in faith. "If any of you needs wisdom to know what you should do, you should ask God, and he will give it to you. God is generous to everyone and doesn't find fault with them. When you ask for something, don't have any doubts. A person who has doubts is like a wave that is blown by the wind and tossed by the sea" (Jas. 1:5-6). We should be sincere and not double-minded (Jas. 1:8).

We should not pray for wrong or selfish reasons. "When you pray for things, you don't get them because you want them for the wrong reason — for your own pleasure" (Jas. 4:3). Our prayers are not to be for gain of things or for longer life to enjoy ourselves aimlessly. James tells us that what we get should be tied to our purpose in life, not for our self-interests. Prayer is to help fulfill our ministry for God, not to enlarge our own kingdom. Our requests are to be for godly, not selfish purposes. "Those who live in me while I live in them will produce a lot of fruit...ask for anything you want, and it will be yours" (Jn. 15:5, 7).

Jesus certainly wants us to ask for earthly things, for He teaches us to pray, "Give us every day our daily bread." However, He also teaches us, "Your will be done on earth as it is in heaven." And so we make these requests within the will of God, acknowledging that the request will be granted on His terms. Spiritual concerns involve asking God for salvation, for granting increase of faith, for deeper insight into His Word, and the ability and willingness to follow Him more closely. It is God's will that we ask Him for such things, and these spiritual requests are to be unconditional. The Lord's Prayer contains petitions that something might happen in our hearts, attitudes and lives.

We are to ask as righteous disciples: "Prayers offered by those who have God's approval are effective" (Jas. 5:16). We are also to ask in faith: "...I tell you to have faith that you have already received whatever you pray for, and it will be yours" (Mk. 11:24). We are to pray without holding grudges: "Whenever you pray, forgive anything you have against anyone. Then your Father in heaven will forgive your failures" (Mk. 11:25).

The Lord's Prayer (Mt. 6:9-13) reveals some distinctive characteristics of prayer: It shows the spirit in which we should pray; it is brief yet profound; it is comprehensive, summarizing all for which we should pray; it has universal application; it indicates the priorities to be observed in prayer; it shows what means to seek and what to avoid.

Full and complete prayers can be especially beneficial when the following pattern is used in this order: Adoration, Confession, Thanksgiving, Supplication, Intercession and Submission. Memorizing these six points (ACTSIS), our prayers can follow this pattern as they include:

Adoration — Specific words of praise that reveal our awe and respect, such as, "holy, almighty, gracious, merciful God." "Praise him for his immense greatness" (Ps. 150:2). Concentrating on His majesty and greatness removes us from the earthly for these moments of prayer.

Confession — Acknowledging our sins, weaknesses, and failures. "I made my sins known to you, and I did not cover up my guilt" (Ps. 32:5). "If we confess our sins, he forgives them and cleanses us from everything we've done wrong" (1 Jn. 1:9). Confession includes genuine sorrow for our sin, admission of wrong against God and of helplessness to correct the wrong and a plea for mercy for Jesus' sake.

Thanksgiving — Thanking God for all the spiritual, material and physical blessings He has given to us and others. "Whatever happens, give thanks, because it is God's will in Christ Jesus that you do this" (1 Thes. 5:18). We say "Thank you" to God because He supplies our needs, protects us from evil that can destroy, hears our prayers, gives us salvation and His Holy Spirit to live lives pleasing to Him.

Supplication — Making requests for our own specific needs. "Never worry about anything. But in every situation let God know what you need in prayers and requests while giving thanks" (Phil. 4:6).

Intercession — Mentioning the needs of our own family, friends, neighbors, community and the entire world. "First of all, I encourage you to make petitions, prayers, intercessions, and prayers of thanks for all people" (1 Tim. 2:1). This should focus on persons, not just problems and diseases or in times of crisis.

Submission — Obedience that says, "Your will be done," to every human request. Let our will and decision comply to God's will.

The Holy Spirit helps us know our weaknesses and for what we ought to pray. "...the Spirit also helps us in our weakness, because we don't know how to pray for what we need. But the Spirit intercedes along with our groans that cannot be expressed in words. The one who searches our hearts knows what the spirit has in mind. The Spirit intercedes for God's people the way God wants him to" (Rom. 8:26-27).

Confession Is Good

Often confession goes no deeper than making a general admission that we sin like everyone else. The confession of sins in prayer should go beyond admitting our general wrongs to God. "So admit your sins to each other..." (Jas. 5:16). It is much easier to confess a sin to God than to one's neighbor. If it fills us with deep shame to confess to a confidant what is easily confessed to God, then our confession to God is in some sense unrealistic.

The encounter with a fellow Christian can help the divine encounter become more realistic and without pretense. Perhaps confession is most therapeutic or healing when the person making the confession no longer cares who knows about his or her sin because it is all taken away.

Confession is good when it opens the way to deliverance and healing through the forgiveness of sins. It is good when it gives us a deeper awareness of the sinfulness of sin. Usually there is no point in the confession being made to a wider public than to the people immediately affected by the sin, except for a confidant.

Give Thanks

It is good to begin our prayers with thanks to God, emphasizing a note of praise to God for His many blessings. "Give thanks
to the Lord because He is good, because his mercy endures forever" (Ps. 118:1). There are more things than can be counted which
give us reasons to thank Him every day.

Our selfish nature causes us to center more on "give-me"
prayers than on thanksgiving. "Whatever happens, give thanks"
(1 Thes. 5:18) suggests that no matter how bad our situation may
be, we have reason to give thanks to God (Ps. 42:5; 63:4; 86:12-13).
If we truly recognize that God is in control of our destinies, praise
will be continually flowing from our hearts and mouths (Ps.
107:8-9).

While prayer is not a means of grace, its power is great, as
we see in Mark 11:24. Yet we must know that God does not always answer "yes," but sometimes He asks us to wait. Sometimes
He says "no" when what we ask would be harmful to us. Often
God makes us the answer to our own prayers through our own
actions.

Give priority to prayer (1 Thes. 5:17). Start each day and
end each day with special prayer, together with meditation on the
Word of God. In all our prayers we are also to confess our sins to
God.

Lord's Prayer

The Lord's Prayer is worth a book in itself, as it is the most
excellent of all prayers by Jesus Himself. In the simple majesty of
this prayer we perceive the type of relationship that should exist
between our gracious God and ourselves. It suggests a closeness
and confidence that permits us to speak honestly and openly, to
share joys and sorrows and all other thoughts.

The tone and content of the Lord's Prayer reveals the spiritual emphasis of a Christian's life and the constant consideration
for others which ought to be reflected through our faith in Jesus.
Of the seven petitions, only one asks for material blessings; all the

rest are spiritual. We are encouraged to pray "Our Father" instead of "My Father" since we pray as part of and for the whole body of Christ and not simply for our own needs.

The conclusion suggests the reasons for asking all these things of God: He alone is the King from whom we seek help; He alone has the power to grant our requests; He alone shall have all glory and praise for all that He does for us. "Amen" is nothing other than an unquestioning affirmation of faith on the part of believers who know that God grants what He has promised. Prayer is asking, talking, speaking, making desires known and seeking a plan from God for our lives, and believing that He will do it.

Go Boldly To The Throne Of Grace

We are told that Jesus as our High Priest encourages prayer, knowing our inmost needs. God asks us to come to His throne of grace boldly: "We need to hold on to our declaration of faith: we have a superior chief priest who has gone through the heavens. That person is Jesus, the Son of God. We have a chief priest who is able to sympathize with our weaknesses. He was tempted in every way that we are, but he didn't sin. So we can go confidently to the throne of God's kindness to receive mercy and find kindness, which will help us at the right time" (Heb. 4:14-16).

Why go to the throne of grace? Life offers some valid and reasonable choices and alternatives. Technology offers plenty. Investments, genius of intellect, government and welfare, bank accounts, extended families —all have something positive to offer. But we come to the end of our resources with Peter and say, "Lord, to what person could we go? Your words give eternal life" (Jn. 6:68).

Only at the throne of grace are our sins washed away and no longer charged against us. There grace and mercy are found, and our guilt is taken away. Only there will strength be available to overcome our weaknesses in daily life. All of our needs — spiritual, physical, mental, emotional, material, occupational, social and all others — are met there.

God encourages us toward prayerfulness: "We pray very hard night and day that we may see you again so that we can supply whatever you still need for your faith" (1 Thes. 3:10); "Morning, noon, and night I complain and groan, and he listens to my voice" (Ps. 55:17). "Jesus used this illustration with his disciples to show them that they need to pray all the time and never give up" (Lk. 18:1). Both the Old and the New Testaments provide examples of many prayers, also many notable prayers of individuals, which demonstrate that prayer should never be underestimated.

We are to go with confidence, boldly. Timidity comes when we misunderstand, or when we try to go in our own strength and wisdom. Timidity comes when we fail to understand God's love and grace and what God offers at the throne of Christ. We have been fully accepted in Christ, and so we have full access to His throne. So we go boldly because all we need is available to us there. We go boldly because it is offered at no other place. We go boldly because there is the solution for our specific needs.

II.

LIVING WITH MYSELF

What kind of persons are we meant to be? How can we become the persons God intended us to be? How can we gain security and happiness with God as our source? The question of what we do with our lives is derived from being sons and daughters of God, growing to spiritual maturity and manifesting the fruit of the Spirit in our lives through God's power working in us. What is God's purpose for our lives and how do we fulfill it? In this chapter we will look at what God's Word tells regarding how the First Century disciples lived under God's grace. We will see the First Century message for 21st Century disciples.

The Christian Calling

Colossians 1:1-18 informs us of who we are by God's grace, to Whom we belong, what has been done for us, the unlimited power available to us, and what the Gospel has to say about the complex issues of good and evil facing us in life. We have been liberated from a self-justifying religion by God's call to be recipients and communicators of the new life in Christ through the Gospel. We are called, appointed, valued, cherished and loved by the God of heaven and earth. As such, we are God's people regardless of our rank, performance or adequacy.

Paul is concerned that Christians understand the blessings of God's call: "Then you will have deeper insight. You will know the confidence that he calls you to have and the glorious wealth that God's people will inherit. You will also know the unlimited greatness of his power as it works with might and strength for us, the believers" (Eph. 1:18-19). Paul continues in Ephesians 4:1: "...I, a prisoner in the Lord, encourage you to live the kind of life which proves that God has called you."

This calling is based upon Christ's righteousness given to

believers. Ever since creation, people have tried to work out their own righteousness and tried to do the kind of work which would make themselves look good in the sight of God. The basic cry of peoples' hearts is to be right before God. Christians, too, are tempted to work to obtain their righteousness. Righteousness is, however, obtained alone from God through faith in Jesus Christ. As seen in Ephesians 4:1, this call is also to righteous living. Everything centers in Jesus, seeking to know, believe, and love Him, and live for Him.

Christians should not ignore the Holy Spirit, nor quench Him (1 Thes. 5:19). We are powerless in our Christian life and work without the working of the Holy Spirit. The call and power of the Holy Spirit is to learn of Jesus, to follow, to be with, and to commit ourselves to Him. To say "no" to God in any way is a contradiction, for there is no conditional discipleship. Dependence upon the Holy Spirit will assure the quality of our response to God's call.

The Christian calling puts everything into focus: the place of the Word, the Message we embrace, our lifestyle and our commitment to service. Christ's call will provide the right answers to the many questions we may have about fulfilling our purpose in life.

Made In The Image Of God

What does it mean to be made in the image or the likeness of God (Gen. 1:27; 5:1; 1 Cor. 11:7; Jas. 3:9)? God's original intent was that we be just like Him, and that is still His goal for us. Being created in the image of God means that we are spiritual beings at our core related to Him, who long for spiritual fulfillment. We are moral beings who by the light of the Holy Spirit can know right from wrong and can make moral choices. We can love or hate, choose to help or harm others. We can show displeasure at sin or at people. With our intellect we have the ability to analyze data. The question is whether we are controlled and empowered by the Holy Spirit or not.

We were created to rule God's creation. Before the Fall,

there was no guilt, since there was no breaking of God's Law; there was no shame or sense of low self-esteem because of the knowledge of any failure, because all was good.

The entire Christian life has to be understood in terms of growing in the likeness of God, having been adopted through regeneration as His sons and daughters. The adoption as God's children is seen in the first words of the Lord's Prayer (Mt. 6:9). This leads to the principle of imitating the Father: "In this way you show that you are children of your Father in heaven...That is why you must be perfect as your Father in heaven is perfect" (Mt. 5:45, 48). This does not mean we can or must be perfect or righteous, but that our actions should glorify the Father (Mt. 5:16) and please the Father (Mt. 6:1).

The strong meaning of being sons and daughters of God was clear to the Old Testament believers, but its depth of meaning seemingly is often lost on us. Unless we understand what it meant to be a son, especially a first-born, we will miss much of what God intended in our relationship with Him. Sonship constituted a person's very identity that shaped his entire life. God wants us to enjoy the kind of loving relationship with Him that typifies the proper relationship between a father and his son, a family resemblance. The same truth includes women as daughters of God.

Our sonship received from Adam was flawed, but Jesus was the way God used to restore us to His original purpose. The first Adam gave us sin, and the second Adam (Jesus) gave us Life: "It is planted as a physical body. It comes back to life as a spiritual body. As there is a physical body, so there is also a spiritual body. This is what Scripture says: 'The first man, Adam, became a living being.' The last Adam became a life-giving spirit...As we have worn the likeness of the man who was made from the dust of the earth, we will also wear the likeness of the man who came from heaven" (Cor. 15:44-45, 49). This is the difference between sonship we inherited through Adam and through Jesus. As God created the human race through one man, He recreated them through the second Man (Jesus), Who came to restore what God had wanted to do for all time through Adam (Gal. 3:26). We experience God's original purpose for us in and through Jesus Christ, which also includes the adoption of His daughters.

The Fall into sin changed this image, but it did not eradicate it. Through regeneration we are related in our inner being to the God Who is perfect love and perfect holiness, a God Who lovingly will not let us go even in our rebellion. The fallen person is still an image-bearer of God. In Genesis 9:6 He tells us that murder is forbidden because man was made in the image of God.

The thought that Christians need continually to grow toward being conformed to the image of God is seen in the Scriptures that speak of putting off the Old Man and putting on the New Man, which is being renewed in the knowledge in the image of its Creator (Col. 3:9-10). Ephesians 4:24 says that we are to put on the new self which is created to be like God in true righteousness and holiness. Even though our image has been distorted by the Fall, we Christians still possess the gifts and capacities with which God has endowed us, though also used in sinful and disobedient ways.

The perversion of this image has affected our functioning in three relationships into which God has placed us with Him: worship (now tempted to worship idols); fellowship (now often using gifts to manipulate others as tools for selfish purposes instead of enriching the lives of others); the relationship between us and nature (instead of mastering the world for God, we now tend to use the earth and its resources for our own selfish purposes).

The renewed image by our new birth enables us to direct ourselves toward God and be empowered to love our neighbor and be good managers of nature. The renewal of the image is continued by the Holy Spirit in our participation of the earthly assignments God has given us. This image means that we are to mirror God and to represent Him, doing what He desires. This renewal of the image is never completed in our lifetime, but it is a process that continues as long as we live. The problems inherited from the Fall remain with us: hiding from ourselves and God and others, rationalizations, and blaming others whenever we can.

The tragic result of the Fall is fourfold: **God-ward**, resulting in alienation from God; **self-ward**, resulting in condemnation and corruption, with the inner nature defiled; **neighbor-ward**, broken relations; **Satan-ward**, resulting in attacks from a subtle, cruel, crafty foe with difficult and endless temptations.

Man, left to himself, repudiates the true God and goes into the "god business" by running his life his own way. He chooses what he wants and decides for himself what is right and wrong. Whenever the big "I" runs himself, man is driven to seek devious devices to deaden his conscience, to fill his ego-needs, to stimulate himself, and to cover up his real intentions.

Our lives united with the life of God through faith in Christ must be strongly related to our eternal destiny in our great hope for the future. Being in the image of God directs our minds to tell us our purpose in what we have to offer the world.

The Devil's Barriers

As the devil once waged the great war against God, so he continues to battle against God's creatures. As the devil caused the Fall of God's original two persons, so he continues to plot the downfall of all human beings today. The devil and the demons are forever making plans to get and keep all people under his control.

As God has made a covenant with us to be our God and our strength, we should make a covenant with Him to submit ourselves to Him and to resist the devil (Jas. 4:7). Such a firm stand against evil desires and temptations is required. This is not a defensive action, but an offensive one which we should adopt as a lifestyle for resisting evil. God promises us that as we resist the devil, the devil will turn and run. We are given power to overcome the enemy as a result of Jesus' victory. "The weapons we use in our fight are not made by humans. Rather, they are powerful weapons from God. With them we destroy people's defenses, that is, their arguments and all their intellectual arrogance that oppose the knowledge of God" (2 Cor. 10:4-5a).

We need to remember that the devil promises the sun, but

delivers darkness. He promises success, but delivers slavery. He promises fame and fortune, but delivers failure. He is the trouble-maker in the world, whom we need to resist.

Human culture tends to be skeptical and apathetic toward the supernaturalism of the Holy God. Man tends to be an easy victim to the evil power of Satan and the demons (all aggravated by modern man's unbelief and skepticism). Many believe that Satan and demons are merely superstition and imagination, and so depraved human behavior must be attributed to sources other than the devil. We have already studied the reality of Satan, who is presented as Lucifer who drew a multitude of angels with him into the kingdom of evil. Now we investigate how his opposition and warfare centers on people and God's purpose for them on earth.

So effective is the devil's disguise that he can gain almost total control of a Christian's life, yet the victim does not suspect the identity of his evil master. His disguise is the mask of self, as his suggestions appeal to our human instincts, which seem to be so natural. We can be used by him and not suspect it, for it is natural to stick up for our rights, put ourselves first, to want a good time, to take advantage of opportunities, to cater to appetites and passions, and to want to get ahead in this world. He uses every natural desire to enslave.

Satan causes Christians to experience bitterness, rebellion, strife, rejection, insecurity, jealousy, withdrawal, escape, depression, and mental illness. He gives them doubt, indecision, self-deception, denial, pride, impatience, addictive and compulsive behavior, gluttony, sexual impurity, occultism, spiritism, cults and false religions.

Scripture reveals the role of demons as Satan's powerful helpers in his opposition to man. It explains how a satanic and demonic destruction is directed relentlessly against man and the earth. The New Testament presents overwhelming evidence for the existence of demons and for their outburst of evil supernatural-ism. It also tells of the devil's invisible army of demons (Jas. 2:19; Rev. 9:20). It describes their nature (Lk. 4:33; 6:18), activity (1 Tim. 4:1; Rev. 16:14), opposition to believers (Eph. 6:10-20), home (Lk. 8:33; Rev. 9:11), and their eternal doom

(Mt. 25:41). Demonic power over fallen man, however, is severely restricted within the limits God has set. When people violate the moral laws of God, they subject themselves to the devil's bondage that brings them under the sway of occult powers in the hidden realm of evil supernaturalism. There is evidence of considerable spiritual warfare being waged in our day. Manifestations of diabolical and occult power are running rampant in our age as practices which were once conducted in secret and abhorred by the average person are now sometimes popularized in the theater, movies, on television and on radio, and in literature.

Jesus distinguished clearly between different causes for human problems: sinful actions; purely physical illness; psychological distresses; and demonic interference. Jesus did not fall into the error of His (and our) day in which some find one cause for every distress, mainly, the devil and demon possession. Matthew 9 shows three different diagnoses and different means of treatment: Jesus encountered a paralytic with a physical manifestation of a spiritual paralysis caused by guilt, and He administered a strictly spiritual cure with the words, "Cheer up, son! Your sins are forgiven"; He provided straightforward physical healing with no suggestion of a spiritual origin of the problem involved; and He faced demonic possession by curing through casting out the demon.

Jesus clearly showed the difference between the power and authority to cast out demons and the ability to heal diseases. He showed the differences between problems which are of spiritual, physical and demonic nature. 1 John 4:1-3 also shows that the problem can refer to doctrine or a spiritual cause rather than demon possession.

These particular paragraphs are presented in order to help you have a healthy respect for our evil adversary, to know how he operates, to have a defense system for protecting our thought-life, and to be equipped with the spiritual mechanics for resisting him and the demons.

The devil's and demons' influence over people in the world and world events are real and ever-present. This influence can also be seen in soothsaying (where the medium is under the direct control of evil spirits or demons to predict the future), sorcery (practice of magic through mystical formulas and mutterings), satanism and occultism, including fortune telling, astrology, palmistry and clairvoyancy.

The tragic activity of astrology and related areas sometimes includes well-meaning but ill-taught Christians who profess to believe and honor the Word of God. Through lack of faith and ignorance of what the Bible teaches, Christians also fall prey to faulty thinking that it must be God at work because Biblical terminology is used. Ignorance of Biblical truth breeds gullibility with the result that some seek spiritual direction from self-claimed leaders and organizations that stress psychic phenomena and experiences. Such people mistakenly seek enlightenment and comfort in the literature of occultism, metaphysics and horoscopes.

We must know that we can be overtaken by demons, but that there is help. We are warned to stay away from satanism, but fill our souls with good things. We should know that it is possible to be deceived.

The chief characteristic of demon possession is a distinct "other" personality within. The demons have a longing for a body to possess (Mt. 13:43; 8:31). They converse through the organs of speech, and give evidence of personality, desire and fear. They also reveal knowledge and power not possessed by the individual or subject. The demon changes entirely the moral character of those he enters, compelling them to act entirely contrary to their normal behavior. Usually oracular utterances are given in jerks and sentences quite unlike the calm coherent sequence of language normally used.

If a believer seems to be inhabited, we can pray in the name of Jesus that the demons depart, and that the demons would be confused and weaken their hold on the person. We also pray that the person would be strengthened in faith to understand his position in Christ and to trust and obey the Word of God. We also pray that the person might recognize the demonic presence together with the power of Christ. The demons are to be resisted by commands in the name of Jesus.

Great care must be taken to avoid any belief or practice for deliverance of various spirits in situations where the problem is fear and various kinds of addictions, or even a lack of repentance over habitual sin. We must beware that we do not treat such problems as sources of demonic subjection. These are not to be treated by casting out demons or deliverance, but by the use of Law and Gospel for repentance and forgiveness.

When we face afflictions, temptations or sin, we should examine our lives in the light of the Scriptures rather than looking for a demon. True confession of sins and repentance with forgiveness is the solution. Even Christians who are involved with the occult or witchcraft are informed by the Bible to repent, not to have spirits cast out of them.

God broke the rule of Satan through the Incarnation of Christ, Who came as the Divine Invader to "destroy what the devil does" (1 Jn. 3:8). "Since all of these sons and daughters have flesh and blood, Jesus took on flesh and blood to be like them. He did this so that by dying he would destroy the one who had power over death (that is, the devil)" (Heb. 2:14). Thus Christ's Incarnation established a permanent beachhead as the fortress against evil that can never be recaptured by the devil. Jesus clearly viewed His mission as including a campaign against evil forces for the sake of the liberation of people from the devil and demons.

The Old Self Overcome By The New Self

Satan's contact with the believer is through the Old Adam or old nature only. He has no access to the new nature received in baptism and in redemption. Any control over the Christian is by permission or by individual surrender to the devil. The Christian is free to choose between control of his two natures.

The center of warfare which Satan utilizes through the old self is our mind, where the thought-life is laid open to his inspection. He seeks to take away the Word of God to introduce his own ideas. He has definite advantages in instant and immediate access to each person's mind to see the complete panorama of our thoughts and imaginations, being familiar with every weakness and

99

strength. He knows our vulnerable areas and our secret ambitions and longings.

We were all born as the old nature in sin. Because the believer is the battleground between two masters, both seeking control, he needs to know the character of both the new self and old self, and the nature of the fight.

The old nature (old man or old self) reveals itself in a lifestyle that is enslaved to sin. The old nature is disobedient, arrogant, undisciplined, ignorant, shameless, haughty, doubts God's Word, lusts after worldly benefits, and is a slave of the devil. The new nature (new man or new self) came into being through our baptism, and reveals itself in a new lifestyle that is joyfully obedient to God. The Christ-identity in us is aware of the truth, alive to Christ, dead to the world, obedient, humble, disciplined and pious. Living the old lifestyle is inconsistent with the new persons we are in Christ. Therefore, Paul calls on believers to make their lifestyles consistent with the new selves they have put on in baptism. "Don't you recognize that you are people in whom Jesus Christ lives?" (2 Cor. 13:5)

The New Nature Victorious Over The Old Nature

Paul gives considerable counsel regarding the old nature-new nature conflict so that the new nature will be victorious over the old nature. This can be seen in the following accounting of the proposals he makes to Christians.

Old Nature (Old Man, Old Self, Sinner Unregenerate)	New Nature (New Man, New Self, Saint Regenerate)	Scripture
Completely sinful and corrupt (Rom. 7:18)	Completely sinless and perfect (Eph. 4:24)	
(100% Spiritual Being)	(100% Spiritual Being)	
Strip off your old self.	Be renewed in the spirit of righteousness and holiness.	Eph. 4:22-24

Follows desires that deceive you.	Put on new self. Created righteous and holy.	
Strip off lying.	Speak the truth.	Eph. 4:25
Do not let the sun go down on your anger.	Be kind and tenderhearted forgiving.	Eph. 4:26, 32
Do not carry out what your flesh desires.	Let the Spirit direct your life.	Gal. 5:16
What the flesh desires is against the Spirit.	What the Spirit desires is against the flesh.	Gal. 5:17
Works of the flesh are...	The fruit of the Spirit is...	Gal. 5:19-22
Sow from flesh... Reap destruction	Sow from spirit.. Reap eternal life	Gal. 6:8
Mind not on earthly things.	Keep minds on things above.	Col. 3:2, 5-8, 10
Kill what is earthly in you...	Put on the new self. Dress yourselves with...	Col. 3:12-13
Get rid of such things...	Bear with one another, forgive.	
Old Self nailed to cross.	Not be slaves to sin any longer.	Rom. 6:6
Think self dead to sin.	Think self alive to God.	Rom. 6:11
Do not let sin go on ruling... do not go on presenting the members of your body to sin as tools of wickedness	Let God use the members of your body as tools for doing what is right.	Rom. 6:12-13
Slave	Free	Rom. 6:16
Wages paid by sin is death.	The gift of God is everlasting life.	Rom. 6:23
Flesh kills...cannot please God.	What the Spirit has in mind gives life and peace.	Rom. 8:6, 8
STARVE	FEED	

We are really two people at the same time — the old man and the new man, sinner and saint. The issue is confused if we talk about the sinners out in the world and the saints in the church. Unbelievers are sinners only, but Christians are simultaneously

101

sinner-saints, old nature-new nature. We are not half and half, but 100% old self and 100% new self, both complete spiritual beings fighting against each other. That is why Paul could say that he was entirely sinful and entirely holy before God, sinner and saint at the same time.

When the ego or "I" is not under the control of God, it manifests itself in self-assertion and wrong doing. At times the old nature shows itself by self-indulgence, through excesses and enslaving habits, even immorality. Another characteristic is self-justification, finding it difficult to admit that he makes mistakes, being slow to apologize, and sometimes vindicating his position. There is also self-sufficiency in which we depend upon our own wisdom, ability and efforts, instead of relying entirely on the resources and grace of God. Another damaging trait is self-will, where we go our own way instead of seeking God's will in every decision and area of life.

The new nature recognizes that God initiates and the person responds, while the old nature believes the person initiates and God rewards. The new nature sees grace making a new creature through baptism into the likeness of Christ as a gift of the Holy Spirit, while the old nature sees grace as a treasury of merits stored up in heaven and earned by good deeds. The new nature focuses on love from God and to others, while the old nature focuses on reward for self now and after death. The new nature emphasizes the internal condition, while the old nature emphasizes external deeds for looking good.

1 Corinthians 3:1, 3 and Romans 8:5 show that we are to be controlled by the Holy Spirit, not to be worldly or carnal. We are not to be spiritually dull or live in slavery to sin. When Christ lives in us, so does the fullness and power of God.

Who will be in control and who will be master? It all depends upon which one we feed — the old or the new nature. If we deceive ourselves and rationalize our lifestyle, we will feed on spiritual garbage and the poison which gushes forth from our culture, its publications and media. The old nature needs to be starved, not fed. Instead, far too many Christians starve the new nature and feed the old.

As we feed on the Word and communicate with God in prayer, we will experience the enabling strength of the Holy Spirit as God will sanctify or make us holy through and through (1 Thes. 5:23). Feeding on the good food of the Word and praying for holiness will help us to put to death whatever belongs to our earthly nature (Col. 3:5). This mortifying of the old self is to destroy the attraction of sin which tries to control our bodies. The issue is not that we will not sin anymore but that we will not be slaves or controlled by sinful habits (Rom. 6:6).

There are no ten easy lessons to gain victory over the old nature and sinful habits or to be trained and disciplined to be godly. The solution is a solid feeding program of the new self by the Gospel. Feeding the new nature involves believing what God has said about the devil, learning how this enemy operates, adopting a definite plan for resisting him, and knowing how to use our resources in Christ.

Whoever Controls Us Develops Our Self-Image

What kind of image do we have of ourselves? Is it a healthy or unhealthy one? Is it one of faith or failure? Is it one of being master or a slave?

Evaluating ourselves makes it possible to act properly in relation to God, others and nature. Those who have an extremely negative self-image, and think of themselves as worthless, will not be able effectively to love their neighbor as themselves. They will not dare to give themselves to neighbors in fellowship since they feel they have nothing worthwhile to give. On the other hand, those with a positive self-image will be willing to give themselves to others intimately, and thus fulfill the Lord's command to love neighbors.

We do not use the words "self-esteem" or "self-love" because they can be misunderstood as though we are to love what we ourselves are by nature, apart from God's grace. The words "self-image" and "self-worth" understood as one's conception of oneself or one's role are neutral terms that can either be positive or negative, lending themselves easily to a Christian interpretation by seeing ourselves not just as we are by nature, but as we are by God's grace.

103

Man's self-image or self-worth was perverted when Adam and Eve wanted to be as big or high as God. Ever since the Fall people have tended to have too lofty an opinion of themselves. Apart from God's grace, they tend to think of themselves as independent or autonomous or as a law to themselves. Christians also look at themselves wrongly when they adopt an inordinately low self-image or view themselves as having little worth. When they realize how far short they have fallen from what they should be, they must then know and accept what God has made of them in their redemption.

Instead of questioning our adequacy, we should question our failure to look at ourselves from God's perspective when we have a poor self-image. Some have an unrealistic or unattainable mental image or standard by which they measure their performance, abilities, looks, character and life. This illusion causes us to think of the perfect husband, the perfect wife, the perfect parent or friend. What we think about ourselves and feel about ourselves may be drawn upon our past: parental neglect, abuse or overbearing authority; fears that were instilled into us; always trying to be right or thinking we are always wrong; did not live in an atmosphere of forgiveness; a hypercritical atmosphere. All of these have a negative effect on our self-worth or self-image.

Our self-image should not be static but dynamic, as we dare never be satisfied with our growth in Christ. The Christian life is one involving perpetual struggle between the Holy Spirit and the flesh: "I say, let the Spirit direct your life, and you will not carry out what your flesh desires" (Gal 5:16).

The standard by which we evaluate our self-image or self-worth is our salvation in Jesus Christ. By forgiving us completely through Christ's sacrifice, God obligated us to forgive ourselves. However unloved and worthless we once may have felt, and however much self-condemnation and self-hate we may have nursed, we see that God gave us high value by loving us enough to redeem us.

When we rest in Christ's unceasing love, acceptance and forgiveness, we are set free from society's rigid standards. Will we believe what society says about beauty, intelligence and status, and live in discouragement? Or will we choose to believe God's grace and mercy, and become all He created and empowered us to be?

Our self-worth is established in our person in Christ, not in our performance. Our human nature seeks to deceive us into believing that success and achieving a high standard of conduct will give us our worth. It invites us to set rules to measure our goodness. But God has given us self-worth in salvation by grace through faith (justification) apart from our ability to perform. By imputing Christ's righteousness to us, God attributes Christ's worth to us.

SELF-WORTH
is established

in our	**not in our**
PERSON	**PERFORMANCE**
(Redeemed)	(Belonging to church)
Who we are in Christ	What we do for Christ
Christ's righteousness	Our righteousness

God has a plan in making us different from everyone else, and as He lives inside us we see how special we are to Him. We will no longer hold a self-image that spawns inhibited or compulsive behavior of all sorts, instability, lack of self-respect, spinelessness, isolation and withdrawal, drug dependence, promiscuity, or any other aberration. We know who we are in Christ, and that self-image directs us toward right living. We are to be prepared for losses and gains, crosses and crowns, and walking tall and fighting hard by the Spirit of God.

God empowers us to make the right decisions. As the Holy Spirit renews us and enables us to renounce sinful pride, we cultivate true humility and gain an honest awareness of both our strengths and weaknesses.

Our attitude towards ourself is extremely important, for our self-concept is the source of our personal happiness or lack of it. It helps establish the boundaries of our accomplishments and defines the limits of our fulfillment. When we dislike ourselves, we tend to dislike others. Consequently we may think other people are our problem, but it is we ourselves who may be the problem.

Reasons why we should love and accept ourselves are that we have a divine heritage, created by the hand of God and in His likeness, and because God created us especially to share in His creation (Ps. 8:4-5). God called us to be fruitful and to multiply and manage the earth (Gen. 1:28). When Jesus told the parable to illustrate the importance of salvation for one person, He used the pearl to communicate the value He places on each of us (Mt.13:45-46). He cares about us so much that He has angels watching over us (Ps. 91:11-12). He has prepared a mansion for us and will come back and take us where He is (Jn. 14:1-3). He has given us positions of influence as salt and light of the world (Mt. 5:13-14). All these are a picture of personal worth and esteem.

Our self-image involves the basic set of attitudes that influence and make up our total personhood. Thus we must be precise when we refer to the ego or the "I," for actually it may have a negative or positive implication. Ordinarily it is used in the negative, but from a scriptural view point we can refer to the old "I" or the new "I." The new "I" should be victorious over the old "I" (2 Cor. 5:17). When the ego is controlled by the flesh, it represents sinful acts; but when the ego is controlled by the Spirit, it refers to good works. The Christian seeks to have the new nature express the proper ego.

Issues Related To Self-Worth And Self-Esteem

Sanctified self-esteem is totally consistent with the humble spirit that Jesus asked His followers to display. To feel bad about ourselves and maintain the lowest possible opinion is not true Christian humility. That can be a spiritual problem which does not take into consideration the image and grace of God. Low self-esteem can be an emotional problem with an inability to receive praise and encouragement because we may feel that we are not worthy of it.

The old self produces a spirit of pride and superiority,

being puffed up, inflated or haughty, which are destructive substitutes for genuine self-acceptance (1 Cor. 4:6, 18, 19; 5:2; 8:1; 13:4). Such superiority may relate to financial resources, appearance, athletic ability, professional position, status in society or even responsibilities in the church. This is sinful self-centeredness.

A strong negative ego can cause us to be so self-centered that we will be individualistic, devoid of any interest in others. On the other hand, we can be so concerned about what others believe and feel about us that we want to conform and be who others want us to be. This means that when we are recognized by others we feel great, and when we are not we feel small. We then feel we must conform to others' expectations of what is valuable in order to feel valuable. This kind of conformism distorts our relationships and weakens or garbles our sense of identity so that we become dependent on other individuals or the group for our sense of worth. Naturally, we have a drive to be recognized, but when it takes the twisted form of conformism, we become insecure, needing to take a poll to see how others are rating us today. This causes us to be chameleons, for how we see ourselves depends on the group of people we happen to be with. We adopt values and tastes from those around us. As we bend and shape our convictions and conduct in order to fit in, it is hard to have deep relationships, and it weakens our ability to stand against the pressures of the world.

With the trademark of the Master Designer upon us, we are a divine original — something special, unique. We are distinct from others and must not try to be somebody else. We must dare to be ourselves. God never intended us to be another person, for trying that makes us phonies. We should never get caught in the comparison games, but accept ourselves for who we are in Christ. If God so loved us, how dare we not love what God loves: ourselves as unique individuals?

We are to love ourselves. We need as much love as our neighbor. We are to love our neighbor **as** ourselves, **not** love ourselves **more than** or **less than** we love our neighbors (Mk. 12:31). Our self-love should see ourselves as image-bearers of God. By looking at our divine origin and destiny as children of God in Christ, we will build an essentially positive concept and self-love. Our self-love should result from seeing ourselves as objects of divine love (Jn. 15:9). Biblical self-love is not an attitude of superiority, self-will or self-centeredness, but seeing ourselves as divine image-bearers, as objects of divine love, and valuing ourselves as equally important members of God's new creation.

We are more than flesh and bones, for we are the product of God's creation. This gives us our spiritual perspective on life and our Christian convictions. We should see ourselves as God sees us and accept ourselves as God accepts us. Therefore, we will not be fearful or timid, which sometimes may come under the guise of humility. What actually is at stake is that we may fear that we may fail or make a mistake, or make someone else upset, and thus make fools of ourselves. We may be anxious about losing love from some people, even though it is something in our mind, not real. Timidity is not a fruit of the Holy Spirit, but self-control is. God does not break Christians down nor diminish their selfhood, but He builds them up. A strong root system in Christ creates a sound character and productivity. Not loving ourselves may come from believing wrong about ourselves on the basis of other people's distortions, or because of a false understanding of forgiveness.

Even with a deep sense of sin, Paul was able to maintain a predominantly positive self-image, which was in God, not in himself. His positive statements about himself reflected his expression of the new nature: "But God's kindness made me what I am, and that kindness was not wasted on me. Instead, I worked harder than all the others. It was not I who did it, but God's kindness was with me" (1 Cor. 15:10). He showed this further: "Christ gives us confidence about you in God's presence. By ourselves we are not qualified in any way to claim that we can do anything. Rather, God makes us qualified" (2 Cor. 3:4, 5). "Our bodies are made of clay, yet we have the treasure of the Good News in them. This shows that the superior power of this treasure belongs to God and doesn't come from us" (2 Cor. 4:7).

Just because his work was not popular to the world, Paul did not brush aside his great achievements, but said: "I worked harder than all the others" (1 Cor. 15:10); "I have fought the good fight. I have completed the race. I have kept the faith" (2 Tim. 4:7). He saw himself as a person on whom God had showered His grace, and whom God had enabled to live a fruitful life for Christ.

With Paul, we can boast of nothing except Jesus Christ: "You are partners with Christ Jesus because of God. Jesus has become our wisdom sent from God, our righteousness, our holiness, and our ransom from sin. As Scripture says, 'Whoever brags must brag about what the Lord has done'" (1 Cor. 1:30-31). There is nothing like the knowledge of the holy and all-powerful God for putting us in our proper place. This grace not only built Paul's character, but also influenced positive change in his personality and temperament. Paul was realistic about his strengths and weaknesses because he had a healthy self-image. He recognized that he and his peers were not perfect, but subject to mistakes. Having accepted his own weaknesses, he was able to accept the weaknesses of others.

Having been accepted into God's family unconditionally and continuing to receive God's love unconditionally, in Christ we are accepted fully and completely. Our sinful minds can keep us from believing that. Too quickly we can believe the deception that we must be unworthy of love, which deepens the pit of rejection. Being rejected, we believe that we are trash and must make an excuse for everything we do — that we are ignorant, always wrong and cannot please anyone. This leads us to believe that we must perform to win love, and if we cannot properly perform, we will be ultimately rejected. The fruits of this rejection are pathetic, because we then believe that we must now compensate for this rejection. The compensation or fruits of rejection are depression, perfectionism, defensiveness, hostility, anger, self-pity, bitterness, workaholism, alcoholism, self-consciousness, self-condemnation and many others.

People who feel rejected grow to protect themselves from further hurts by erecting their own defenses or masks. They keep their distance from others and hide their real selves by a veneer of shyness or aggression, of confidence or joking, and become experts at cover-up. The result is superficial relationships.

The spirit of rejection is rooted in the person of Satan, who models rejection in every move he makes, and it is reflected in a negative system of thought, life and action. Rejection grows more severe with every successive cycle of negative thought unless there is miraculous intervention by God's means. This rejection, which short-circuits love and confuses communication, can be resolved only in Jesus Christ and the Gospel.

The Gospel leads us to forgive those who have rejected us, to give up bitterness, resentment and rebellion because we know we have been accepted in Christ. We will stop belittling ourselves because we are God's handiwork: "Who do you think you are to talk back to God like that? Can an object that was made say to its maker, 'Why did you make me like this?'" (Rom. 9:20). It is not humility when we falsely criticize or wrongly value or devalue ourselves as Christians, but it is rebellion against God.

Performance-Based-Acceptance

The results of experiencing or even perceiving conditional love and of being rejected is that sometimes persons may live by what some have termed, "Performance-Based-Acceptance." Then we seek our value in **what we do**, since our identity is tied to our actions. The result is that the promise of self-worth is never realized because we can never do enough. Life is reduced to actions and results, which become the only tangible means we can use to measure our value. Such activism makes busyness, not God, the goal of the Christian life. Real needs go unfulfilled and the misguided ones believe that God calls us to busyness, not purposefulness.

The love of God and His acceptance of us is based on grace, not on our ability to impress God through our good deeds. Christ offers us unconditional love and healing even of our emotions. We do not have to please God in exchange for His acceptance. Our perception of failure is at the root of our poor self-concept. Even in failure, the repentant Christian is deeply loved by God, completely forgiven, totally accepted by God and complete in Christ.

110

Performance-Based-Acceptance (PBA) is an ugly intrusion into the free grace of God and the unconditional love of Christ in the forgiveness of all our sins. It is a terrible perversion of grace and of the precious Gospel of Jesus Christ. If not recognized and not stopped, its many tentacles will begin to develop in our lives until our whole life is based on Performance-Based-Acceptance (PBA).

The insidious nature of PBA is that it never answers the questions: How much performance is necessary? Who sets the measures, and how will the performance be measured? Will the standards always be changing or are they set and rigid? How will we know when we have achieved acceptance? What will we have to do tomorrow and the next day to achieve it? How long will what we have worked to achieve today last?

PBA is actually a form of "salvation by works." It programs us to be manipulators as we are in bondage to those that we seek to manipulate for acceptance. This creates depression and anxiety which is humanly unbearable. It hurts us emotionally and psychologically. It cripples us with fear, stress and pressure.

Why should we carry this heavy load when the Holy Spirit, the ultimate Spiritual Therapist, desires to solve our personal problems: "Why are you discouraged, my soul? Why are you so restless? Put your hope in God, because I will still praise him. He is my savior and my God" (Ps. 42:11).

David A. Seamands in his book *HEALING GRACE, Let God Free You from the Performance Trap*, states that the lie of performance for salvation "insists that everything depends on how well we perform —

Our salvation and status — Our relationship with God

Our sense of self-worth — Our relationship with ourselves

Our sense of security and belonging — Our relationship with others

Our sense of achievement and success — Our relationship with society around us.

111

"Performance-oriented Christians represent a wide range of humanity. There are the very young in the Christian life, who are struggling to believe in a grace which just seems too good to be true. There are those who, like the Galatians, started out living by grace, but now are mixing law (performance) and grace (gift). There are the perfectionists who feel sure nothing they do is ever good enough for God, others, or themselves." Seamands writes that there are those who will die **for** their Christianity, but the real question is why they seem to be almost dying **from** it. Seamands says that "performance-grounded Christians do not feel good about themselves as persons, in spite of what they may have accomplished."[3]

PBA totally contradicts Ephesians 2:8-9, "God saved you through faith as an act of kindness. You had nothing to do with it. Being saved is a gift from God. It's not the result of anything you've done, so no one can brag about it." Grace and grace alone is, and always will be, the basis of our relationship with God. We are saved by grace through faith plus nothing. Grace is undeserved, for if we deserved it, it would not be grace. It cannot be earned, and it cannot be repaid or the grace-base would be changed into a performance-base.

Seamands writes, "Grace is God's love in action toward those who do not deserve it. And this love is manifested as grace, offered us in the life and death of Christ. Hence, God did not say,

I love you **because**...
I love you **since**...
I love you **forasmuch as**...
or
I will love you **if**...
I will love you **when**...
I will love you **provided**...
I will love you **presuming**...

"Any such statement would make His love conditional, would mean His love was caused by something in us — our attractiveness, our goodness, our lovableness. The reverse of this

112

would mean that there could be something in us which would stop God from loving us. God's love for us is unconditional; it is not a love drawn from God by something good in us. It flows out of God because of His nature. God's love is an action toward us, not a reaction to us. His love depends not on what we are but on what He is. He loves because He is Love."[4]

The solution lies in repentance and forgiveness. We should first repent for believing lies about ourselves and trying to turn God's gracious love into a series of deals to be made with Him. Let us admit that we have a problem and honestly face the influence that our PBA attitude has on our relationships with ourselves, with others and especially with God Himself.

Take responsibility for all our actions and accept God's unconditional love and acceptance of ourselves as His children, asking Him to take away the guilt which has built up. We need to study God's Word daily, which describes our true identity as God's children. We must allow this Word to reprogram our faulty thinking and let this Word produce the liberating process in our lives. Then we will accept the healing of our spirit and the wholeness God gives.

What To Do?

Never surrender to negative emotions or ideas. Every time a negative idea comes into your mind, replace it with a Biblical and positive one of God's unconditional love for you. Learn to tell yourself the truth about yourself when negative thoughts attack you. Locate your misbeliefs about yourself and replace them with the truth. Such misbeliefs are learned, and they can also be unlearned. Don't believe the misbeliefs that others can be happy and change, but you can't. As long as you are convinced that you cannot change, you will not try or resist change. It has been observed that the way people think influences the way that they act. Christ, who is the strength of our life, said, "What you have believed will be done for you" (Mt. 9:29).

When we have God's love and truth in our value system and expectations, that truth will set us free (Jn. 8:32). We can learn this truth about God's love as a way of life which leads to wholeness, restored functioning, and freedom from anxiety and emotional disturbances. Look for God's goodness and the good He gives in life, and you will find it. Give thanks in everything. "Keep your minds on all that is true, all that is noble, all that is right, all that is pure, all that is lovely, all that is appealing — on anything that is excellent or deserves praise" (Phil. 4:8). Express thanks, appreciation and warm feelings to others. Keep repeating, "God has a plan for my life. His love and grace is sufficient for me. He will bring good out of every bad situation, and He will continually forgive me. He is with me in providential and gracious care, and His angels watch over me. Nothing is impossible with God."

You will want to have the same attitude that Christ Jesus had (Phil. 2:5). What we could not buy or deserve, God gave us freely. Just accept it. Knowing that we are pardoned, accepted and affirmed by God in Christ's righteousness is the dynamic that makes possible our acceptance of ourselves. This shifts the emphasis and the center of our attention from ourselves to God. That shift of attention will be kept alive by the Indwelling Christ Who will continue to shape us more and more into His image (Gal. 4:19).

Everything Is Resolved In Repentance-Forgiveness

The Christian solution to wrong-doing and broken relationships is revolutionary. Human approaches alone never work, as they often pretend it did not happen, or avoid the person wronged, or hope no one noticed, or try to be extra nice. These tactics simply do not repair the effects of the wrong that has been done.

What has been broken or destroyed by our wrong actions and attitudes can only be repaired by God's loving process of repentance, forgiveness and reconciliation. This means that we stop excusing or claiming that our intentions were good, stop the euphemisms (substituting agreeable or inoffensive expressions for the ugly truth) and start admitting the reality of the situation and taking responsibility. Such repentance involves renouncing what is bad.

Renunciation begins with godly grief over our wrongs. Renunciation also means to denounce our false actions and state it decisively, being specific and vigorous.

Repentance involves a true reckoning of the past with a change of mind, of the heart, and of conduct, turning over the controls to God. Sorrow over sins is insufficient, for there needs to be a change in the inward condition of a person as the mind and heart are altered by grace. People can be sorry at being caught and of being deprived of the pleasures of sin, but that is not repentance.

There's a great distinction between worldly and godly sorrow. Worldly sorrow or grief leads to death and pain, whereas godly sorrow produces repentance that results in deliverance from evil (2 Cor. 7:10) and leads to salvation. Worldly sorrow leads us to believe that we can somehow contribute something to our own moral goodness and that we can deserve some of God's favor, whereas godly sorrow shows us our total spiritual and moral depravity and inability to do anything about our bankruptcy. Worldly sorrow encourages us to try to repay for our sin or our lack, whereas godly sorrow causes us to confess our inability to repay God, and joyfully to declare that Jesus has already done it.

Worldly sorrow causes us to recognize that punishment is required, so we may try to punish ourselves. Godly sorrow recognizes that Jesus has already taken our punishment, and that there is no more punishment needed. Worldly sorrow knows that justice is required, so we attempt to justify ourselves. Godly sorrow recognizes that we cannot justify ourselves, as God has already justified us.

Worldly sorrow fails to recognize the grace of God despite our sinfulness, while godly sorrow leads us to know that not only will we not get the bad we deserve, but we will get more than we deserve by God's grace. Worldly sorrow is person-centered, while godly sorrow is God-centered. Worldly sorrow produces self-pity, while godly sorrow produces true humility. Worldly sorrow allows relationships to continue to suffer, while godly sorrow produces good relations that grow through love.

Genuine repentance does not involve the mere giving up of sins, but includes ceasing to be slaves to sin. It is a change of heart and mind, not just of words and acts. "Turn to God and change the way you think and act, because the kingdom of heaven is near" (Mt. 3:2). This is a continual process for the Christian. Repentance does not just tie down the lid on the garbage can, but it cleans the can.

Forgiveness will be difficult when we focus on the problem and the person instead of God. An unforgiving person looks strictly from a human perspective and believes the problem is with the other person, never with himself. That worldly view will be overcome only by opening ourselves to the love of God.

No amount of human striving can earn God's forgiveness and blessings. Our do-it-yourself world needs to learn that human efforts are utterly worthless and are never a substitute for the Gospel. Belief in human worthiness and in our deserving good and wealth in this world is self-righteous and arrogant, since it is rooted in the goodness of human nature rather than in the goodness of a loving God.

Forgiveness is gained not because we deserve it, but because a loving God wants to give it to us. That kind of love is His nature. That is what Luther experienced when he learned "The person who has God's approval will live because of faith" (Rom. 1:17). Wesley, like Luther, had built his hope and pride in religious forms, but when he also recognized justification by faith, the assurance that his sins were forgiven and that he was a child of a loving God, he said he felt his heart strangely warmed as he trusted in Christ alone for salvation, saving him from the law which gives sin and death.

Confession of sin and faith in Christ unloads guilt from us. David did not blame the pace of life for his problems, but he blamed his guilt and so confessed his sins (2 Sam. 12:13; Ps. 32 and 51). Confession and faith are the keys to recovery from sinful habits and rebuilt relationships. Confession and faith break the deadly and exhausting cycle of hiding behind compulsive habits and addictions. Through forgiveness a person enters a cleansing process that is life-renewing and energizing.

"God is faithful and reliable. If we confess our sins, he forgives them and cleanses us from everything we've done wrong" (1 Jn. 1:9). Confession and faith cause us to dispose of our spiritual garbage.

Forgiveness of all our sins is a promise of the Father, a provision of the Son, a proclamation of the Holy Spirit in the Word, and a required practice of the Christian. When forgiveness is not sought, a minor offense becomes a major issue. Broken laws and broken fellowship produce broken lives. God's love and forgiveness pays our debts and restores us to a healthy relationship with Him.

Judson Cornwall shares these precious words, "Let us enjoy forgiveness. We have been restored to a whole new life. Let's live it...Let's stop punishing ourselves trying to 'help God out' but start enjoying our release from sin's penalty, pollution, power and guilt. We have been justified; let's enjoy it. In Christ we have been sanctified; let's savor it to the fullest. We are being glorified; let's delight in it. Let's stop listening to our memory circuits, and reprogram our minds to enjoy our new status as forgiven and loved people.

"The handcuffs have been removed. Rejoice!

The contract has been canceled. Sing!

The debt has been paid. Shout!

God's love has triumphed over His law. Enjoy it!

Let's enjoy forgiveness!"[5]

The Flow Of God's Great Grace

Titus 2:11-15 shows grace to have a double dimension — grace for salvation and grace for sanctification: "After all, God's saving kindness has appeared for the benefit of all people. It trains us to avoid ungodly lives filled with worldly desires so that we can live self-controlled, moral and godly lives in this present world. At the same time we can expect what we hope for — the appearance of the glory of our great God and Savior, Jesus Christ. He gave himself for us to set us free from every sin and to cleanse us so that we can be his special people who are enthusiastic about doing good things. Tell these things to the believers. Encourage and correct them, using you full authority..." This shows the flow of God's great grace for redemption **and for doing good works**. It reveals grace to have two dimensions of effects and influence.

The message of Titus 3:4-8 reveals **the Flow of God's Great Grace**, especially for sanctification in verse 8. Titus chapters 2 and 3 carry messages that might be named, **the Gush of God's Great Grace**, because it is more than a flow. It is a gushing forth of God's extravagant love for justification **and sanctification**. The flow or gush of God's great grace is seen in the faithful sayings of Paul to Titus, including this one: "However, when God our Savior made his kindness and love for humanity appear, he saved us, but not because of anything we had done to gain his approval. Instead, because of his mercy he saved us through the washing in which the Holy Spirit gives us new birth and renewal" (Titus 3:4-5). That's redemption. "This is a statement that can be trusted. I want you to insist on these things so that those who believe in God can concentrate on setting an example by doing good things. This is good and helps other people" (Titus 3:8). That's sanctification.

Paul presents no one-dimension Gospel that stops with redemption but fails to provide power for love and righteous living. Indeed, listen to what he says in 2 Timothy 3:16-17: "Every Scripture passage is inspired by God. All of them are useful for teaching, pointing out errors, correcting people, and training them for a life that has God's approval. They equip God's servants so that they are completely prepared to do good things." Or, Ephesians 2:8-10: "God saved you through faith as an act of kindness. You had nothing to do with it. Being saved is a gift from God. It's not the result of anything you've done, so no one can brag about it. God has made us what we are. He has created us in Christ Jesus to live lives filled with good works that he has prepared for us to do." That's power for justification and sanctification...the flow of grace, a double focus of Gospel power.

The dynamic nature of grace for living the Christian life is offered also in 2 Corinthians 9:8, "Besides, God will give you his constantly overflowing kindness. Then, when you always have everything you need, you can do more and more good things." This assures strength for our weakness to serve God.

Grace is our only hope for dealing with any problem or sinful habit, the only power that can destroy and conquer the destructiveness of any bondage. Grace is the advocate and force of freedom. Any unresolved slavery is an enemy of grace. Grace is the bridge to transformation and reformation to get away from the land of slavery where we try repeatedly to consecrate ourselves on our own terms.

Even when choices are destructive and their consequences hurtful, God's grace is seen in His loving us regardless of who we are or what we do. The problem is that we are often so preoccupied with attention to our compulsions and blinded by our attachments that we cannot see evidences of God's love. Nothing in our culture prepares us for the radical reality of grace.

The facts of grace are simple: Grace is a pure gift which always exists. It is always available and good, coming often at surprising times to catch us off-guard when our manipulative systems are working furiously to achieve our own desires and goals. Such amazing grace simply will not allow us to be normal, but often will drive us to radical choices of taking risks of faith. Grace cannot be controlled, for it is God's love in action. This is true because grace is the dynamic outpouring of God's loving nature that flows in and through the believer in an endless flow of mercy, healing and power.

We cannot accept grace if our hands are full of earthly things to which we are enslaved. If our minds and hearts are filled with cultural influences, they are polluted and permeated with things that shut out grace, occupying and congesting spaces where grace should flow. Hearts, minds and hands can be emptied of these destructive things only through repentance and forgiveness. Repentance means to stop clinging to these harmful objects, which hinder our reception of grace.

Paul did not present a cocoon Christianity, that is, going from baptism to a future salvation, encapsulated all the way to heaven, not allowing God's great grace to cause us to flower forth in love and good works here on earth to His glory. More is involved than a spiritual dump truck to load our minds with sets of theological formulations to which we give assent. Faith is not just something to be preserved, but it is to be expressed and to be shared by the power of the Holy Spirit.

Obviously, we are to avoid two extremes. One is **Law** motivation for good works or moralisms, and the other is **Gospel** for redemption **only**, acting as though sanctification will flow automatically without the Word which strengthens us for the good works.

Some years ago, empirical research in the *Study of Generations* revealed that over 40% of Lutherans were not certain of their salvation. In spite of often quoting Ephesians 2:8-9, we spend too little time on verse 10, which is attached to grace also. People can quote "By His grace you are saved through faith," but still live by Performance-Based-Acceptance, hoping that performance will be acceptable by God even while they quote the proper Scriptures. They can answer questions about eternity, but are fearful about life and are weak in values and real love. Their doubts and confusion about life-issues raise questions about a denial of faith. They fail to see grace at work in their good works. Not only is the flow of grace our only hope for salvation, but it is also the only hope for a vigorous and loving spiritual life.

If some point to their human weakness, we appeal to the power of the Holy Spirit. If some plead inabilities, we put forward the extravagant ability of God in His love and mercy. We need to tap God's grace for every challenge of life.

Pieper certainly made all this very clear so that we can see God's grace both in justification and sanctification in better perspective. He wrote, "God has instructed the teachers and watchmen in His Church to give attention not only to the quality but also to the quantity of the works performed by Christians. Titus is to make it his business to 'insist on these things so that those who believe in God can concentrate on setting an example by doing good works' (Titus 3:8)...In urging the members of the churches to become 'rich in good works,' pastors should not be deterred from doing this boldly and resolutely, without any fear or faltering, by the thought that this insistence on good works might crowd out of its central position the doctrine of justification without works. Only if one does not know the Scriptural doctrine of justification by faith will he be timid in asking for a multitude of good works...According to Scripture the only motive for good works is the pure grace of God, which we have experienced in Christ Jesus. St. Paul knew of no other incentive to good works: 'I beseech you by the mercies of God.'" 6

This is the flow of God's great grace, gushing from a two-dimensional Gospel.

Flow Of Grace For Salvation And Living For Christ

Justification (Salvation)	Sanctification (Christian Living)
Position (unchanging)	Practice (changing and growing)
What we are in Christ	What we do in Christ
Faith established — saving faith (Rom. 1:17)	Faith expressed — sanctifying faith (Mt. 6:30; 8:26; 14:31; 17:20; Lk. 17:5)
New life (2 Cor. 5:14)	Walk in the new life (Rom. 6:4; Eph. 5:15; 6:13)
You are called (Eph. 1:18)	Fulfill your calling (Eph. 4:1)
Receive grace (Rom. 5:1-2)	Grow in grace (2 Pet. 3:18)
Receive love (Rom. 5:5; 1 Jn. 2:5)	Love! (1 Pet. 1:22; 4:8; Jn. 13:34 1 Jn. 3:18)

Abounding Grace For Christian Living

Sanctification is a life that not only finds us breaking free from the bondage of sinful habits but also loving and living the life of servants. Basic to breaking the link to past sinful actions of our carnal nature are confession, repentance, cleansing and restitution. Through the renewal of the mind, there will be fruit developing and growing by the Spirit.

Justification and sanctification, conversion and discipleship are meant to function together. There must be a move from

faith to virtue to knowledge to self-control to steadfastness to godliness to brotherly affection to love (2 Pet. 1:5-7). We do not
know where the path of discipleship will lead, but we know that
the journey is a lifelong process of spiritual growth and development. We know that our lives can be changed, should be altered,
and are being transformed by God's grace into Christ's likeness.

Sanctification dare not be focused on rules instead of on
the character of God in His love, power and will. The good
works of Christians are God's work — God's action (Phil. 2:13;
2 Cor. 3:5; 1 Cor. 12:6-11; Eph. 2:10). The great encouragement in our Christian life is that God is love and that our sanctification is reflective of that love. This means that we must be preoccupied with God, not with ourselves, as the norm and power of
our pursuit of personal holiness.

The holiness of God, the all-consuming fire, is threatening
only if we keep our religious experience centered on our own
person rather than allowing it to be a flow of love from the character and work of God to us and others. Anything other than a
sharp focus on God will cause us to center on superficial externals.

Good works are those which God has commanded and empowered as part of our Christian calling or vocation (Jn. 15:16).
Justified by faith, our call is to walk in faith, lead a godly life,
love and serve our neighbor, in obedience to our Lord. We should
willingly place ourselves entirely into God's service with everything we have.

Disciples should not be satisfied with performing single
works in response simply to requests by church leaders for church
programs, but respond to God's calling by doing many good
works daily (2 Cor. 8:7, 20; 9:8, 11). They are not to wait to be
asked, but should seek opportunities and be "enthusiastic about
doing good things" (Titus 2:14; 2 Cor. 8:4), and never "tired of
living the right way" (Gal. 6:9). Serving God should not be something they do when they find time, but that should be their avo-
cation in every avenue of life — occupation, family, civic responsibilities, social and recreational activities.

Disciples are admonished to make the most of their short
stay on earth by performing many good works (Gal. 6:10; Eph.

5:16; Col. 4:5). The Word of God commissions them to serve, and it gives the strength to do so. (2 Pet. 1:3-4) In the power of grace we can act in faith and love, but, because of our old nature, we will never fully fulfill the demands of faith and love.

The pursuit of holiness centers in the Lordship of Christ and the power of the Holy Spirit, leading to the obedience of faith. A radical dependence on the Holy Spirit produces obedience to Christ. God calls His people to be holy as He is holy (1 Pet. 1:15-16; 1 Cor. 1:2). To be holy means to be sanctified, to express our faith actively by the Holy Spirit (Heb. 12:14; Eph. 4:1).

The pursuit of holiness is a joint venture between God and the Christian disciple, God being the designer, motivator and power while the disciple is the instrument. Disciples must understand what they are to expect of God and what they are to do.

When Paul tells us "In the same way continue to work out your salvation with fear and trembling. It is God who produces in you the desires and actions that please him" (Phil. 2:12, 13), that is the New Testament sense of sanctification in which God is working in us what He also wants to work out of us to serve and witness. Sanctification and holy living are not for salvation, but are a result of salvation. This is not a trade-off of our works for God's good gifts as traders in a celestial market. Nothing in our moral and spiritual good can ever be computed as "earned income" for salvation.

Let there be no timidity or cowardice in seeking to do good works, for that reflects poorly on the power of God and on our confidence and faith in Christ and the Holy Spirit. As we trust God for the forgiveness of our sins, we are assured that He will help us to defeat the evil forces in our lives and to bear abundant fruit. God is strong enough to deal with whatever we find in our lives. This will get us far beyond the surface and our "comfort zone" or self-sufficiency. A death blow must be struck against spirituality that is built on pretense of our own adequacy.

Divine power will give us more than just mere relief from frustrating situations, but will produce change and transformation.

We need to look inside, beneath the surface of life, and not worry whether we will like what is in there. More effort is not the way, but changing from the inside out causes maturity. This will cause a radical transformation and restructuring of how we approach life.

Human nature always tempts us to rearrange our deeds rather than making substantial change inside, which effects our actions. Focusing on achievements takes us through life only by trying to cope, not to make real change. Core problems involving who we really are remain only partially addressed by merely adjusting what we do. We can easily join the Pharisees in specializing in looking good and preserving our image rather than in making fundamental changes. Real change requires an inside look, not only an outside look.

If we, like the Pharisees, reduce sin to manageable categories and expend all our energies in maintaining the standards we set, then spirituality will be measured by avoiding negatives rather than pursuing loving acts of service.

Focusing on measurable, shallow, superficial behavior serves to divert attention away from deeper realities of our lives. The result is that change is largely external, increasing a sense of pressure, not the freedom which Christ gives. We can become rigid moralists who push ourselves and others to keep carefully crafted standards rather than be growing Christians living by the grace of God. We easily become increasingly vulnerable to follow anyone who convincingly holds out the promise of more through the latest spiritual fad or program.

Renewed From The Inside Out

We change from the inside out, not the outside in. Inside change worked by the Holy Spirit will lead to breaking bad habits and will aid us to recognize subtle sins, and to develop passion in our pursuit of God. This is followed by change in our outward direction and relationships, which began in our very being or character.

How much we center on external factors at the cost of internal quality can be seen when we ask the question, "How are you?" People's answers will be affected by their health, financial situation, work and busyness. The answers will be determined to a large degree by the external environment. However, how you are on the inside greatly affects the way you can answer the question, "How are you?" What happens in your inner space probably determines more than anything else how you are.

People may have lots of things — health, wealth, leisure, etc. — and yet be very miserable. Little in the external environment needs to be changed, but on the inside people may feel low self-image, a sense of worthlessness and failure or even of enormous guilt. Or people may be selfish, greedy, fearful, hateful, lustful, or gloomy inside. No matter what things are like on the outside, what's inside will manage to make the person feel rotten or great.

How we feel inside determines how we are, so it is vital to discover the full potential of Christ's Spirit which creates deep changes in the innermost recesses of our person. The Holy Spirit recreates our innermost environment so that we can survive our external environment.

The rich fool who tore down barns to build bigger for selfish physical satisfaction, forgetting the needs of the soul, elevated the temporal and diminished the eternal (Lk. 12:16-21). Often people like him usually see reality through external matters. The external involves more than material, but also social relations and politics. Our systems of belief which embrace these two issues, together with our religious view, determine what we believe to be possible in our lives.

Many wrongly perceive the Christian faith and discipleship to be a behavior pattern instead of an inner regeneration which flows from the inside to the outside. This can be seen as we study this graph representing mankind's **World View**:

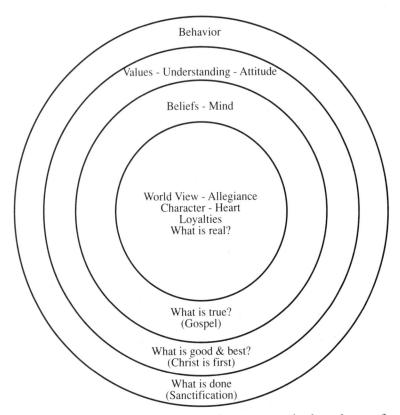

Behavior

Values - Understanding - Attitude

Beliefs - Mind

World View - Allegiance
Character - Heart
Loyalties
What is real?

What is true?
(Gospel)

What is good & best?
(Christ is first)

What is done
(Sanctification)

Whatever is in our inner being — our attitude and way of looking at things (mental map or world view) — is seen in the inner circle as reality to us. This reality depends upon the beliefs that we have, for they are related to our sense of reality. Our beliefs and inner reality will be the source of our strength and will establish our values, which in turn will dictate our behavior. Behavior for the Christian will thus be a reflection of the inner reality and the belief in Jesus.

The inner circle is our character, our heart, our roots, which is also related to our mind and beliefs. Our character and beliefs determine our attitudes and values, which are the father of our behavior. Our behavior is the fruit of the roots.

Jesus enunciated this truth clearly in His words recorded in Mark 7:20-23, "What comes out of a person makes him unclean. For from within, out of people's hearts, come evil thoughts, sexual sins, stealing, murders, adulteries, greed, wickedness, cheating, shameless lust, a jealous eye, slander, pride, foolishness. All these evils come from within and make a person unclean."

The reason why our external situation is never the last word or never brings real satisfaction is because the world is alien territory to us. This world is only a transitory home. Heaven is our home. Ever since God expelled Adam and Eve from the Garden, we have lived in an unnatural environment, a world in which we were not designed to live permanently.

Something is wrong, and we know it, both within ourselves and in our world. Our old nature causes us to desire what we do not have and what we cannot have until Christ returns and restores us and everything to the way it was meant to be, and that will be heaven. In the meantime, we often try to pretend things are better than they are or we insist on things that may destroy us.

We struggle against looking inside because it is too frustrating or threatening to face the necessity of deep internal change. We desire to face what we believe we can manage and control rather than penetrate into our deeper recesses and make fundamental changes. We live with the delusion of doing the right thing by correcting our ways just a bit to ease our consciences. We would rather say 100 times that we are sorry or say "the devil made us do it" than sincerely repent of a sinful act which will gain inward renewal. Thus we act superficially on the outer behavioral level rather than respond to our real need of inner change. It is much easier to dust off the surface of our lives than to endure the inner cleaning process of repentance which through forgiveness takes out the poisons which are destroying us.

We have often been looking in the wrong places, pulling rotten fruit off the tree to make things look better instead of digging and fertilizing the roots, and spraying the limbs to make healthy fruit. When we understand how to recognize and deal with sin in the heart instead of only in the mouth and hands, then the shift from sinful to godly behavior will reflect an inner change that makes the real and lasting change.

Spirituality cannot be measured by a code of conduct, even though it is important to exhort people to abandon sinful practices and to develop good habits. A focus on conformity to specific standards of right and wrong can easily lead to a disastrous neglect of deeper sins against relationships. Merely giving up wrong and disciplining ourselves is not the best way to achieve the desired change that God wants.

What is required is to take a painful look and face our real sin. The solution lies in our willingness to search the realities of our own internal life and allow God to do His sanctifying work. Christ's loving sacrifice allows us to accept the sinfulness and weaknesses coming from our old nature. Every step of maturing is progress, but there is a long way to go. We will continually say with Paul: "...This is what I do: I don't look back, I lengthen my stride, and I run straight toward the goal to win the prize that God's heavenly call offers in Christ Jesus" (Phil. 3:13-14). This is the spiritual process into which God has placed us by our baptism and redemption. We must be willing to accept our disappointments and pains by changing from the inside out, or life will be little more than stagnation, pretense and delusion.

Many Christians do not deal honestly with their lives. Catch words about love and the power of God are repeated piously, with little evidence of the Word's life-changing impact. Doctrinal affirmations concerning the role of the Holy Spirit in changing lives readily substitute for compelling witness about what God is actually doing in a dramatic fashion. It is much easier to talk about spending more time in prayer than to grapple with the messy issues of life by speaking the Word of Law and Gospel to each other. The way of change and of love is more often discussed than displayed.

While we may have kept our distance from God so that He does not penetrate too deeply, He has not kept His distance from us. He deals with life as it is, not as we wish it were. He is ready to open our eyes to whatever is true, however unsettling it may be. He alone will give us hope when things seem terribly wrong and when we feel most alone. His grace, love and forgiveness are penetrating and rich. He will replace our pretended satisfaction and false certainty with real Christian faith, hope and love.

The pain of life may overwhelm us, but it will never over-come us. The inner working of grace will display the outer manifestation in the world of who we truly are in Christ, in our relationships with others, and in our interactions with the events and circumstances of our lives. That is the heart-soul-mind level of "being," out of which our "doing" must flow.

The inner change involves knowledge, understanding and attitude. God increases our knowledge and understanding to change our attitudes. Change of behavior and of relationships always begin with a change of knowledge, understanding and attitudes. Being changed by the Holy Spirit is the only way to change the church and the world.

Not Slaves, But Free

Our service to God is not under the Law, but under grace. What does this mean? How can we experience freedom in Christ and yet be obedient to His will? To have freedom means that we are not under the power of anything or anyone but Christ. It means that our conscience is not answerable to human authority, but to God. It means that every area of our lives should be under the lordship of Christ, who sets us free from all human slaveries.

God intended that Old Testament Israel should see the Law not as their redeemer but as their teacher. It was a standard of the right way to live if they desired to be free, a standard which comes from Christ's righteousness. That which sets the limits of freedom is not the freedom itself, but it is the Son of God who sets people free, who forgives and restores love and trust. Not only the freedom but also the strength to maintain that freedom comes from Jesus Christ.

Freedom in Christ is freedom from human regulations (Col. 2:6-23), from sin's domination (Col. 3:1-17), and from lawless rebellion (Col. 3:18—4:6).

Freedom means many things to many people: freedom to a philosopher may mean wisdom; to the poor, wealth; to the student, the 3:00 o'clock bell; and to a convict, escape from prison. In all these cases the person is thinking like a slave, who is in bondage in some way. Jesus gives us another kind of freedom which is available to all people, yet so few possess it. His is freedom from the slavery of sin, and from rules and regulations for earning his acceptance.

Man's freedom, which he lost in the Fall, is restored in redemption and experienced in the process of sanctification. He is delivered from the bondage of the human will, now free to do God's will, and now he is free indeed (Jn. 8:35-36). The heart of the Gospel is the freedom from the need to keep the Law in order to earn our salvation.

Freedom from bondage means to be released from whatever prison is holding us, from whatever is binding us spiritually, mentally and emotionally. Freedom frees us from pride, resentments, jealousies, obsessions and oppressions which may be eating away at us.

We must not insist on extra-biblical standards of behavior to be acceptable in Christ, for we cannot do one thing to earn more acceptance than His sacrifice which gave us full acceptance. Spiritual prohibitions which may seem sensible will not resolve issues if they are not Biblical, for a heavy emphasis on external rules represents a lapse back under the Law.

Church rules which encroach upon Christian freedom tend to create a rash of contradictions and hypocrisies, for they cater to craving for acceptance by human standards and efforts. For example, to insist dogmatically that something Jesus created and drank in His day is now sinful for all Christians contradicts the freedom Christ has given us. He gave severe warnings against drunkenness, but not against drinking. What Jesus sought was an internal discipline which controls external use. When it can be established by medical evidence that normal use of any substance is harmful instead of helpful, then use should be rejected.

Legalism And Pharisees

Jesus ran head-on into what someone has called the world champion nit-pickers, the Pharisees. Although the law of Moses allowed an afternoon snack, which Jesus did in taking some grain to eat, the Pharisees became terribly upset as they accused Jesus of violating the Sabbath rest. Thus they gave fanatic attention to external details, which Jesus rejected by saying, "The day of worship was made for people, not people for the day of worship. For this reason the Son of Man has authority over the day of worship" (Mk. 2:27-28). Jesus did not allow them to use the Sabbath as a test to see how many little rules they could keep to protect their religiosity and prove their spirituality. This was ridiculous legalism.

The Pharisees' rule-laden mentality manages to get footholds into our lives, too. No matter how free God's grace is, some want to take us back under the Law with them. The reason for legalism is that we do not want to be told that we can do nothing to merit God's approval, so we try to design a lifestyle that gives us at least a little credit. This leads to a false security which rests in human deeds rather than God's finished work of salvation.

The Pharisees shared many of Jesus' beliefs, taking seriously the Biblical doctrine of God's government of the universe. Their legalism caused their interpretation to be faulty, building it on a body of traditions which became as holy as the Law itself. It is easy to give traditions higher value than God's will, since all of us have some of the Pharisee within us. Jesus harshly criticized them for honoring the traditions of men over the Law of God. Jesus differed from them in what they regarded as important, what it meant to be holy, and what it meant to know and obey God.

The Pharisees were less concerned with the messages of the prophets, which correct man, than they were with the priestly ceremonial laws. Their religious activity was not pleasing to God as they offended His relationship with them. Jesus did not accept the pecking order or lordship of man which they held sacred. Rather, He required servanthood (Mk. 10:42-45; Jn. 13:1-20). Thus Jesus revealed the nature of God and the tremendous value He places on human life and relations, reaching out to others in love to mirror the very nature of God Himself. Christianity is a call to love as God loves, not to obey the traditions of men.

Jesus taught the same lesson of love and relationships in His conversation with the lawyer reported in Luke 10:25-37. When the lawyer wanted a religious discussion apparently to appeal to his human instincts and to intellect, Jesus turned it into a concrete lesson about spiritual realities and about the basic truths of life. Jesus summed up life in terms of love to God and to our neighbor. Jesus took the Law seriously, but He showed that love was intertwined with it in an integral manner. He showed that if they had understood the whole of the Law, they would have understood the call to loving relationships. God's call to holiness was not to avoid association with others, but to have association with others on godly terms of love.

While the Pharisees understood holiness in terms of rituals and ceremonial actions and separation from sinners, Jesus showed holiness through His image of God as Reconciler and His radical difference from the world through a life of love. The Pharisees depended on outer props instead of inner vitality.

People could not know what God is like by looking at the Pharisees because they could see no love in them, for love shows what God is like. The Pharisees also showed that knowledge is not enough, for they considered themselves righteous because of their great knowledge. They appeared to be overeducated and undertransformed.

The legalist, like the Pharisee, is dangerous because he carefully builds his own pattern of living and tries to make it normative for all Christians, making others prisoners of his expectations. He insists on being both the judge and jury for the rest of the Christian community. Legalism creates man-made fences which restrict others from living with consciences free from human bondage. The rules of legalism are usually cultural in their origin rather than Biblical.

By keeping the letter of the Law and missing the intent, legalism fails to develop real maturity and Christian moral character. It can lead to pride in one's obedience to a set of rules.

Legalism is a man-made religion which negates the vitality and strength that God's grace brings to life. Such a "rules-religion" will fence us out from the spontaneity of the

Gospel and the maturity it gives. The fact is that man-made rules and legalisms simply do not help us discipline our sinful desires: "These things look like wisdom with their self-imposed worship, false humility, and harsh treatment of the body. But they have no value for holding back the constant desires of your corrupt nature" (Col. 2:23). Here God reveals the inadequacy of rules and self-effort which are elevated to divine imperative. At the same time, God uses the Law to provide principles which give structure and order to what otherwise would be anarchy in our lives.

Ethics And Values — Shaping Character

Ethics relate to what is right in conduct, habits and customs. Values are the worth we set on ourselves and things — how we prize them.

The basic presuppositions of Biblical ethics and values include the fact that God is by nature ethical and men are responsible to Him, and that God values us highly in Christ and that we are to value life highly. The Christian life relates to moral decisions and ethical actions from a holy God, and there is constant tension between the ideal (God's will) and the actual (our actions). The Holy Spirit is active in every phase of the Christian's ethical decision-making. God has made His church responsible for influencing the social order by Gospel dynamics, not by politics.

Christian ethics looks to the Bible for ethical norms and principles. Social sciences have value for analysis of the issue and the context, but not to set the standards.

Emphases which are prominent in the ethics of the Bible are: 1. The will of God — God expects believers to do His commands; 2. Godlikeness — the character of God is to be the pattern for the character of man; 3. Love — God is love and His people are to love, which is the supreme virtue; 4. Covenant — God set forth specific obligations in faith for His people; 5. Community — the ethical requirements are for a community of persons, not merely individuals, for they are intended to be the people of God, not isolated persons.

133

Jesus Christ is the moral standard for Christian ethics, and our Christian belief is to determine our ethics and values. Every moral decision and all human behavior must be weighed against this standard. A Christian expectation of ethics and values starts from a new character, a divinely-given existence through regeneration which we possess in Christ. Biblical ethics are rooted in establishing the moral life and putting to death the old self and being renewed, putting on the new self. Those who do not grasp the radical nature of this truth will misunderstand the way in which Christian ethics transcends human weaknesses. We are no longer under Law, but are now directly under the Lawgiver, Who by His grace regenerates us and grants us the strength to live by the Spirit to follow the Law as a guide. This gives the joy of serving beyond the obligation of the Law.

As Christians, our primary task is not merely the cultivating of moral or religious values, but remaining faithful to the Gospel in a culture that is secular in varying degrees. Christ in Scripture, not ill-defined love, is the infallible norm for ethical action.

The way we value ourselves will determine the direction of our lives. A wrong standard of value will drive us in the wrong direction. People who have bitterness and hate will place a low value on others and will be blind to true love and beauty. This becomes a vicious circle as those who are treated badly, feel badly, and then act badly. And if they act badly, they will be treated badly, and so goes the circle. We must pay careful attention to value, for the heart pursues value, pays attention to what it values, provides for what it values, and protects what it values.

Devaluation exists because of sin, for sin distorts value as it changes the price tags. The devaluation of man begins with the devaluation of God, succumbing to an attack upon the character of God. Devaluation of people can always be traced to a devaluation of God. "Who am I?" must lead us back to God our Creator, where our true identity and value is learned.

After refusing to glorify God, some people "exchanged God's truth for a lie. So they have become ungodly and serve what is created rather than the Creator, who is blessed forever.

Amen!" (Rom. 1:25). Separated from God, man's darkened mind devalues himself. Rather than responding appropriately to the true value of God, man tears down God's character. As he alters his concept of God, he will even change the demanding Ten Commandments to be "Ten Suggestions."

Donald G. Bloesch presents God as Reconciler, Sanctifier and Civilizer. He writes, "The cultivation of the arts and sciences would not be possible apart from the work of God as Civilizer. It is God Who educates and enlightens so that people realize their potential for culture and wisdom. It is God Who leads people beyond provincialism and tribalism into a social existence that makes room for human sublimity...Unless people learn to know and fear their Creator and Lord, their efforts to build a just society will ultimately be self-defeating. Sanctity is necessary before education, for otherwise people will misuse the skills and knowledge they acquire. Repentance is necessary before there can be real peace among peoples.

"No enduring civilization or culture, in the highest meaning of the terms, is possible apart from the light of the Gospel and the leaven of the church. It is the church that provides the spiritual and metaphysical foundation for culture, and it is the Spirit working through the Gospel Who endows people with the motivation and the power to pursue peace and justice." [7]

God the Civilizer, as Donald Bloesch states, is the source of all ethics. Ethical standards not derived from God will be filled or supplied by human opinions. Moral standards depend upon something that transcends the earthly. The world's values are in sharp contrast to God's values.

Our goal as Christians is to bring people into a saving relationship with Jesus Christ. The weapons of the church are spiritual, not legal. The world needs a prophetic church, not a politicized one. The mission of the prophetic church is also to be a servant church. Through the Gospel, the church should be a leaven that turns the world in a new direction by changing attitudes, ideas, hopes and goals.

Destructive to Christian ethics are antinomianism (living without the law), legalism (divine will reduced to rules), and relativism (there are no absolute standards). Relativism and situation ethics contend that the only criterion for right and wrong is humanly-defined love, often based on whether it feels good. However, love needs an anchor, and the only absolute criterion is the law of Christ. Situation ethics does not have adequate emphasis on the seriousness of sin, and does not take God or the Bible seriously. It assumes that people can act responsibly because of some unanchored good will, but it fails to acknowledge the value of principles, guides and rules.

Humanism where we are the measure of all things is a law to itself and denies God as Civilizer and Reconciler, as it looks to man to establish standards for himself. However, humanism never takes evil seriously, for it proposes that people behave badly, cruelly and selfishly for economic, political and psychological reasons. It allows no extra-human source of goodness and compassion, and no healing and rehabilitation by the Spirit of God.

Humanism has provided unlimited license for destructive thought. Humanists have failed to understand both human nature and God. They are lost in a sea of utter confusion where they will never find meaning to life, authority or God. Proclaiming itself as guide, the humanistic way of thinking finds no task higher than the attainment of delusive happiness on earth because it does not admit either the existence of evil in man or the holiness of God. Charles Colson wrote: "What people once expected from the Almighty, they now expect from the almighty bureaucracy. That's a bad trade for anyone; but for the Christian, it's rank idolatry."[8]

Christian values differ radically from all others because God is seen as the ultimate source of truth and authority and Jesus Christ as Lord of all areas of life. Furthermore, the Bible is God's special revelation and the sufficient authority for man, who was created by God.

Our values are our blueprint for living. Someone has said, "Sow a thought, reap an act; sow an act, reap a habit; sow a habit, reap a character; sow a character, reap a destiny."

It is vital, therefore, that we seek Biblical values and think Biblically every time we make a decision. In doing so, we should identify and question each alternative by comparing it to God's standard on the matter. Then define the issue or problem by the guidance of the Holy Spirit and apply Biblical perspectives to make the decision. Always ask, "What is the Biblical response to the challenges that face me?"

Values based on the nature and will of God are eternally relevant. Eternal and universal values are revealed by God in the Ten Commandments which are necessary for social order in any society.

The Ten Commandments As A Blessing And Grace Event

While the Ten Commandments reveal God's Law which shows us our failure and rebellion, it is important that we see the love that caused God by His grace to give His Commandments as protection from harming ourselves and others, and as freedom from slavery. The Law condemns us for our own sin, but it is also a guide for the Christian to do the will of God. Grace is evident because God cared enough to give the Ten Commandments as a danger signal and as a guide for Christian conduct.

Learn of the love of God as He makes a covenant, and He promises to do wonders: "I'm making my promise again. In front of all your people I will perform miracles that have never been done in any other nation in all the world. All the people around you will see how awesome these miracles are that I will perform for you. Do everything that I command today. Then I will force the Amorites, Canaanites, Hittites, Perizzites, Hivites, and Jebusites out of your way" (Ex. 34:10-11).

The Ten Commandments should not take the freedom out of life, but help give stability and orderliness. They give positive direction to Christian faith that can spare us from harmful ways and free us from stupid things which cause us shame. Because of God's love, the Commandments are protective in their intent. Through obedience to them by faith and by Gospel power we are protected from self-destruction and preserved from inflicting unnecessary harm on others. They point the way to lives that give honor and praise to God.

The Ten Commandments are a blueprint or a map for us believers to guide our thoughts as we make our daily decisions and choices. They are meant to be safety shields to protect us from the devil's war against us.

The first three of the Commandments govern a person's relationship to God Himself. When we look beyond the negatives, God is teaching believers that He loves us so much that He gives Himself to us. There is no other God and He alone gives us wholeness. He wants nothing to come between His relationship with us. Since He has given us His name, we will value His name and not profane it. He wants us to set aside a day weekly to celebrate His relationship with us, and to give our bodies and minds rest, remembering whose we are and who gives us all we have.

The other seven commandments show that God loves His creatures so much that He wants them to experience love from and to each other, too. Life is sacred, and God wants it preserved and respected. He desires loving relationships among all, beginning in the family. He makes ownership a privilege and responsibility and so entrusts us with possessions and property, and He wants us to respect everyone's right to ownership and work. God shows that our relationships succeed only when truth prevails and trust is built, avoiding all lies and falsehoods which harm anyone's reputation.

Hear of the love and mercy as well as warnings against sin which God proclaims to Moses: "The Lord, the Lord, a compassionate and merciful God, patient, always faithful and ready to forgive. He continues to show his love to thousands of generations, forgiving wrongdoing, disobedience, and sin. He never lets the guilty go unpunished, punishing children and grandchildren for their parents' sins to the third and fourth generation" (Ex. 34:6-7).

As He brought His people out of bondage in Egypt, so He will deliver us from our sin and slaveries: "I am the Lord your God, who brought you out of slavery in Egypt" (Ex. 20:2). It is significant that the Ten Commandments follow this reminder of deliverance from bondage, an act of grace and love. For us, they show how to be delivered from slavery to our own sinful nature.

The Ten Commandments Considered

"Never have any other god.

"Never make your own carved idols or statues that represent any creature in the sky, on the earth, or in the water. Never worship them or serve them, because I, the Lord your God, am a God who does not tolerate rivals. I punish children for their parents' sins to the third and fourth generation of those who hate me. But I show mercy to thousands of generations of those who love me and obey my commandments.

"Never use the name of the Lord your God carelessly. The Lord will make sure that anyone who carelessly uses his name will be punished.

"Remember the day of worship by observing it as a holy day. You have six days to do all your work. The seventh day is the day of worship dedicated to the Lord your God. You, your sons, your daughters, your male and female slaves, your cattle, and the foreigners living in your city must never do any work on that day. In six days the Lord made heaven, earth, and the sea, along with everything in them. He didn't work on the seventh day. That's why the Lord blessed the day he stopped his work and set this day apart as holy.

"Honor your father and your mother, so that you may live for a long time in the land the Lord your God is giving you.

"Never murder.

"Never commit adultery.

"Never steal.

"Never lie when you testify about your neighbor.

"Never desire to take your neighbor's household away from him. Never desire to take your neighbor's wife, his male or female slave, his ox, his donkey, or anything else that belongs to him" (Ex. 20:3-17).

Jesus taught His followers to teach and obey the Commandments (Mt. 5:19). God gave the Law and the Ten Commandments for three purposes:

1. A **curb** or restraint: God's Law helps us to preserve order in the world by keeping the wicked actions of ourselves and

139

all peoples within bounds. Just as a curb marks the boundary of a street or road, so God's Law shows us what is out of bounds. It is to discourage us from disobeying God. This is for our outward lives (1 Tim. 1:9-10; Ps. 119:120; Rom. 2:14-15).

2. A **mirror**: God's Law works in the hearts of people to show them God's hatred and condemnation for their sin and their need of a Savior (Rom. 3:20; 7:7). Just as a mirror shows us what we look like, so God's Law shows us the naked truth about ourselves and allows us to see the mistakes of which we are guilty in attitude and actions. We might apply some kind of spiritual make-up to deceive our fellow men, but God cannot be fooled. He looks at the heart, not appearance. We are shown how selfish, proud or deceitful we may be.

3. A **guide**: God's Law tells Christians, blinded by sin and living in a sinful world, the deeds and way of life which is pleasing to God (Ps. 119:9, 105; Rom. 12:1-2; 2 Cor. 5:15; Deut. 10:12-15; 1 Jn. 5:3-4). The Law tells us how we should put our faith into practice. Here we are shown the directives and ideals we are to follow. It provides the boundaries for acceptable human behavior, a blueprint, a pattern for life. It reveals a code of ethics. This is called the third use of the Law — a guideline for believers. Biblical norms are a source of positive prescription and of establishing boundaries, revealing God's will and pointing to the road of freedom in Christ.

In our study of the Ten Commandments, we will look both at the threat and the promise of the Law given by our gracious God. His promise shows that He is serious about wanting us to keep every one of His Commandments, and that He wants to keep us safe in this life and hold us as His own throughout eternity. His promise to bless our obedience is an undeserved gift. His gracious promise should lead us to love and trust in Him and gladly obey what He commands.

God's commandments are rooted in His very being as His loving will for us is to love and to be holy. They reveal the character of God. These commandments are eternal truths revealed by God for Christian living to those He created and redeemed. The Commandments establish God's place in our lives, and the priorities and values we are to adopt.

The Ten Commandments as a goal for godliness provide the foundation upon which Christian character is built. Godliness is composed of the essential elements of the fear of God, the love of God, and the desire for God. The power for godly character comes from God, but the responsibility for decisions in developing and displaying that character is ours.

The Ten Commandments are a description of reality by the One who created the world and us. These are guidelines for governing human behavior which are meant to enable us to live the very best and most fulfilling life on earth under God's grace. It is important to look beyond the surface negativism of the Ten Commandments to learn something of the loving and gracious nature of God's laws to encourage reverence to God and fellow men.

The first three Commandments deal with our relationship with God, and the last seven Commandments treat our relationship with other people. The Biblical revelation concerning love for God and fellow men undergirds the Ten Commandments, for they belong together (Mt. 22:39).

A lawyer asked the question: "Teacher, which commandment is the greatest in Moses' Teachings?" (Mt. 22:36). Jesus answered him, "Love the Lord your God with all your heart, with all your soul and with all your mind. This is the greatest and most important Commandment. The second is like it: 'Love your neighbor as yourself.' All Moses' Teachings and the Prophets depend on these two commandments" (Mt. 22:37-40; Deut. 6:5). The terms heart, soul, strength and mind are used to stress that man is to seek to love God with his total being:

1. With all our heart, all our powers of the will, informed by God's Word so that we might know what we should and should not do;

2. With all our soul, all our powers of emotion, developing Christlike qualities in service to God and others;

3. With all our strength or physical powers, keeping fit to be living sacrifices of God for our servant work;

4. With all our mind or powers of intellect, being equipped through knowledge and understanding to be edifiers of our fellow men.

First Commandment

NEVER MAKE YOUR OWN CARVED IDOLS OR STATUES THAT REPRESENT ANY CREATURE IN THE SKY, ON THE EARTH, OR IN THE WATER. NEVER WORSHIP THEM OR SERVE THEM... (Ex. 20:4-5).

The main goal is to glorify God as we fear or revere Him, love Him, and trust Him. We give glory to God above all things by placing His Word and command above that of anyone else, by considering Him as more dear to us than anyone or anything else, and by relying on Him for help more than anyone or anything else.

The principle is that God is sovereign and the command is that no divided loyalty is allowed. Jesus gave a New Testament version of the First Commandment in Matthew 4:10: "Worship the Lord your God, and serve only him." We give adoration to one God, not many. A god is whoever or whatever a person gives loyalty to, looks to for good things, and runs to for comfort and help in trouble.

False gods give promise of big hopes which they cannot deliver. Whatever promises they make are phony, making them humanly fabricated faiths. The false gods manipulate people by offering counterfeits of what the divine, eternal God has to offer. Instead of the "heaven on earth" which they offer, the opposite is gained: shame, alienation, rejection, death.

There is no support available from a false god. People who run on energy derived from an unregenerated ego that attaches itself to a god which is no more than human illusion are disconnected from the divine support system. This leaves them helpless and hopeless, alienated from the true God.

False gods do not give freedom, but slavery. They do not give glory or share glory because they have nothing to offer. The eternal God shares the glory of His Son Jesus Christ with His children. He trusts us with the management of our lives, our possession, and even of His Church by the guidance and power of the Holy Spirit.

False gods cannot communicate with us. We learn about them only by communication from those who have been deceived by them. They cannot hear or listen. They cannot relate to us, and they cannot offer grace and forgiveness.

Since false gods are a false image of God, they give their worshipers a false image of themselves. False gods give people a distorted self-view. Only the God who created man in His own image can provide a true self-image to people. That image has promise only as the Creator and Redeemer God shines into our regenerated hearts and minds and then loves through our lives and speaks grace and peace through our lips. False gods destroy all of this. Only the God of heaven and earth is worthy of glory, honor and majesty.

The Old Testament gives vivid descriptions of an uncompromising denunciation of the idolatry which seduced God's chosen people. The true God is a divine Person in heaven, while earthly gods have mouths, eyes and ears, but they cannot speak, see or hear (Ps. 115:3-8). Isaiah exposed the vanity of idolatry and the misguided zeal of idol makers when he wrote, "All who make idols are nothing. Their precious treasures are worthless. Their own witnesses do not see or know anything, so they will be put to shame" (Is. 44:9). John tells all about Jesus and then ends with a warning, "Guard yourselves from false idols" (1 Jn. 5:21).

Love and priority to another god displaces and dethrones the true God; this is misplaced allegiance and idolatry. People sin openly against God when they give glory to idols (idolatry) and when they give glory to the Father without giving equal glory to Jesus and honor to the Holy Spirit. People can be guilty of private idolatry when someone or something takes first place in their hearts before God. Some worship their minds, bodies or themselves by putting their own ideas before God's Word. An idol is anything or anyone that usurps God's place in our hearts. An idol can be a habit, person, sex, possessions, a religious tenet, TV, or spectator sport that gets between God and man.

Involvement with false gods is a most serious violation of God's love or will, and it is referred to as spiritual adultery in the Old Testament. These false gods wear all kinds of masks, using deceptive techniques to seduce and destroy us. They ultimately destroy their worshipers.

God is true reality, the only God we will ever need. We cannot tolerate inferior representations of Him, for we need only Him. We have a wonderful gift of a direct, personal relationship between Him and us. Value it and do not destroy it.

Therefore, we gladly place God's Word before all other words spoken, no matter how wise. We place Him before all the books which explain that He is a god of another age. We place Him first in our minds before all the interesting things which clamor for our attention. We place Him first in our time schedules when we have all kinds of other demands.

The Second Commandment

NEVER USE THE NAME OF THE LORD YOUR GOD CARELESSLY. "The Lord will make sure that anyone who carelessly uses his name will be punished" (Ex. 20:7).

God's name is every expression which He uses to refer to Himself. He revealed Himself to us in His Word, and by its use He blesses and saves us (Ex. 20:24; Rom. 10:13). God's name displays what He has to offer in His relationship with us. Our use of His name affects our relations with Him. To worship God is to love and honor His name.

When we are adopted into God's family, we are identified with His name. He is Father of the family of which we are members by faith in Jesus. Our language and the use of His name declare our reverence of Him, and the value we place upon our relationship with Him.

If words or names can turn us off or on, we can readily understand why we value the name of God and how we use it. We dare no more misuse God's name than abuse the names of our spouse, children or friends. Abuse of a name is demeaning, whether it is God's or yours. To dishonor God is to dishonor ourselves who are created by Him.

By telling us His name and His Word, God makes it possible for us to know Him and to communicate with and worship Him. The way we treat His name indicates our attitude toward

Him. Thus thoughtless references to Jesus Christ or God Almighty are as demeaning as angry cursing in His name.

Exodus 20:7 shows that cursing is a sinful misuse of God's name and will not be tolerated. Swearing is a sin when we use God's name to verify a lie (Lev. 19:12; Mt. 26:74). Taking an oath or swearing is also wrong when we do not know what we are promising to do, as Herod did in uncertain things (Mk. 6:21-28). God's Word is not to be used superstitiously, treating it as if it were magic by doing witchcraft or contacting spirits.

God's name stands for everything He is and does. It is different from all other names because He is set apart as the only perfect and infinite being. As we use God's name with the respect it deserves, we will use it to pray, to give thanks, to praise Him, and to honor His name.

He loves us so much that He has given us His name, for we are known as His people. Valuing that privilege, we will not misuse His name by profaning our spiritual Family name or by not living as God's people. The Second Commandment is violated also by meaningless religion in which Christians want to be identified with God without being committed to His will and cause, to be "religious," yet irreligious in their actions and attitudes. Another way in which we break this commandment is by being casual in things meant to be sacred or to be flippant in matters of faith.

The Third Commandment

REMEMBER THE DAY OF WORSHIP BY OBSERVING IT AS A HOLY DAY. "You have six days to do all your work. The seventh day is the day of worship dedicated to the Lord your God. You, your sons, your daughters, your male and female slaves, your cattle, and the foreigners living in your city must never do any work on that day. In six days the Lord made heaven, earth, and the sea, along with everything in it. He didn't work on the seventh day. That's why the Lord blessed the day he stopped his work and set this day apart as holy" (Ex. 20:8-11).

Sabbath means rest. The Sabbath day (which was a Saturday) was used as a holy day of rest and worship. Colossians 2:13-17 shows that the exact day is not commanded for Christians, as was prescribed in the Old Testament. It is still God's will that Christians keep one day holy and also gather for worship and rest to honor God.

All the commandments are about relationships. This one is about worshipful communication with our Creator-Redeemer-Sanctifier. Communication lines should be open and used actively between us and our God. Since relationships can be corrupted, they can weaken or be disrupted if there is not steady contact. The temptation is always present to give attention and devotion to earthly competition, which takes time away from our one essential relationship.

Christians have two tasks or works: glorifying God through our occupations and worship. This is what we are created to do as beings made in the image of God and saved by the blood of Christ. The prime sin against the Third Commandment is a failure to do these works of glorifying God. There is a laziness that avoids Creator-attention and creature-awareness, as we busily divert our attention from God to ourselves.

We may think we have kept the Sabbath (worship and rest or pray and play) by Sunday church-going or pew-sitting for one hour. While this day was intended to get us into step with the rhythm of the Triune God through worship and relaxation, we find ourselves on the run, watching the clock to the extent that we can barely unwind for one hour while the rest of the day is focused on material things and physical activities rather than spiritual.

Puritan America of two centuries ago was good at Lord's Day worship and prayer, but ruled out play. Our culture today is strong on Sunday self-centered play, but is weak in worship and prayer. By trivializing worship and prayer, our lives have been devalued to the extent that we often end the Lord's Day more fatigued than refreshed.

We apparently have not been aware that the world is conspiring to steal our Lord's Day, leaving us hurrying after fantasy and pleasures, and losing much of God and our dignity at the same time. Keeping of the Lord's Day cannot be imposed, but it can only be realized by believers who catch a sense of reverence of a great God worthy of worship and meditation. The intention of the Third Commandment is that we gain an intimacy with God through Bible study, worship and relaxation which provides weekly meditation that melds and weaves our beings into greater unity with the Divine Being.

We despise God's Word when we let anything in the world crowd worship out of our lives, and if we don't do what God's Word says. We worship God because He is worthy as One who created us, saved us, gave us faith, and made us His own through Baptism. In worship we show His worth and remember the mighty things He has done, that He has rescued us from sin's slavery and forgiven our transgressions.

Stress and tension which block communication must be relieved by rest. One day of quiet, rest, relaxation, and worship is obviously the solution to avoid the modern jungle of cars, buses, commerce, concrete and technology. Only within our church are we shielded from the telephones, ghetto blasters, insults from people, racing motors, and other indignities. There we relax in an atmosphere conducive to communication with One who knows us and loves us with an undying love. Here we communicate and build a closer relationship with Him. Here our emotional batteries are recharged, attitudes realigned, and our faith strengthened.

God must be worshipped in spirit and in truth, and He should be reverenced in all our deeds and words. In teaching us to pray in the Lord's Prayer that God's name be kept holy, Jesus encouraged all to honor the name of God.

The Third Commandment reveals that God wants us to gladly hear and learn His Word. We do this by attending Bible classes and public worship regularly, by listening carefully to God's Word and believing it, and by supporting the teaching and preaching of it.

God has given us a beautiful world in which to live, work and enjoy many things. Our bodies need rest, and our spirits need constant refreshing through Bible study and worship.

The Fourth Commandment

HONOR YOUR FATHER AND YOUR MOTHER, SO THAT YOU MAY LIVE FOR A LONG TIME IN THE LAND THE LORD YOUR GOD IS GIVING YOU. (Ex. 20:12).

This commandment establishes parents as God's representatives and shows the order of proper family life. It reveals that parents and parental authority in the family should be respected.

God commands children to honor and to obey their parents (Col. 3:20) by respecting, obeying, loving, serving and caring for them. They are not to despise their parents by making fun of them, by speaking or acting disrespectfully, by rebelling against them, or by causing them sorrow. God has given a special rank of distinction to fathers and mothers, higher than all other ranks in life.

God calls special attention to our parents because through them He gives us many blessings such as food, clothing, and shelter for our bodies, instruction in His Word and spiritual guidance for life. Our obedience to our parents and all those who govern us is a service to God, not men, and it pleases God and honors Christ (Col. 3:20; Eph. 5:20-21).

God adds a special promise to this commandment by emphasizing that He will bless us as we honor them (Eph. 6:2-3). He forbids us to disobey, dishonor, or anger our parents or others in authority (Deut. 21:18, 21; Prov. 30:11, 17; 2 Tim. 3:1-2).

God wants His representatives to rebuke and instruct patiently those who sin against His commandment and to discipline them when necessary (Rom. 13:2-4). Such discipline is a blessing, for it is designed to prevent a person from falling under God's terrible judgment (Prov. 19:18; 23:13).

At the same time, we live in an age in which some parents are disobedient to God and treat their children badly, giving emotional, verbal, spiritual, and even physical and sexual abuse. Such children become emotional cripples and spiritual orphans. Those who experience this should take great care to avoid self-pity or to transfer their alienation to God. They should get their self-worth from God, not their parents. We cannot change what has happened to us, but we can control our reactions and depend on God, our Heavenly Father, to give us what our earthly parents do not give. If we cannot depend on parents, we can depend on God.

If we have no family or are alienated from our family by no fault of our own, then we can attach ourselves to a "family." We can build family relations where there is respect and honor. We should not tolerate demeaning, insulting, negative "put-downs." We should make our family a place where each person's honor is protected and treasured.

The Fifth Commandment

NEVER MURDER (Ex. 20:13).

Human life is so sacred to God that He commands protection of body and life as His gift to every human being (the crown of His creation). The most valuable possession is life. The most appalling crime is to take it away. "...I will demand the life of any person who kills another person. Whoever sheds human blood, by humans his blood will be shed, because in the image of God, God made humans" (Gen. 9:5-6). God's call is to respect and reverence life, restore and revive it when in danger, and release it from any threats of damage.

Man's span of life is so important because once a person dies, his time of grace is ended, and he faces judgment. Life is so important that only God or His appointed representatives in government have the right to end a person's life (Deut. 32:39; Ps. 31:15; Gen. 9:5-6; Rom. 13:4).

Accidental killing, justifiable homicide, killing in war, and capital punishment were not considered murder in the Old Testament (Num. 35:23; Ex. 21:12ff; 22:2). Murder is violating a person's existence and his relationship with God. It is an attack upon the image of God in man. God has invested His creative self in the world and, specifically, in the design of our bodies, which are fearfully and wonderfully made (Ps. 139:14).

The negative side of this commandment is that we must

not take the life of another person, harm our own body, hurt or hate our neighbor in any way, or take our life or destroy it by a degenerate lifestyle. This includes avoidance of taking foolish risks and being cruel toward people or animals. We are to protect life as a precious gift of God, show kindness to our neighbor and help him in every possible way. We are to help those in need, forgiving those who do us wrong, trying to live at peace with others.

What about the unborn? Are they pre-human, just a fetus which has only future value and must wait for human recognition from fellow men? There is no distinction made in the Scriptures between babies in the womb and those already born, as the same Greek word is used to describe Elizabeth's baby before birth in Luke 1:41, 44 (even giving the unborn a name) and after birth in Luke 18:15. In Thayer's Greek-English Lexicon **brephys** means both an unborn and newborn child, an embryo or an infant, a fetus or a baby.

David's Psalm 139 speaks about the glorious creation of his and our body both before and after birth: "You alone created my inner being. You knitted me together inside my mother. I will give thanks to you because I have been so amazingly and miraculously made. Your works are miraculous, and my soul is fully aware of this. My bones were not hidden from you when I was being made in secret, when I was being skillfully woven in an underground workshop. Your eyes saw me when I was only a fetus. Every day of my life was recorded in your book before one of them had taken place" (Ps. 139:13-16).

Because all our days were selected by God and were written in His book of life before any part of us was formed in the womb (Jer. 1:5), God forbids the destruction of the unborn child (Ex. 21:22-23). This is true because God creates each person to know and resemble Himself as a child does a father. Because of this, nobody has a right to kill a baby in the prenatal home any more than one does to kill an adult in the family home. God designed the womb to be the safest refuge, as a home is for a person. Yet abortionists have made the womb the most dangerous place for a human being to be.

No one can question that the development of a new individual begins at fertilization. The question is what we identify it to be, and how we value it. At every stage of its development, human life is valued by God. As we are required to respect the lives of adult human beings, unborn and born babies are entrusted to our care as precious human lives. The Fifth Commandment shows that we are forbidden to participate in activities which cause unjustified killing. Ours is the limited role of a creature, not of a deity or God. Thus the Fifth Commandment restricts freedom related to ending the creation of a human being, no matter what stage of development.

The act of abortion clearly is a refusal to honor God as the Creator and to value life as He values it. We know too much about the unique features and identity of the unborn child to make the mistake of improperly calling a baby a "part" of the mother's body as though it is a disposable organ. The unborn human being is undergoing a time of growing in the environment in which all human beings are developed. The unborn child developing within the mother's body is clearly a human being entitled to care and protection by the mother and all society.

The human body is a precious resource for productivity and enjoyment in life. Each of us must set priorities in establishing and maintaining health and strength to serve God and our fellow man. Many experience mediocre or poor health, weight problems and lack of strength and vigor for a truly productive life because of abuse or misuse of their bodies.

God, the Giver of life and health, wants us to avoid doing whatever needlessly destroys, harms, shortens, or endangers life and health. This means that we should promote quality and length of life through good nutrition, exercise and adequate sleep. There is cause and effect in choosing our food and life-style.

Contributing to ill health and physical weaknesses, cardiac difficulties, and other physical problems are some refined foods and additives, caffeine, alcohol, and smoking. In view of the scientific facts and Biblical principles, Christians should take appropriate action, such as refraining from harmful habits and encourage others also. Disciples are to set a good example for others, and be patient, understanding and helpful to those who have developed bad health habits.

God, Who in love created, redeemed, and regenerated us, wants us to avoid whatever hinders our service, shortens our time on earth or that destroys or wastes anyone else's life.

God gave life its enormous worth. We are to respect it and hold on to it, and protect the lives of others also. God's love in our lives is to be poured into the lives of others as ourselves to aid release from any sinful or destructive slaveries against our bodies or lives.

The Sixth Commandment

NEVER COMMIT ADULTERY (Ex. 20:14).

Sex is a good gift of God. The purpose of the Commandment is to keep God's gift of sex pure in our bodies and to keep marriage holy. It is designed to protect the sanctity of family life, requiring purity of the sex life before and after marriage on the part of all.

Adultery is the breaking of a commitment and a relationship with God and another person. Only death causes more pain than adultery, which leaves emotional scars and physical diseases that afflict the guilty and innocent ones alike.

Jesus emphasized the character of this commandment by applying purity even to the heart, equating even the sexual look outside of marriage as an act of adultery (Mt. 5:28). It has a degrading effect on human character. It is a breach of faith and trust between people. Our choices carry lasting consequences.

God created us as sexual beings, making men and women so that they could live together as partners in marriage. He blessed them with the ability to have children, making them His partners in the creation of life.

The sex urge is one of the strongest instincts which in itself is not wrong, for God has given it to us. Because of sin, however, sex easily gets out of control to become an evil, harmful thing in our lives. Adultery or fornication is the choice of a god of pleasure, which distorts the reflection of God's image in one's life. It is also stealing trust, love and purity from another person.

According to God's Word marriage is a life-long union of one man and one woman (Gen. 2:24; Mt. 19:5-6; Rom. 7:2). This is a union and companionship in which the man is the head and the woman the partner (Eph. 4:24-25; 1 Cor. 11:3). Sex needs marriage, and marriage needs sex. God reserved sexual intercourse exclusively for this relationship.

God's Word concerning sexual purity is clear: sexual activity that degrades the humanity or dignity of others is wrong. The act of sexual union is to be experienced only within the security of the total commitment of marriage. In 1 Corinthians 7, Paul clearly tells us that marriage is to be a life-long one man-one woman relationship, and that sexual faithfulness is a part of that arrangement.

Strong sexual thoughts and desires for someone outside of marriage jeopardize our relationship with God, because impure thoughts are acts of disobedience against His standard of holy living. Uncontrolled thoughts with sexual fantasy erode our relationship with others.

The marriage relationship prior to and during marriage is broken down by lusting (Mt. 5:28), by unwholesome obscene talk and coarse jokes (Eph. 4:29; 5:3-4), by improper or suggestive clothes (Prov. 7:10; 1 Tim. 2:9), by giving in to fleshly desires (1 Pet. 2:11; Eph. 5:12), and by changing natural sex into unnatural actions like adultery, homosexuality, and lesbianism. The New Testament totally repudiates all outside-of-marriage and unnatural intercourse. The judgment against fornication and adultery in the Old Testament was very harsh.

Problems with sex flow from the Fall, and Paul traced this tragic development in Romans 1. As people turn God's good gift into sin and get farther from God, they become more debauched and morally corrupt. Sexual sins are worse because they are more damaging personally and socially, and they stain the deepest personal and relational identity. They produce guilt that cripples faith and a desire for God's forgiveness. They assault Christ's Lordship in one's life, for Christ will not be united with a fornicator (1 Cor. 6:19).

Sexual sins are sins against one's own body (1 Cor. 6:18). That means that we lose respect for our body, as well as for the body of the one with whom we may be involved. Losing respect leads to a warped view of love, centering our definition of love around the physical, getting caught in a deceitful illusion of seeking love merely in a sexual relationship. This becomes a game of shame.

God created us to be total beings, and we are not to take sex out of the context which God established. True love displays love for the whole person, while counterfeit love in the form of premarital sex is detrimental to the whole person. Sexual immorality harms the emotions and clouds the mind to make godly decisions. Outside of marriage the enjoyment of sex is short-lived. It is like looking for another fix to appease one's lust, much like a drug addict craves another shot.

There is a need to develop standards of sexual behavior which will direct this gift of God toward its most rewarding fulfillment. Christian standards ask, "What is right?" rather than "What do I want?" The world gives advice and sets an example which makes it more and more difficult for us to distinguish right from wrong: birth control methods are inexpensive and easy to obtain; most venereal diseases have an easy cure; abortions are legal and safe; adultery is common and acceptable under many circumstances; and divorce is an acceptable way out of a not-so-happy marriage. This is a new morality which promotes so-called freedom.

But how free is the teen-ager with an unwanted pregnancy? How free is the man who has contracted AIDS? How free is the child who is lost in the turmoil of a broken home? Without God and His perfect love, people are not free. The spread of tragic sexual disease together with death for the unborn does not speak of love or civility, but of barbarism and destruction. Fornication and adultery defile people (Mt. 15:19-20).

Christians should experience the freedoms of restraint or abstinence: the freedom from outside-of-marriage pregnancy and sexually transmitted diseases, abortion, pressure to marry too soon, exploitation of others, and the guilt and rejection that come from an illicit sexual affair. There is also the freedom to be in control of our bodies, to know our dating partners as persons rather than toys or things to be exploited. Christians should look forward to marriage to choose and be chosen by the kind of person one would want for the father and mother of one's children.

The Sixth Commandment also involves avoiding pornography, which destroys the image of God in mankind and hurts women and children. Pornography destroys normal human relationships and is addictive, rotting the fabric of society. It pulls people away from that which is good and godly.

While the world propagandizes and debates, God condemns homosexuality as sin (1 Cor. 6:9-10; Rom. 1:26-27). God leaves no doubt about the fact that homosexuals receive in themselves the due penalty for their perversion and that He condemns their moral behavior. The God of love does not turn us loose on each other to destroy our bodies and ruin our lives by forbidden sexual acts separated from marriage and from godly love.

The homosexual lifestyle is not an alternative lifestyle that is acceptable to God. The only appropriate responses are repentance, confession, forgiveness, healing and restoration. Arrogance will lead to self-destruction, whereas brokenness in heart through true repentance will result in the gracious forgiveness of Christ. Jesus said all are to come to Him, including those guilty of homosexuality and adultery, but on His terms, not on theirs.

God reminds us that our bodies are the dwelling-place of the Holy Spirit and that we should glorify God in our bodies, keeping away from people and places which tempt us to sin against this commandment (1 Cor. 6:18-19; Prov. 1:10).

The deepest human relationship possible is marriage, as God created it to solve the essential loneliness in the hearts of people. We must value that relationship highly and save sexual intimacy for its rightful place for reproduction and enjoyment in the family situation. Adultery is never an option.

The Seventh Commandment

NEVER STEAL (Ex. 20:15).

Here God speaks of the proper attitude toward His property placed into man's care. Personal property is a sacred trust from God. Not only are we not to take any property away from anyone else, but we are also to make sure that adequate wages are fully paid (Deut. 25:14; Jas. 5:4), that we share honestly (Deut. 25:13), and give to the poor (Deut. 15:7-11). Jesus emphasized generosity to the needy (Mt. 5:42). Lying about products we sell, bribing officials, evading taxes, and swindling dare never be allowed to masquerade as legitimate business methods.

The positive side of this commandment stresses the commitment to unselfish work, the importance of earning, the obligations that go with owning, and the sacred stewardship of managing possessions and property.

God gives to whom He pleases, giving more to some and less to others. All are to be faithful caretakers of what has been entrusted to them (Deut. 8:17-18; 1 Cor. 4:2; Prov. 22:2).

Our possessions have been given so that we might have the necessities of life (Ps. 145:15-16), provide for our family (1 Tim. 5:8), find satisfaction in our work (Ecc. 5:18), share with those in need (Eph. 4:28), cheerfully give for the work of the Lord (1 Cor. 16:2; 2 Cor. 9:11), support the work of the government (Lk. 20:25; Rom. 13:6-7), and express thanks to God (Eph. 5:20; 2 Cor. 9:12-13).

There are three ways in which we may gain possessions: by working diligently for them (2 Thes. 3:10-12); by paying for them (Prov. 31:16); and by having them given to us (Mt. 7:11). Sometimes we may even gain something by finding it and not being able to find the owner.

We should always be satisfied with what God gives and be content (1 Tim. 6:6-7). We should always help a neighbor to care for his property (1 Cor. 10:24).

There are some things which we should avoid: failing to thank God (Lk. 17:17-18); taking advantage or cheating others (1 Thes. 4:6); paying low wages (Jas. 5:4); wasting possessions (Lk. 15:13); charging too much (Lk. 3:13); robbing God and giving leftovers (Mal. 3:8); being lazy and not working to earn an income if possible (2 Thes. 3:10).

As stewards or caretakers, we are responsible to God for the way we use the possessions He has asked us to manage. God warns against covetousness or greed, which is a perverted sense of man's God-given right to own things. God warns in Ephesians 5:5 that a greedy person, like an immoral one, will not have any inheritance in the kingdom of Christ and of God. Greed causes excessive love for luxury, gambling, using fraud or dishonesty in dealing with others, calling stinginess thrift, hoarding unreasonably, or using questionable methods to obtain things.

God entrusts us with property, which is a great privilege and responsibility. God expects dividends from these investments for Him.

The Eighth Commandment

NEVER LIE WHEN YOU TESTIFY ABOUT YOUR NEIGHBOR (Ex. 20:16).

Here God protects His gift of our good name. This means speaking and listening to the truth, being truthful, and refusing to listen to slander, tale-bearing, gossip or character assassination. Rumors (unreliable stories that cause anxiety or confusion about events or things) and gossip about people are harmful to the individuals involved. "Triangling" is a vicious attempt to get people caught in the middle between them and someone else.

A good name is important because it determines whether or not other people will respect us or trust us. This commandment forbids anyone to lie about another person (Prov. 19:5), to say anything which will give another person a bad name (Jas. 4:11; 1 Tim. 5:13), and betray another person's secrets (Prov. 11:13; 25:9).

God wants us to defend the good name of others, speak well of them, and accept words and actions in the kindest possible way. We are forbidden to gossip (Prov. 16:28), use careless words (Mt. 12:36), judge or condemn others by our own standards (Mt. 7:1; 1 Cor. 4:3, 5). Taming the warring tongue is vital for the Christian. The tongue has power to communicate both good or evil (Jas. 3:5-10).

Any accusation against anyone must first be brought to the one who is accused. Any other approach of sharing it with others is sinful, if it is designed to destroy the reputation of the other. This rule of God is designed to protect both the accuser and the accused in case there is a misunderstanding, and at the same time to allow corrections to be made through proper repentance and forgiveness if that is necessary. Christ has established guidelines in Matthew 18 for dealing with differences between people, whether real, imagined, or misunderstood. Paul said that when we listen to accusations, we are first to establish the facts with two or three witnesses (1 Tim. 5:13, 19), and that we are to bear with each other and forgive whatever grievances we may have against one another who repents, forgiving as the Lord forgives (Col. 3:12-13).

Gossip and false witness are ugly. They tamper with truth, malign people's character, and ruin the reputation of the innocent. Victims of slander were Joseph (Gen. 39:7-20), Jesus (Mt. 11:19), Stephen (Acts 6:11-14), and Paul (Acts 24:5-9). Every report that cannot be adequately proven is false witness. What is secret should be allowed to remain secret, including correction in secret.

Precautions to help prevent us from bearing false witness include the evaluating of the sources of information, resisting exaggeration and avoiding half-truths. Be willing to deal directly with the source of information or misinformation.

The tongue may pollute the entire being of a person, as James describes how it can lead to the evil of evils as it soils the whole body, sets on fire the whole course of our life, and is set on fire by hell (3:6). An unknown author wrote:

A careless word may kindle strife;
A cruel word may wreck a life;
A bitter word may hate instill;
A brutal word may smite and kill.

The poet shows the blessings the tongue may give:

A gracious word may smooth the way;
A joyous word may light the day;
A timely word may lessen stress;
A loving word may heal and bless.

We need God's help so that we may protect others from evil talk and support them in love. Let every Christian adopt the principle, "If there are any criticisms, talk **to** people, not **about** people."

Relationships only succeed when they are governed by telling truth about each other in love (Eph. 4:15).

The Ninth And Tenth Commandments

NEVER DESIRE TO TAKE YOUR NEIGHBOR'S HOUSEHOLD AWAY FROM HIM. NEVER DESIRE TO TAKE YOUR NEIGHBOR'S WIFE, HIS MALE OR FEMALE SLAVE, HIS OX, HIS DONKEY, OR ANYTHING ELSE THAT BE-LONGS TO HIM (Ex. 20:17).

Coveting is the sinful desire for anything, wanting something that we have no right to have or seeking to get it in a sinful way. Coveting can lead to sins against the other commandments and destroy our relationship with God and with other people. God is impressing on us that He condemns not only our sinful words and actions, but also our sinful thoughts which lead to sinful actions (Rom. 7:7-8; Jas. 1:14-15).

Coveting finds Achan dying because of his desire for money (Josh. 7:20-21). It is Aaron and Miriam envying a superior's position (Num. 12:2). It is Absolom scheming to gain his father's power (2 Sam. 15:1-6). It is David killing another man for his wife (2 Sam. 11:2-5). It is you and me always seeking something bigger and better, or simply demanding something new and different. It is the desire which brings evil with it: "Then desire becomes pregnant and gives birth to sin. When sin grows up, it gives birth to death" (Jas. 1:15).

Coveting may lead us to undertake certain strategies or procedures which are legal and acceptable by society's standards but violate the spirit of these commandments. It leads some to lawsuits in an attempt to get something away from a neighbor.

Covetousness is desire that has become uncontrolled, wild — normal desire gone wrong. It drives people to steal, sacrifice or even kill. It causes us to rivet our eyes on something we do not have, rather than praising God for what we do own.

These Commandments take us back to the First Commandment because covetousness puts a false god in the place of the true God in our lives, for greed seeks first the kingdom of things, not the Kingdom of God. Rather than scheming to get something which is our neighbor's, God teaches us to be content always with everything so that we do not covet anything that belongs to our neighbor (1 Cor. 7:17; Heb. 13:5).

We should be satisfied with the gifts God supplies to meet our basic needs, and be happy for our neighbor when he has something we do not have. We should help our neighbor keep his property, as we hope in God and His loving promises.

We are to desire only that which is within the will of God. People are always more important than things, so we are to **love people while using things** for the good of others, too.

Not all desires are bad. The desire to be more Christlike, to have a stronger faith, to be more fruitful and faithful in our Christian lives, and to be more bold in witnessing are good because they are the will of God for us. To desire the higher gifts (1 Cor. 12:31) is to want to be available to God for service as His stewards. We should also desire the fruit of the Spirit (Gal. 5:22-23).

The Conclusion To The Ten Commandments

God calls any breaking of His Commandments sin (missing the mark), transgression (crossing the forbidden line), and iniquity (failing to measure up perfectly). God threatens to punish on earth and in eternity all those who disobey His Commandments. This threat tells us that God is jealous and serious about wanting us to keep every one of His Commandments. He promises grace and every blessing to those who love Him and keep them.

God's gracious promise should lead us to love and trust Him and gladly obey what He requests. We all confess that we are sinners who have broken God's Commandments and pray for and accept Christ's forgiveness. Under grace we look to these commands as freedom from slavery and protecting us and others from harm.

Paul helps us chart our course toward spiritual wholeness in supplying the following guidelines for our instruction to maximize our potential in living for God. He lists these behaviors and attitudes in Ephesians 4, which we have put on two sides of the ledger:

VIRTUES COMMENDED	VICES CONDEMNED
A renewed attitude of mind (v. 23)	Futility of thinking, darkened understanding, ignorance (v. 17-18)
Righteousness (v. 24)	Hardness of heart (v. 18)
Holiness (v. 24)	Loss of sensitivity (v. 19)
Speak truthfully (v. 25)	Uncontrolled sensuality (v.19)
Righteous anger (v. 26-27)	Impurity (v. 19)
Honest work (v. 28)	Lust for more and more (v. 19)
Wholesome talk (v. 29-30)	Bitterness (v. 31)
Kindness (v. 32)	Rage and anger (v. 31)
Compassion (v. 32)	Brawling (v. 31)
Forgiveness (v. 32)	Slander and malice (v. 31)

WHOLENESS TO SEEK	WRONG TO SHUN
Right thinking (Christian world view)	Wrong thinking (distorted world view)
Warm relationships ("giving and receiving" as a lifestyle)	Uncontrolled sensuality ("taking" as a lifestyle)
Speech which is wholesome	Speech that tears down
Honest work	Time wasting and laziness

New Steps To Security And Happiness

There are deep, yearning emotional needs that we all have in common, regardless of our uniqueness and individuality: the need to be loved, to know we are forgiven, to experience security, and to have adequate hope. We are all created this way by God who only can fulfill these needs. Other people cannot satisfy them. No person has enough love, forgiveness, security or hope to share with us in the amount that we need. Only the God who created us can fill the emptiness of our emotional needs through fellowship with Him. All that the world has to offer cannot fill that emptiness. Only Christ can do that.

Created as social beings, another need is to be related to people and to God. We will remain lonely no matter how many people are around is, if we are not related to Jesus Christ. We find security only in God's love and Christ's forgiveness.

Far too many people seem to be afraid of life and fearful to open themselves to God and others. They seem to be afraid of what they are and what they might find. Openness is necessary if we are to be honest in taking responsibility for choosing and defining our lives. What does life mean to us? What do we really want out of life? What will we put into it? How will we attain the security and happiness we seek?

Are we truthful enough at this time to follow the advice of Paul: "With them we destroy people's defenses, that is, their arguments and all their intellectual arrogance that oppose the knowledge of God. We take every thought captive so that it is obedient to Christ" (2 Cor. 10:4b-5). This requires assessment of our situation with integrity, as we recognize all of the devil's temptations and reject them in Jesus' name, replacing all harmful and negative thoughts with the Gospel of God's love and the Heavenly Father's protection. This portion of the Bible study is written as a reminder "refresh your memory" (2 Pet. 3:1).

Introduction To The Twelve Steps

The Twelve Steps of Alcoholics Anonymous have a basis of confession and forgiveness which are very beneficial to Christians when we add the Gospel emphasis at strategic points. We offer a Christian version which should help all Christians who experience various forms of obsessions, compulsions, addictions, or any kind of sinful habits.

There are many cravings and habits which hamper us in our spiritual life and growth that can be solved by faithful use of the Twelve Steps. Whether we are food-aholics, choc-aholics, alcoholics, soft drink-aholics, spend-aholics, gossip-aholics, temper-aholics, nicotine-aholics, curse-aholics, complain-aholics, caffeine-aholics or any other "aholic," the Twelve Steps can help us clear the deck and gain a clear conscience through confession of our sins and forgiveness in Christ.

A review of the Twelve Steps from a Christian perspective affirms that only God can heal us through Jesus Christ, whom we acknowledge as Savior and Lord. With God's help, we will make a fearless moral inventory of our lives and admit all of our faults to ourselves, to God, and to at least one other person. We will repent, receive forgiveness, and ask Christ to break our sinful habits. We will list people whom we have offended and become reconciled with them, making restitution when appropriate. By God's grace, we will make a commitment to a lifelong process of living in the light of Christ through confession, repentance and forgiveness.

Human ways of dealing with sin are barriers to gaining freedom from sinful habits and addictions. Pretense, which tries to hide failures and sins from self and others, results in being uncomfortable in the presence of God, Who knows us as we really are. Denial, assuming that sinful habits are "normal," causes us to put new labels on sinful acts to cloak them in respectability. This increases involvement in the immoral life, and shuts out God.

Excuses, which seek someone or something to blame for our own failures, leads to an inability to see or deal with reality, and to a loss of fellowship with God. Accusations, blaming ourselves or others for sins, result in a type of sense of guilt that may lead to self-punishment, and an inability to believe that a relationship with God is possible through Christ's forgiveness. All these end in continued slavery and disaster. Fully admitting to ourselves and to God that we are guilty of a specific sin is a big step to peace with ourselves and with God.

There are barriers to overcoming sinful habits and to gaining a clear conscience; We may depend upon our own strength, adding this to our faith in God. We may confess Jesus as Lord but not feel we need to do everything He says. We may excuse ourselves for doing some evil things because of our temperament, background, or claim it is other peoples' fault. We may feel that God cannot forgive us or heal us of our habits. We may believe that our problem is only a small thing. We may maintain that others are as bad or more wrong than we. We may also fear to face what other people think if they hear of our weakness.

All of these attitudes indicate that we have taken control of our own lives by ourselves, and are closing God out in some way. We must recognize that we are not God, not absolute, not infinite, not all-powerful. We must recognize that we are not in control of the world, and sometimes not even in control of ourselves. The first step toward recovery is the admission and acceptance of that fact. Half measures will prove to be useless. We stand at the turning point and need to throw ourselves under God's protection and care with complete abandon.

To be whole again, we must admit that we have limitations and that we are not God. We are dependent upon God, which is a safe place to be. If we are to eliminate sinful habits from our lives, we must develop humility and look to God to control and empower us. We need to avoid deceiving ourselves and others. People who have some kind of compulsion or addiction often refuse to believe they have a problem, and live double lives. Their consciences have become weakened and they seem unable to understand the harm they inflict on themselves and others.

Required is the adoption of absolute honesty and unselfishness, seeking what is right and true in every situation. God's love motivates us to seek purity of mind, body, emotions, and heart in reordering our lives. The Gospel shows us that God breaks the power of canceled sin.

The Twelve Steps offer us relief from addiction and freedom from compulsions. They help abusers of all kinds to face their helplessness and to admit their dishonesty. The Twelve Steps provide a detailed plan and roadway to freedom. They provide a basis for a supportive, non-judgmental, caring community where those addicted feel at home and at ease.

Our addiction, compulsion or sinful habit, whatever it may be, may be a symptom of the real problem — an outer expression often underlying inner spiritual weakness or illness. The problem is that the compulsive or addictive behavior brings no relief, no blotting out or coping with the real pain. We will continue to be driven compulsively until we deal with the real spiritual issue.

Continuing in a bad habit encourages self-centered delusions, rationalizations and escape that make it easy for denial of the real problem. If our difficulty is some obsession, we can delude ourselves into thinking of ourselves as not really having a problem at all by comparing ourselves to alcoholics or sex-aholics. Through denial, we can rationalize and trick ourselves into thinking we are not exactly giving up our values, nor are we guilty of transgressions.

The great discrepancy between our behavior and our own view of ourselves is not easily seen by ourselves. We tend to dump our frustrations and feelings on others, projecting our guilt as the fault of other people. By this time, we cannot admit being wrong and may have an exaggerated need to be right. We usually have a distorted picture of ourselves and our actions.

We need to recognize that the excessive use of such things as tranquilizers and sleeping pills, smoking, drinking, working, television, sex and caffeine are crippling people who in other ways may be normal. They honestly do not believe that they have a problem. They will react with anger when someone speaks to them about it.

Paul urges a life of self-control. A life out of control, where indulgences are rampant, is not a life of freedom, but a life of chaos. Wholeness does not just happen, but comes from study of the Word and prayer to God.

Here are the original *Twelve Steps of Alcoholics Anonymous*
1. We admit we are powerless over alcohol — that our lives have become unmanageable.

2. We have come to believe that a Power greater than ourselves can restore us to sanity.

3. We make a decision to turn our will and our lives over to the care of God as we understand Him.

4. We make a searching fearless moral inventory of ourselves.

5. We admit to God, to ourselves, and to another human being the exact nature of our wrongs.

6. We are entirely ready to have God remove all these defects of character.

7. We humbly ask Him to remove our shortcomings.

8. We make a list of all persons we have harmed, and become willing to make amends to them all.

9. We make direct amends to such people wherever possible, except when to do so would injure them or others.

10. We continue to take personal inventory and promptly admit when we are wrong.

11. We seek through prayer and meditation to improve our conscious contact with God as we understand Him, praying only for knowledge of His will for us and the power to carry that out.

12. Having had a spiritual awakening as the result of these steps, we try to carry this message to alcoholics and to practice these principles in all our affairs.[9]

We derive a Christian version of the Twelve Steps from the original twelve:

1. The First Step For Change in Lifestyle—Give Up Control:

We admit we are powerless over our habits, compulsions and addictions — that we cannot manage or control our lives by ourselves.

2. Hope For Change Or Recovery—Power to Regain Control:

The Holy Spirit has caused us to believe that only a Power greater than ourselves (the Triune God, Father, Son and Holy Spirit) can change us and restore us to stability — that only Jesus can lead us to fullness of life.

3. A Complete Change—Turn Away From Addictions To God:

We make a decision by the Spirit to turn our wills and our lives over to the care of God through forgiveness in Jesus Christ as Manager of our lives.

4. Look At Ourselves Honestly—A Moral Inventory:

We make a searching and fearless moral inventory of ourselves, of our strengths and weaknesses.

5. Guide To Healing And Reconciliation:

We admit to God, to ourselves, and to another human being the exact nature of our wrongs.

6. Stop Holding On:

We have repented and are entirely ready to have God remove all these defects of character and give us healing through Christ.

7. Ready To Let God Make Necessary Changes:

We humbly ask God to remove our shortcomings and to forgive us through Jesus, renewing our minds and transforming our lives.

8. Restore Relationships:

We make a list of all persons we have harmed, and are willing to make amends to them all.

9. Reconcile And Build Bridges To Others:

We make direct amends to people we have harmed wherever possible, except when to do so would injure them or others.

10. Keep On The Road To Abundant Living:

We continue to take personal inventory and promptly admit when we are wrong.

11. Maintain Spiritual Health And Strength:

We seek through prayer and meditation on God's Word to improve our conscious contact with Him, praying for knowledge of His will for us and the power of the Holy Spirit to accomplish it.

12. Live And Share These Truths:

Spiritually awakened as the result of these steps, we are determined to share Christ's healing and freeing message of love with those still in slavery and addicted (whether to great or small things), and to practice these principles in all parts of our lives as the Holy Spirit leads and empowers.

Be A "Twelve-Stepper"

In order to live righteously, we need to repair our wrongs and stop emotional manipulation. Whatever our problems or habits, we need to assume accountability for them, evaluate the damage, and immediately eliminate the causes. The **Twelve Steps** provide us with a powerful Biblical process of repentance and forgiveness, which help remove the obstacles on the road to security and happiness.

While we have **The Twelve Steps To Be Free, Secure and Happy**, the devil gives us the ten commandments of self-defeat. Satan has his own commandments by which he tries to destroy any chance for happiness and living in peace with other people. His way will give us regular doses of depression, anger, fear, and worry.

What the devil desires for us is that we should blame our neighbor for our problems and that we never admit mistakes. We should excuse ourselves for our problems because we are trapped by our past, for which we can never forgive or accept ourselves. The devil wants us to expect things to be different than they are, while being preoccupied with everything that bothers us. We should seek the approval of everyone for everything we do, and depend mostly on them for our happiness.

In contrast to this, we should make spiritual healing a lifelong process, applying the Gospel of forgiveness day by day in every situation. As we continue in open communion with God through His Word, the Holy Spirit will teach us and release the wounds, hurts, negative attitudes and self-defeating ideas. The Holy Spirit wants to make us aware of our doubts and deceits, our painful relationships, dishonesty, defense mechanisms and manipulations. The real hurt in our lives is that which we hide from ourselves. God prescribes repentance and forgiveness.

We need to stop rationalizing our failure to forgive others as we say, "I can't forgive...I can forgive, but I can't forget...I have forgiven, but the pain will always stay there." It is not that we cannot do it, but that we refuse to do it. Sometimes there is the need to take the log out of our own eye instead of talking about the splinter in our neighbor's eye. We need to ask for God's grace to flood our hearts so that repentant tears will wash the splinter out of our eyes (Lk. 6:41-42).

As God's Truth shapes our lives, we will gain victory and overcome what our enemies — the devil, world, and our sinful flesh — are doing to harm us and even to destroy us. They will seek to dull our consciences which allows us to excuse sins. There should be no doubt, however, that sin is sin, no matter how we rate its ethical seriousness: "There are six things that the Lord hates, even seven that are disgusting to him: arrogant eyes, a lying tongue, hands that kill innocent people, a mind devising wicked plans, feet that are quick to do wrong, a dishonest witness

169

spitting out lies, and a person who spreads conflict among relatives" (Prov. 6:16-19).

As the Holy Spirit guides and strengthens us, Satan will no longer be successful in distracting us from God, in attacking us through doubts, in causing us to believe his lies, or to fall into temptation. The world will no longer draw us into love of money and sinful pleasures, or living with unChristian values. Our old nature will no longer lead us to live self-directed lives, to complain against God, to pity ourselves, or to have an "anything goes" attitude. Our Christian faith will no longer be a bunch of disconnected Biblical facts, but it will be an integrated understanding of God's Word connected as the Way, the Truth and the Life (Jn. 14:6). We will stop valuing trivia, but pursue the pearl of great price wherever the search leads. Truth will be unveiled to us.

God's forgiveness reminds us that He will remember our sins no more (Jer. 31:34); our sins are separated from us as far as the East is from the West (Ps. 103:12). By God's grace we will see forgiveness blocking Satan's designs (2 Cor. 2:10-11).

Now our lifestyle will be one of following Jesus (Lk. 6:7ff), and we will seek to love our enemies. We will do good to those that hate us, bless those who curse us, offer the other cheek to the person who strikes us. We will do unto others as we would like them to do unto us. We will not judge, and we will not accept the uncharitable human judgment of others. We will not condemn, nor allow ourselves to be condemned.

We will forgive, and we will be forgiven. God's power will work through us to be dead to the old life, and to refrain increasingly from self-effort. We will allow God to direct and empower us, and to make ourselves available to Him for His purposes. We will live as true disciples, overcoming the enemies of our lives.

No Promise Of Heaven On Earth

People who misunderstand the human situation and who feel that God should reward their good intentions with a conflict-free life, often ask, "Why would God allow this to happen to me?...How could a loving God allow such suffering to exist?...Why me, God?"

The sin of Adam and Eve brought pain and death into the world, and we feel the consequence: "He said to the woman, 'I will increase your pain and your labor when you give birth to children'...Then he said to the man, 'The ground is cursed because of you. Through hard work you will eat food that comes from it every day of your life. The ground will grow thorns and thistles for you, and you will eat wild plants. By the sweat of your brow, you will produce food to eat until you return to the ground, because you were taken from it. You are dust, and you will return to dust'" (Gen. 3:16-19). When man breaks the moral and spiritual laws of God, he often suffers terrible consequences. When others sin, we sometimes suffer because of their sin.

Human sinfulness causes much suffering, such as war and man's inhumanity to man, which harms many innocent people. James gives an exact source and origin for this: "What causes fights and quarrels among you? Aren't they caused by the selfish desires that fight to control you? You want what you don't have, so you commit murder. You're determined to have things, but you can't get what you want. You quarrel and fight...You have lived in luxury and pleasure here on earth. You have fattened yourselves for the day of slaughter. You have condemned and murdered people who have God's approval, even though they didn't resist you. Brothers and sister, be patient until the Lord comes again. See how farmers wait for their precious crops to grow. They wait patiently for fall and spring rains. You, too, must be patient. Don't give up hope. The Lord will soon be here." (Jas. 4:1-2; 5:5-8).

The suffering of Jesus is shown to be an example for believers, providing right perspective on the meaning of suffering in our experience: "...Christ suffered for you. He left you an example so that you could follow in his footsteps" (1 Pet. 2:21). Suffering is not only rooted in our human condition, but also something that God uses for good in our lives. Jesus, "...a man of sorrows, familiar with suffering" (Is. 53:3), experienced suffering as

171

part of His divine mission on earth: "He will see and be satisfied because of his suffering. My righteous servant will acquit many people because of what he has learned through suffering. He will carry their sins as a burden" (Is. 53:11). In a similar sense, we as God's servants exist in the light of human existence, aware that our suffering is in a sense "redemptive."

Following Jesus' example, we surrender ourselves to the will of God: "But let your will be done rather than mine" (Mt. 26:39). By God's grace, our suffering gives birth to much good: "...We also brag when we are suffering. We know that suffering creates endurance, endurance creates character, and character creates confidence. We're not ashamed to have this confidence, because God's love has been poured into our hearts by the Holy Spirit, who has been given to us" (Rom. 5:3-5).

James also shows the value of trials: "My brothers and sisters, be very happy when you are tested in different ways. You know that such testing of your faith produces endurance. Endure until your testing is over. Then you will be mature and complete, and you won't need anything...Blessed are those who endure when they are tested. When they pass the test, they will receive the crown of life that God has promised to those who love him" (Jas. 1:2-4, 12).

Paul told how his prison chains were a part of God's plan to advance the Gospel, telling how this encouraged others: "I want you to know, brothers and sisters, that what happened to me has helped to spread the Good News. As a result, it has become clear to all the soldiers who guard the emperor and to everyone else that I am in prison because of Christ. So through my being in prison, the Lord has given most of our brothers and sisters confidence to speak God's word more boldly and fearlessly than ever" (Phil. 1:12-14).

Paul adds good advice when we experience persecution and suffering: "Live as citizens who reflect the Good News about Christ. Then, whether I come to see you or whether I stay away, I'll hear all about you. I'll hear that you are firmly united in spirit, united in fighting for the faith that the Good News brings. So don't let your opponents intimidate you in any way. This is

God's way of showing them that they will be destroyed and that you will be saved. God has given you the privilege not only to believe in Christ but also to suffer for him. You are involved in the same struggle that you saw me having. Now you hear that I'm still involved in it" (Phil. 1:27-30).

John 15, with its message that Jesus is the Vine and we are the branches, certainly reveals God's use of problems and trials in our life: "...He removes every one of my branches that doesn't produce fruit. He also prunes every branch that does produce fruit to make it produce more fruit...You give glory to my Father when you produce a lot of fruit and therefore show that you are my disciples" (Jn. 15:2, 8). It is obvious that fruit-bearing is tied to our purpose in life and our ministry for the Lord. His pruning process is to make us more fruitful. This means that care must be taken when we pray and how we pray in the midst of difficulties: "When you pray for things, you don't get them because you want them for the wrong reason — for your own pleasure" (Jas. 4:3). For what purpose do we pray to God to save our lives? To pile up more money and to have more pleasure? To serve Him faithfully and to be His effective managers of all His resources on earth? What is our motive for praying to God for relief from trials and tribulations?

Why does suffering continue? One reason is "because of free will." God refuses to program us for actions and decisions, but wants us to choose good and right, with freedom to choose the wrong. Because of our freedom, we often make wrong choices, blunders, and mistakes. God could take away all suffering and sorrows, but this would take away our freedom of choice, and we would be robots.

As difficult as sufferings are, they remind us of our weaknesses and dependence upon God. To run away from God is disaster. Pain and suffering remind us of our frailty and teach us humility, as Paul reminded: "...especially because of the excessive number of revelations that I've had. Therefore, to keep me from becoming conceited, I am forced to deal with a recurring problem. That problem, Satan's messenger, torments me to keep me from being conceited" (2 Cor. 12:7). Paul recognized that

God's grace was sufficient for him, and that his strength came from recognizing his weakness which made him depend upon God.

Pain serves to discipline us: "You have forgotten the encouraging words that God speaks to you as his children: 'My child, pay attention when the Lord disciplines you. Don't give up when he corrects you...We don't enjoy being disciplined. It always seems to cause more pain than joy. But later on, those who learn from that discipline have peace that comes from doing what is right" (Heb. 12:5, 11).

A person who has no sorrow in his life sometimes is immature in faith. Job showed this refining influence of suffering: "I can't find him because he knows the road I take. When he tests me, I'll come out as pure as gold" (Job 23:10). Isaiah quoted God: "I have refined you, but not like silver. I have tested you in the furnace of suffering" (48:10).

Peter gives this assurance: "You are extremely happy about these things, even though you have to suffer different kinds of trouble for a little while now. The purpose of these troubles is to test your faith as fire tests how genuine gold is. Your faith is more precious than gold, and by passing the test, it gives praise, glory, and honor to God. This will happen when Jesus Christ appears again" (1 Pet. 1:6-7).

Suffering presents us with eternal values. Too often our material blessings blind us to our spiritual needs. Suffering may help demonstrate life's true values: "God, who shows you his kindness and who has called you through Christ Jesus to his eternal glory, will restore you, strengthen you, make you strong, and support you as you suffer for a little while" (1 Pet. 5:10).

God's purpose is not to give us pain, but lovingly to make us His faithful servants and to guide us on productive paths: "He renews my soul. He guides me along the paths of righteousness for the sake of his name...Certainly, goodness and mercy will stay close to me all the days of my life, and I will remain in the Lord's house for days without end" (Ps. 23:3, 6). Suffering tells us, "Prepare for the day of the Lord." There are many things we do not understand about suffering, but one thing we need to recognize: "We know that all things work together for the good of those who love God — those whom he has called according to his plan" (Rom. 8:28).

Beyond suffering is hope. Paul encourages, "Be happy in your confidence, be patient in trouble, and pray continually" (Rom. 12:12). The positive note in Romans 5:3-5 heartens us, "But that's not all. We also brag when we are suffering. We know that suffering creates endurance, endurance creates character, and character creates confidence. We're not ashamed to have this confidence, because God's love has been poured into our hearts by the Holy Spirit, who has been given to us."

Being Content

One of the great battles of life is to be pleased with what God gives and does. Sometimes we may even think that God is unfair. Being content with our life does not mean absence of problems or afflictions. Nor is contentment opposed to experiencing some weeping, sighing and groaning at times.

Contentment is not mere human optimism. Nor is it simply a strong and sturdy spirit. Being content comes from a deep faith in God and a willingness to let Him direct our lives. The Christian who earnestly prays, "Your will be done, not mine," will find contentment while the one who insists on getting all his wants met now will have considerable discontent.

Contentment is tied to being satisfied with the necessities of life: "As long as we have food and clothes, we should be satisfied" (1 Tim. 6:8). Paul told the secret, "I've learned to be content in whatever situation I'm in" (Phil. 4:11). Knowing that God's promises are sure and that He will never forsake us will help us to be content with what we have (Heb. 13:5).

Contentment means to have quietness of the heart, to be at peace with God and with oneself. It means that we freely submit to and take pleasure in God's way. It is an acknowledgment of God as gracious, loving, merciful in good and bad circumstances, even difficulties. Contentment means that we resign ourselves to God in difficulties and patiently wait upon him for deliverance.

175

Contentment does not mean that we do not have a feeling of affliction or have some mourning, which are human emotional feelings. Contentment is opposed to complaining against God or to be consumed with cares. It is opposed to a constant attitude of discouragement.

Contentment means to have faith that God has grace for us in every situation. We do not surrender to any situation, but are above circumstances by practicing godliness and righteousness, becoming "more than conquerors."

Being content means that we should be satisfied with the simple things of life and learn not to desire more possessions. It means to adopt a reasonable standard of living. It is important to cultivate a thankful heart. Being content means that we discern our needs from our wants.

Bearing The Fruit Of The Spirit

One of the struggles of the Christian life is to avoid trying only those things which we can easily do with our own strength. What are we daring to do that only God's power can accomplish? Without full reliance on the Holy Spirit, our lives will be limited, cautious and unfruitful. Not only does God offer the power of the Holy Spirit, but He also gives the fruit of the Spirit. "But the spiritual nature produces love, joy, peace, patience, kindness, goodness, faithfulness, gentleness, and self-control" (Gal. 5:22-23).

These are not a number of separate traits which exist and operate independently nor are they merely a collection of exquisite jewels, but they are a single reality — the fruit of the Spirit with many facets. The fruit of the Spirit is a result of a life conformed to Jesus Christ. This fruit is what grows in us as a result of the Holy Spirit living in us, the result of His work in us. These character traits, like the ones stated in Ephesians 4:1-3 and 2 Peter 1:5-7, describe what God is like **and what He wants us to be like..** There is no need to struggle for it, but it is a **gift** of the Holy Spirit for which we pray.

Love

Love is divinely ordained for all personal relations. What really is love? All the poems and popular songs about love give us many emotions people feel about it, but very little about the real character of Christian love. Much of it is about the need to be loved and to want to love others for personal gain.

The world reduces love to a warm feeling or emotional reaction, or a positive response to a relationship that makes us feel good, very different than genuine Christian love. Romantic and self-centered love pleads, "If you love me, you will have sex with me." Biblical love says, "If you love me, you will respect my convictions and will not push me into something which I consider wrong and do not want to do."

There's also a dependency love which justifies making enormous demands on others, and there is logical love which emphasizes the practical values of a stable relationship. There is friendly love, which is mutually supportive.

Christian love must be expressed in spite of feelings. It has a Christlikeness about it, for we are told to "love...as Christ loved" (Eph. 5:2, 25). This love is not only done individually, but also as part of a body, a community of believers relating to each other, and building each other up in love as Christ loved (Eph. 4:16). It also encourages us to speak the truth "with love" (Eph. 4:15). Christians together can do functionally what individuals cannot do, for they also have corporate strength in love.

Love cannot be easily defined, but true love can be recognized. The English language uses one word "love" to express a number of dimensions of love, while the Greek language uses basically four:

1. **Eros**, which is an act of the emotions and it seeks only to gain advantage for itself. It is basically a response to the attractiveness of the other person and often has sexual connotations.

2. **Phileo**, which is basically a companionship, and it responds to the stimulus of attention or kindness on the part of others.

3. **Storge** is a kind of affection practiced in family circles and can be seen in the love of parents and children.

4. **Agape** flows freely to serve the needs of others without expectation of return. It needs no stimulation for its action, but it fills a need which is seen. It describes God's love for mankind and the love people should have for one another.

1 Corinthians 13 tells what love (Agape) is and what it is not: It does not envy, boast, and is not proud or rude or self-seeking. It is not easily angered, and keeps no record of wrongs, nor does it delight in evil. Love rejoices in the truth, always protects, trusts, hopes, perseveres, and reflects maturity.

The directive to love others is one of the most repeated exhortations in the entire New Testament, and it is often a direct command: "Love your enemies...Love your neighbor as you love yourself...Love each other...Do everything in love...Serve each other through love...Live in love...Love your wives...Pursue love...We must show love through actions that are sincere, not through empty words" (Mt. 5:44; 22:39; Jn. 13:34; 1 Cor. 15:14; Gal. 5:13; Eph. 5:2, 25; 2 Tim. 2:22; 1 Jn. 3:18).

Love does not ask **whether** it shall express itself, but seeks only **how** and **when** and **where** for the advantage of others.

The individual listings of the fruit of the Spirit begins with "love," which is the pre-eminent Christian virtue because it most characterizes God, for "God is love" (1 Jn. 4:8). This is God's description of Himself, and it is to be our nature. Jesus linked loving God to loving man (Mt. 22:37-40). Such love gives even at a great cost to itself. We cannot think of it as a noun, but rather as an active verb, of actions rather than mere thoughts or emotions.

Christian love is a supernatural love, which causes a person to be more interested in God than in the material kingdom. It is not limited to temperament. It is a fruit of the Spirit seen in action.

Joy

We are commanded to rejoice always (1 Thes. 5:16; Phil. 4:4). Being happy is not enough. We are to be full of joy and grow in joy. Despite the problems of pain, grief and difficulties, in Christ we experience real joy because of His love. Yet there are real stumbling blocks to be avoided, which can hinder joy in our lives: sin that is not confessed (Ps. 51:12); misplaced confidence in the flesh or in our own works or religious attainments; chastening or disciplining if we lose sight of its intended purpose, which can lead to self-pity.

Joy is not limited by outside circumstances, for joy endures in spite of situations. We rejoice because our situation is good in God, grounded and secure in Jesus Christ.

Peace

Peace is a gift from God. Peace with God refers to the condition when we are not in conflict or rebellion against Him. This peace reflects the inner tranquility which we have because Christ lives in us, and when God is in charge. Peace with others is experienced because we have acquired by God's grace the peace of and with God.

God is the author both of personal peace as well as peace among people. Peace manifests quiet tranquility within us and also in our relations with others.

Jesus tore down the wall of hostility that divides people. Jesus said, "Blessed are those who make peace" (Mt. 5:9). Paul warned against hatred, discord, dissensions, factions, and devouring each other. Paul said, "So let's pursue those things which bring peace" (Rom. 14:19), and "Also, let Christ's peace control you. God has called you into this peace by bringing you into one body" (Col. 3:15).

We are to take the initiative to restore peace when it has been disturbed or destroyed (Mt. 5:23-24; 18:15). We are never to seek revenge, but always to leave justice to God.

Patience

How difficult it is to practice patience. A poster reads: "Lord, grant me patience, and I need it right away!" Rather, we should first of all be even-tempered, slow to anger, and forgiving (Col. 3:13).

The occasion for practicing patience may even be wrongs done against us, which may include ridicule and insults. Patience from a human viewpoint means bearing pains and trials calmly or without complaint. From a spiritual viewpoint, patience is calm determination to endure, a perseverance to live like a child of God. God's grace rewards endurance and patience (Lk. 21:19; Rom. 2:7; Jas. 1:12).

Patience is love that tolerates frustration, and suffers mistreatment if need be. It does not respond wrongly to provocations. It tolerates the weaknesses of others (Col. 3:13).

Kindness And Goodness

Kindness is love exercising compassion and forgiveness while true goodness is being gracious and generous. Both are love's service and behavior. Goodness is kind but just, tender but tough, fair but firm. Goodness is kindness in action.

God shows kindness to all, regardless of who they are, whereas our natural inclination is to show kindness only to those with whom we have some natural relation or feeling. Paul tells us to "do what is good for everyone, especially for the family of believers" (Gal. 6:10). Opportunities for doing good are almost unlimited, so we should be untiring and not become "tired of living the right way" (Gal. 6:9).

Faithfulness

Faithfulness is love keeping its promises and sticking to its commitments. It is reliability, dependability, loyalty with integrity. This begins with faithfulness to God by opposing everything that opposes God or what is false.

Every aspect of our Christian life rests upon the faithfulness of God, as we have His firm promise. The entire Bible is all about the faithfulness of God. As His children, we also are to be faithful and trustworthy.

Gentleness

Gentleness is love refusing to be harsh or demanding, when it has every right to push its own interests. Paul says, "As holy people whom God has chosen and loved, be gentle" (Col. 3:12), which is how we should treat others. This gentleness is born of strength, not of weakness, displaying a sensitive regard for others and being careful never to be unfeeling to others.

Gentleness, which shows respect for the dignity of others, will result in avoiding blunt speech and an abrupt manner. We will treat others considerately.

Self-Control

Self-control is love voluntarily stopping actions that may be harmful to ourselves or to others. It is control of ourselves and governing our desires.

God has given us natural desires, which can be healthy or harmful. These desires must be controlled, lest they become unruly or exceed proper limits. Problems with emotions, compulsions and addictions have already been studied under the **Twelve Steps**. Self-control means that all aspects of our lives are to be brought under the mastery of the Holy Spirit characterized by discipline. We are to be temperate and be able to restrain our natural desires. Jesus tells us to deny ourselves (Lk. 9:23).

The key to self-control is to avoid anger. Anger, a lack of self-control, is the cause of many problems, causing people to lose their temper (Prov. 12:16). Anger may lead to seeking revenge against others (Prov. 24:29), and to physical harm of others (Gen. 4:5). It causes people to make bad decisions (1 Sam. 18:8-9), and disqualifies them for spiritual leadership in the church (Titus 1:7).

Anger is a negative emotion that is aroused when a person's self-centeredness is threatened. We are responsible for controlling anger so that it will not conflict with God's Word and will (Eph. 4:26). An angry person fails to take responsibility for his actions, justifying his conduct by blaming situations, people and things.

181

Anger devastates us physically and poses a threat to our own relationship with other people and with God.

Anger takes various forms, such as being irritated, violent, vengeful, disgusted, quarrelsome, hostile with screaming, slamming doors, throwing things and storming out of rooms.

All who have a problem with anger and temper should seek God's grace to break the pattern and to control it. They need to admit that it is contrary to God's will (Eph. 4:31-32). Uncontrolled anger causes people to lose their integrity.

As our inner strength is exerted through sound judgment by the power of the Holy Spirit, "We take every thought captive so that it is obedient to Christ" (2 Cor. 10:5). This includes not only refusing to allow sinful thoughts, but also focusing our minds on what is good.

If we are to grow in self-control, we must desire it as a fruit of the Spirit, a gift from God, and make a conscious decision for it and work at it. We will insist on order in our lives, have faith in God, and seek help and encouragement through His Word.

The result and progression of experiencing God's power for godliness, self-control and love is seen in 2 Peter 1:5-11, which shows God's grace at work in us to make our calling sure: "Because of this, make every effort to add integrity to your faith; and to integrity add knowledge; to knowledge add self-control; to self-control add endurance; to endurance add godliness; to godliness add Christian affection; and to Christian affection add love. If you have these qualities and they are increasing, it demonstrates that your knowledge about our Lord Jesus Christ is living and productive. If these qualities aren't present in your life, you're short-sighted and have forgotten that you were cleansed from your past sins. Therefore, brothers and sisters, use more effort to make God's calling and choosing of you secure. If you keep doing this, you will never fall away. Then you will also be given the wealth of entering into the eternal kingdom of our Lord and Savior Jesus Christ."

Peter here not only tells us how to escape the corruption in the world, but also suggests the spiritual fruit that is to be added to Christian knowledge. These verses can be outlined in the following manner:

Escaping the Corruption of the World and
Making One's Calling Sure

```
                                    | Love
                                 | Brotherly kindness
                              | Godliness
                           | Patient endurance
                        | Self-control
                     | Knowledge — learning daily
                  | Excellence — moral goodness
               | Faith — God's purpose outweighs human factors
            | Every bit of energy
```

2 Peter 1:5-11 shows us how we may reach God's goal for our lives. It might be named "the steps for maturity in our Christian faith." We cannot expect real love when Christians are immature. Possessing these qualities in increasing measure, Peter says, will make us effective and productive believers, growing and maturing in our knowledge of Jesus Christ. Peter tells that it begins with a commitment to consistent discipleship by use of every bit of our energy, then trusting God, followed by seeking excellence, and knowledge. This ladder of sanctification next has the rungs of self-control, patient endurance, godliness, brotherly kindness, and the greatest of all virtues, love.

Living As Disciples

The disciples of Jesus were very ordinary people, having all the human faults and weaknesses which we have — sometimes weak in faith, fearful, selfish, impatient, weary, immature, ambitious, argumentative, proud, slow to learn and quick to forget. The people Jesus selected to follow Him were called disciples.

The Bible shows that all Christians are disciples. There are faithful and unfaithful disciples, and strong and weak ones. A faithful disciple is a Christian learning, growing, maturing, and

183

shaping in the image of Jesus Christ, being strong in the Word to edify Christians and to evangelize non-Christians. Jesus said that when a disciple is fully mature, he will be "like his teacher" (Lk. 6:40). Luther referred to disciples as "little Christs."

Our goal as Christian disciples is to become mature in faith (Eph. 4:13-14; Col. 1:28). Maturity in Christ is not restricted to being active in religious events, but refers especially to our witness and relationships in our homes, at work, in leisure, in our involvement in our community, indeed, our whole style of living.

The following is a list of factors which may be hindrances to Christ's Lordship in your life. In which of the following areas do you find it difficult to let Christ rule?

( ) Setting priorities (Mt. 6:33)
( ) Things— clothes, stereos, cars, TVs, house, etc. (Lk. 12:15)
( ) Social status (Mt. 20:26)
( ) Power (1 Pet. 5:5,6)
( ) Pride (Rom. 12:3)
( ) Family (Lk. 14:26)
( ) Escapism — drinking, drugs, etc. (Eph. 5:18)
( ) Social life (Prov. 29:25)
( ) Selfishness (Lk. 12:21)
( ) Fun (Mk. 4:19)
( ) Money (Eccl. 5:10,11)
( ) Sex (1 Cor. 6:18-10; Mt. 5:27-28)
( ) Worry or anxiety (Rom. 8:28)
( ) Pride in good works (Rom. 4:4-5)
( ) Robbing God by poor giving (Mal. 3:8)
( ) Fear (2 Tim. 1:7)
( ) Thought life (Prov. 23:7a)
( ) A critical spirit (Mt. 7:1)
( ) Bitterness (Heb. 12:15)
( ) Gossip and unruly tongue (Jas. 3:2)
( ) Envy (Prov. 14:30)
( ) Bad temper (Prov. 16:32)

These obstacles to Christ's will in your life can be viewed in a positive way, as opportunities for growth in your relationship with Christ.

Every Christian disciple should be willing to grow spiritually. Some of the most important traits of a disciple involve a willingness to:

1. Learn and be teachable. "You've heard my message, and it's been confirmed by many witnesses. Entrust this message to faithful individuals who will be competent to teach others" (2 Tim. 2:2). Be knowledgeable. Regularly read the Bible and Christian books.

2. Listen (Lk. 10:38-42).

3. Be trustworthy and faithful (1 Cor. 4:2; Mk. 11:22).

4. Submit to authority and be quick to obey (1 Thes. 5:12; Heb. 13:17; Lk. 5:4-9).

5. Don't be controlled by unwarranted fears (2 Tim. 1:7).

6. Be humble (Phil. 2:3-4).

7. Serve and be a servant (Mt. 20:26-28; Jn. 13:17).

8. Follow the Spirit's leading, making changes and adjustments as God requires (Ez. 36:27; Jn. 14:26; 1 Jn. 3:24).

9. Be forgiving (Lk. 17:14; Eph. 4:32; Col. 3:16).

10. Avoid being a perfectionist, or self-righteous or judgmental (James 3:2; 1 Jn. 1:8-10).

11. Share faith with others, witnessing (1 Jn. 1:1-3; Acts 1:8).

12. Avoid gossip or being a busybody (Jn. 21:21-22; 1 Tim. 5:13).

13. Adopt God's priorities (Mt. 6:33; Acts 6:2-4).

14. Rejoice in the Lord and have a joyful attitude (Phil. 4:4).

III.

LIVING WITH MY FAMILY AND FELLOW MEN

God made the family the basic social institution on earth, providing an example of the way society should be. The family is based upon marriage and the sacred union which creates and sustains family life. Parents are to be models which will help children grow into maturity. The basic family unit is a married couple — husband and wife, augmented with children.

The Bible shows the source of marriage and the family, its purpose, nature, foundation, form and model, and its customs. Old and New Testament truths give 21st Century disciples insights into the 1st Century family and about how men and women are to function together.

Marriage — Sanctified Sexuality

The Bible shows that the love of a man and a woman was God's idea. Sexuality is woven into the very creation of man. Genesis declares that God deliberately created "male and female" (Gen. 1:27). After having created man from dust, God formed a woman from Adam's rib, and He Himself "brought her to the man" (Gen. 2:22).

The first two chapters of Genesis clearly show that God created the sexual capabilities for intimacy, bonding and procreation. Their sexual relationship was intended to bring them closer together, provide an intense emotional tie, and enable them to give birth to children and thus perpetuate the race. God had a purpose for a sexual relationship between the first couple: "Be fertile, increase in number" (Gen. 1:28); "Be united...become one flesh" (Gen. 2:24).

God even intervened in the reproductive process to fulfill His purpose in the case of Abraham and Sarah (Gen. 21:1-7), Isaac and Rebecca (Gen. 25:21), Jacob with Leah and Rachel (Gen. 30:17, 22), Elkanah and Hannah (1 Sam. 1:19ff), and Zechariah and Elizabeth (Lk. 1:24). All this shows that married sex is more than a mere physical act, and that the sexual relationship is intended for marriage.

Married love is intended to be personal, warm, caring, intimate, sensitive, joyous, intelligent, purposeful and meaningful to both partners, not impersonal, mechanical, insensitive, exploitive or abusive.

The Source And Partners Of Marriage — Man And Woman

Marriage succeeds only when done God's way. It exists for the sake of service to God and His people. It functions best in the context of the Christian community.

The source of marriage and the family is grounded in the nature of men and women. The first ones (Adam and Eve) were created in the "image of God" (Gen. 1:26-27). Men and women are made for physical, social, emotional, psychological and spiritual intimacy with each other (Gen. 2:18-25).

When God created human beings, He made us male and female. None of us is merely a person, for each of us has a gender. The distinctiveness of being male or female reaches to the very core of our identity. Whatever we do, we do first as a man or as a woman. Our distinction is far greater than anatomy, voice pitch, clothing, and hair style. Gender, masculinity and femininity, which is a vital part of the true self and personhood, is rooted in God.

Wrong identities, distortion or imbalance in identities, influence the health of an individual, society or an entire civilization. The Bible shows a need for recognizing and affirming the distinction between male and female, and also the proper balance in their relationships. We must possess our gender identities strongly if we are to function in a healthy manner.

Cultural confusion has been seen recently in unisex ideas

that cloud our gender identities and keep us from being whole. God has polarized us into two genders (masculine and feminine), which fact should be recognized and acted on accordingly. Failure to do so has tragic consequences.

Being in proper relation to God and functioning according to His design as male and female, we will have a rich enjoyment of our sexual identity. Giving fully what we have to give as man or woman allows us to function naturally to complement each other in marriage and in the family and also in society. It is just like using the right tool for the right job. This goes far beyond the sex act itself.

Men were designed to enter their world strongly, providing for their families and leading them under God to fulfill their purpose in life. The woman is relational and feels an internal calm, giving courageously her wisdom, talents, intellect and kindness, allowing herself to be supported in love. "Wives, place yourselves under your husbands' authority as you have placed yourselves under the Lord's authority. The husband is the head of his wife as Christ is the head of the church. It is his body, and he is its Savior. As the church is under Christ's authority, so wives are under their husbands' authority in everything. Husbands, love your wives as Christ loved the church and gave his life for it. He did this to make the church holy by cleansing it, washing it using water along with spoken words...So husbands must love their wives as they love their own bodies. A man who loves his wife loves himself...That's why a man will leave his father and mother and be united with his wife, and the two will be one" (Eph. 5:22-26, 28, 31).

God's Word shows that husband and wife have a difference in function, but not in worth or dignity. The pattern of the husband's spiritual leadership and the wife's submission is the pattern of Christian marriage. This actually provides an umbrella of protection for the entire family. It is the same kind of relationship that God has ordained in the church through Christ.

Demands which conflict with the will of God through cultural influence (Acts 5:29) force us to choose between God or man. When submission is interpreted to make the woman inferior,

189

it creates destructive results. Neither men nor women need to be emancipated from their God-created role, but perform their roles in the will of God. Man is to leave his father and mother, and cleave to his wife, while the woman is a partner and helper suitable for him.

Many passages of Scripture support male spiritual headship and leadership and proceed from a common assumption of God's divine design for relationships in creation (1 Cor. 14:34ff; 1 Tim. 2:11ff; Titus 2:1-5,15; 1 Pet. 3:1). Someone has to be given the responsibility of spiritual leader, and God has given it to the husband (1 Cor. 11:30). Paul's teaching was based on God's command, not on his personal opinion or cultural tendencies (1 Cor. 14:37). While maintaining New Testament sexual identities and role differences for men and women, it does not contradict the many functions and responsibilities men or women individually have.

Christ is the head of the man, and man is the spiritual head of the woman, as Christ is Head of the Church. The husband's headship requires commitment to his wife, unselfish sacrifice for her, the spirit of a servant, affirmation and reinforcement of her unique qualities, and active love in nourishing, cherishing, and providing for her (Eph. 5:21-25; Col. 3:18-19; 1 Tim. 3:11-12; 1 Cor. 11:3; 14:34-35; 1 Pet. 3:7). Being head means that the husband not only has spiritual authority over his wife but, along with her, also has authority over the children.

The husband first sets an example by the way he loves and respects his wife. Fathers carry the primary parental responsibility for representing God to their children. Fathers are the main source of personal identity for children to be Christlike. They must provide love and discipline (Rom. 11:22). They are to protect their children spiritually, emotionally, morally, socially, and physically (Prov. 19:18). They are to challenge their children to mature in the faith, and encourage them along the path of life (Col. 3:21). This does not weaken the mother's responsibility and role to participate fully in rearing children.

Because of human cultural conditions, the relationship between husband and wife has become one of the vital issues of the crusade and struggle of what is called the Feminist Movement. Some of the rhetoric accompanying it leaves wrong impressions on both sides. There is sinful sexism practiced in culture, but the Bible and church liturgies and songs cannot be rewritten in a neuter gender to suit human misconceptions. Strong womanhood can relate meaningfully to God our Father just as woman relates deeply to an earthly father. But Scriptures dare not be rewritten in order to correct real or perceived mistakes of sexism in our culture.

When Paul talks of headship in the home, he is talking about final spiritual authority in the home, not authoritarian, arbitrary or dictatorial dominion over a wife. Final spiritual accountability is the responsibility of the husband. This is not a military chain of command nor a political bureaucracy which requires unthinking obedience, but it is a sensitive and delicate love relationship, like the pattern of Christ loving His Church, and the church obeying Christ.

As seen in Christ's example (Phil. 2:5-8; Eph. 5:21; Heb. 13:17), spiritual submission is a voluntary act of the will which surrenders self-interest and gives preference to others and to God-given leadership in obedience to God. Submission does not mean inferiority or inability, but rather is a reflection of God's desire for harmony, order and peace in relationships. God's role for a husband and wife is to help develop greater spiritual maturity in every believer.

Christ is our example, both in subordinating Himself to the Father while on His earthly mission and as Head of the Church. As Christ was subordinate and gave up His rights (Jn. 5:19; Phil. 2:5-8), so must man. Jesus' objective was to glorify God (Jn. 13:31-32). He trusted His Head, the Father, implicitly even when all was going against Him (Lk. 23:46). He did not please Himself, but pleased the Father (Rom. 15:3). He was totally resigned to the requirements of His Father's authority (Lk. 22:42).

Christ as Head maintained the heart of a servant (Jn. 13:13-14). He demonstrated self-sacrificing love (Jn. 13:1). His patience and kindness shows that He sympathizes with our weaknesses (Heb. 4:15; 2 Tim. 2:13). He assumed responsibility for

His disciples and met their needs, seeing those under His authority as a sacred trust from God (Jn. 17:6; 10:29). He taught them to love one another, to love their neighbors, and even to love their enemies (Jn. 15:12; Mt. 19:19; 22:39).

What is the servant role that husband and wife exercise to follow the example of Jesus? The husband is to fulfill his duty to his wife (1 Cor. 7:3) and give up his authority over his own body and not to defraud her (1 Cor. 7:4-5). He is to please her (1 Cor. 7:33) and to love her with a self-sacrificing, unselfish love even as Christ loved the Church (Eph. 5:25). He is to love her as his own body (Eph. 5:28). He is not to be harsh (Col. 3:19), and he is to live in an understanding way, to honor her and not to lord it over her (1 Pet. 3:7).

The wife, on the other hand, is to fulfill her duty to her husband (1 Cor. 7:3) and also to give up her authority over her own body. She is not to defraud her husband (1 Cor. 7:4-5). She is to please him (1 Cor. 7:34), and be subject spiritually to him as the Church is subject to Christ, and she is to show reverence to her husband (Eph. 5:22, 24, 33). She is always to do what is right (Col. 3:18). She is to show a meek and quiet spirit (1 Pet. 3:1-6). **This does not allow for male domination!** It is not slavery for women, but rather freedom to the highest degree.

The Scriptures have not shortchanged women by giving them the less desirable roles of submissive "helpmates" and nurturers, while the men have the more desirable positions of leaders and providers. Any discussion of desirable roles reflect our society's values more than that of the Scriptures. There is no replacing the wife or mother any more than replacing the husband or father.

Any change of function in male or female or in husband or wife is a deviation from the Biblical direction of our very being and of our created order. Attempts at change arise because of our sinful nature and worldly desire. Since the Fall, all men and women struggle to regard themselves as fully male and female. This is the source of the struggle over sexual identity.

When Paul wanted to show the great need for the Gospel in Romans 1, he described people that were determined to live

192

according to their own design with the consequence that God gave them over to their sinful desires for destruction. The first result of taking complete control over themselves without reference to God was in their sexual desires. People without an awareness of masculine or feminine design created in their own being cannot live according to God's plan.

When God removes His restraining hand, the first thing that they pursue is sexual pleasure, even desiring homosexual relations (Rom. 1:26). This leads to all kinds of sinful practices that harm their bodies and corrupt their relations (1:29-32).

When corruption enters our sexual identity, we try to compensate in one way or another. When males become aware of their weaknesses, they compensate by emphasizing whatever they find in themselves or they generate a counterfeit sense of masculinity through aggression, rebellion, and exaggerated independence. In some cases, they retreat passively to demand that others take care of them. Females quickly feel violated and unsafe since their trust has been betrayed. At that time, they feel the shame and fear that is attached to the loss of their clear identity as male or female. Then males lack the healthy confidence that they are fully male, while females lack exhilaration that they are secure women.

When roles are confused, men pursue defensive strategies to compensate, and so dominate their families or neglect them. Women exaggerate their physical appeal, while some become docile and accept the demeaning control of someone who will take care of them. Various measures are taken to protect themselves from further harm.

Living in repentance and forgiveness in Christ is the only liberating power for men to be strong and tender in properly representing Him, and for women to be secure and giving, living out God's design. Redirection of our spiritual lives will help to solve whatever difficulties there are in role identification.

A serious consequence of men's or women's failure to be affirmed in their masculine or feminine identity is that they will suffer from low self-worth. They will be unable to accept themselves, for they know that they are not what they ought to be.

193

Then the man cannot become the head of the house, and the woman will not know how to submit. They will be immature in their tasks and become increasingly passive or rebellious, and unable creatively to act according to their individual design.

When men are healed, the healing of women will naturally follow. It is the father who affirms sons and daughters in their sexual identity and as persons. A gender is not a thing to be learned, but a God-given quality to be experienced. When sons are not affirmed as male, they become cripples like their fathers, and generations may follow where the male identity is lost. Although a mother's love and affirmation are imperative, usually she cannot by herself get the message across as well as a good father to her son and daughter that they are man and woman. Just as the mother is very vital in the first months of life, so the father also plays an important role as the children grow up. When there is loss of identity of the father, the young will look to their peers for affirmation and acceptance, which means a loss of God's design.

From the Scriptures, we need to learn what it means to be a man or a woman, a husband or a wife, a father or a mother, a son or a daughter.

The Purposes Of Marriage And The Family

Marriage is for companionship. God said that it is not good for the man to be alone, so He made a helper suitable for him (Gen. 2:18-24). Marriage is also for procreation and bearing of children (Gen. 1:28; Ps. 127:3-5). God also made marriage for sexual fulfillment (1 Cor. 7:3-5).

Sex is described as a spiritual union. It has implications far beyond the physical. Ephesians 5:31-33 refers to the "mystery" of the marital union, symbolizing a spiritual relationship that includes the symbol of the church. Since sex and marriage have a sacred quality beyond the physical aspects, the Bible condemns sex outside of marriage (1 Cor. 6:18; 1 Thes. 4:3-4,7-8; Ex. 20:14).

194

Another purpose of marriage and the family is for nurturing the faith and for promotion of the kingdom of God (Eph. 6:1-4). Christian nurture is implicit in the loving relationship of a husband and wife and also in the training of the children. Marriage is for the stabilizing of society. There is a promise for obedience by children, that they may live long (Ex. 20:12). Those guilty of sexual sins were warned especially of the curse on their acts (Lev. 18:24-29), which is very evident in modern society in the scourge of sexually transmitted diseases, including the catastrophe of AIDS. The great blessing of obedience is especially promised in Proverbs 3:1-4, 4:1-22, and 22:6.

The Nature Of Marriage

Marriage is to be a natural union (Gen. 1 and 2) of one husband and one wife (Gen. 2:24). It is a physical and intimate union (Gen. 2:24; 1 Cor. 6:16; Mt. 19:5).

Marriage is an exclusive union. It does not include parents (Gen. 2:24) and other partners (Heb. 13:4). Thus marriage is for oneness through loving, which is expressed in unrestricted giving of mind, emotion, will, body and soul to a spouse as if given to Christ Himself. Harmful to this oneness is sin which causes the marriage union to degenerate into conditional love, inability to listen or to be open in sharing, hidden agendas, manipulative behavior, and being judgmental.

This God-ordained union (Gen. 1:26-28) is ideally a Christian coupling. We are not to be unequally yoked together (2 Cor. 6:14-18). This suggests honesty and being vulnerable to one another and not hiding anything but having open communication. It suggests love that initiates action, not waiting for the spouse to make the first move. This love is not a 50-50 proposition where one will meet the other half way, but it is a 100%-100% proposition where each spouse is not concerned about doing a share but is ready to be a total servant regardless of the response of the other.

Marital roles and relationships include: husband and wife must seek first the kingdom of God, loving Him with all their

195

hearts, minds and souls; husbands must learn to love their wives as Christ loves the church; in loving their husbands, wives are to love their husbands and be submissive to them as unto the Lord; parents should love their children, maintaining discipline while not provoking them to anger; children need to honor their parents.

Husbands and wives should be committed to one another and to the primacy of marriage and family. Both should find their main fulfillment within the home. Parents are to accept children as a gift of God and therein see an opportunity to invest their lives for future generations in a godly way. Loving discipline by the parents helps direct the will of the child to obey the will of the authorities God has put over them.

The Foundations Of Marriage

Jesus affirmed the sacred relationship of the principle of monogamy (one husband and one wife) in marriage, telling couples that God had put them together and that no person shall separate them (Mt. 19:4-6). Jesus here showed another principle which was the principle of permanent marriage just as Paul taught (1 Cor. 7:10). God also established the principle of faithfulness to each other in a lifelong agreement (Heb. 13:4), insisting that there be no adultery or sexual immorality. Paul also enunciated the principle of mutual and submissive love that is expressed in trust, mutual helpfulness, commitment, forgiveness, and fairness (Eph. 5:21-33; Col. 3:18-21, 23-24).

Husbands and wives have the responsibility to forsake all others, provide mutual sexual satisfaction and remain faithful to each other. Husbands are to show love, patience and understanding, honor, support, leadership, and complete commitment. Wives are to show love, respect and submission.

The Customs Of Marriage

The Old Testament showed restrictions regarding marriage to relatives. Being engaged or betrothed was equivalent to marriage in the Old Testament, even though the marriage was not as yet consummated (Gen. 29:21; Deut. 22:23-24). This showed the seriousness of getting engaged. The marriage ceremony, which apparently was a private affair of families, was a time of festive celebration (Is. 61:10; Jer. 7:34; 16:9). The marriage itself was not final until its consummation (Gen. 29:23).

Homosexual marriages are a gross sin and are therefore forbidden (1 Cor. 6:9; Rom. 1:27).

The Problems Of Divorce And Remarriage

God clearly shows that His original intent in marriage is one man and one woman joined for life. Therefore, divorce is marriage failure or missing the marital target.

Jesus' teachings on divorce are stated four times:

1. Jesus compared the Old Testament Law with His teachings and stated that divorce makes the wife an adulteress as well as the one who marries a divorcee. (Mt. 5:31-32)

2. In Matthew 19:3-12, referring to the Law in Deuteronomy 24:1-4, Jesus affirmed the principle that all divorce is wrong: Moses accommodated himself because of the hardness of hearts; God's ideal is no divorce; divorce without cause involves the breaking of the Sixth Commandment.

3. In answer to the Pharisees' question and following His statement on the establishment of marriage, Jesus stated that "Whoever divorces his wife and marries another woman is committing adultery" and the same is true of a wife. (Mk. 10:2-12)

4. Jesus restated the same principle in Luke 16:19. He condemned the guilty but not the innocent party, and He allowed for divorce in the case of infidelity.

Paul provides a lengthy discourse on marriage, marital difficulties, and divorce in 1 Corinthians 7:1-16. There were many problems in Corinth and this advice is as vital to them as it is to our culture today. He strongly stresses marital duties and obligations, providing guidelines and many cautions. There is an emphasis on mutual responsibility. Paul introduces the idea of malicious desertion, besides infidelity, as cause for divorce.

God issues a very severe warning about a man breaking

faith with his wife, insisting that in flesh and spirit they are His, and He has made them one. So in Malachi 2:14-16, God says to guard ourselves in our spirit and not to break faith with the wife of our youth; He states: "I hate divorce!" Notice the emphasis that the breaking of the marriage agreement is a breaking of faith.

The modern era has presented us with the situation of divorce within the church and Christian families. Forgiveness which we have dealt with very much in detail in this book is central to situations where divorce has occurred and has become a reality. If a marriage can be restored again, it is imperative that every step be taken to accomplish that.

If one of the parties has remarried, then forgiveness must heal the wounds. At the same time, Scriptural conditions must be followed in such people's restoration and leadership in the church. When Biblical principles are followed, there will be loving solutions to situations where divorce has occurred.

Turning Marriages Into Families And Houses Into Homes

The family receives its authority and identity from God. God wants to bless the world through Christian families. His name and glory are to be communicated through the family. Society and the church are only as strong as their families and homes. The "church in your house" was a central factor in early New Testament Christianity.

One of the outstanding blueprints in God's Word for the Christian home is found in Ephesians 5 and 6: 1) a right relationship to God; 2) walking in love and abstaining from evil; 3) using time as a gift from God; 4) seeking the right relationship with the Holy Spirit; 5) worshiping; 6) holding father, mother and children in high regard; 7) using the Lord's weapons to fight spiritual battles. The bond to hold the family together is a meaningful, loving and honest commitment to God's Word.

When the church and its educational efforts do not influence in making proper family choices and decisions, then TV, VCR's, movies, friends, culture and other forces will. Taking Christian communication seriously, the Christian home should be a nurturing center where a family of Christian priests unite in Bible study, worship and prayer.

There are more basic family functions and needs than protection, economic security, education and status. The most important functions of a family are relational. A family must provide love, nurturing, and healthy, intimate relationships. When these deepest relational needs of its members are not met, the family will function improperly and be crippled. Where unconditional love and nurturing are not supplied, there will be individuals who are hurt. A family breaks down when its members search elsewhere for loving and helpful relations. A family must not be so involved in providing financial needs that they forget the importance of love in family life.

Some maintain an image of rigid religiosity in public, but hide the fact that the family is fractured and has devised all kinds of cover-ups for individual failure. We must look beneath the disguises which conceal the fact that one or another is sinning against the others or that the members of the family do not talk openly about crucial matters, do not trust each other because they do not keep their promises, and suppress their feelings because they have been abandoned or treated badly.

Healthy families display deep spirituality, providing caring and nurturing. This spirituality leads to such practical aspects as recognition and appreciation of the value of routine and ordinary life, of allowing the space needed for individuality to grow and mature, of creating a deep sense of dependency and interdependency in the appreciation for others, and the value of playing together. Christian direction is offered in matters of morality and values. A living model for children is provided for what marriage is to be. A healthy marriage helps members of the family to discover God and commit themselves to Him. It gives an ample opportunity to practice the art of forgiveness. Marriage should facilitate the experience of parental "letting go."

Healthy Christian families model healthy relationships, and encourage hope in Jesus Christ. Some of the healthy family traits include good communication and good listening, acceptance of a sense of right and wrong, and enjoyment of a shared faith. Such traits involve teaching respect for one another through affirming and supporting one another, valuing service and shared responsibility toward others, seeking help with problems, having interaction with each other while respecting privacy, and sharing leisure time.

Healthy families provide godly role models, establish clear rules and boundaries for the family's security and protection, applying these rules equally to every family member. Appropriate consequences are established for violating rules that are consistent and fair. Trust and openness are developed.

A time and place is provided for family prayer, devotions, worship and celebration. Wholesome, meaningful family traditions will be developed. The family will want to avoid performance orientation, letting everyone know that they are loved unconditionally.

Family members will refrain from trying to buy love or control and manipulate others with things. They will live by a mutually-agreed-upon covenant with loving accountability, making vital commitments to each other. They will accept problems as being a normal part of life, and comfort one another in failures, mistakes and losses. There will be celebration of one another's joys, accomplishments, and growth, always giving encouragement and positive reinforcement.

The differences between a healthy and unhealthy family are as follows:

Healthy Family	**Unhealthy Family**
1. Members are open and in touch with one another with communications which is flexible and shares feelings and activities.	1. They are isolated and out of touch with each other, being rigid and are talking only about events and things.
2. Appropriate love and affection is displayed.	2. Love and affection are external or a payoff.
3. There is trust of each other.	3. Very little or no trust.
4. Consistency.	4. Inconsistency.

5. There is unity, togetherness, support.	5. They are detached, alone, isolated (survivors).
6. Clearly defined boundaries and rules.	6. Poorly defined or no boundaries rules.
7. Tolerate truth.	7. Denial, lies, anything but the truth.
8. They have internalized responsibility and control.	8. They need external control and rule to gain a semblance of normality.
9. Interdependent.	9. Co-dependent.

Christian parents should seek to make the home a **school** for learning the essentials about relationships with Christ and our fellow man, where everyone is open to learning truths about God, oneself, and one's fellow man.

The home should also be a **hospital** where parents give loving care and healing to wounded members of their family who may have fallen into difficulties or strayed. Such a hospital-home invites openness and treatment for the ills that life inflicts. The home should produce healthy members of the family and offer peace in instructive, positive relationships, using strength to build up relationships instead of tearing them down.

Crises in all relationships are inevitable, and they provide valuable opportunities for growth when they are handled well. Healthy homes with bonds of love work through crises, and can pass through temporary weakness and fragility. This is how bonding and growing together happen, with no retreating into individuality or distancing between members of the family.

The home should also be an **evangelism center** where non-Christian friends and neighbors feel welcome and experience the love with which Christ has enriched the family, and which He desires to pour upon all humanity.

We need to look to the church for the primary support unit of the family. At the same time, the family has to remain the focus for Christian education. The church must be viewed as assisting the parents to train the children rather than allowing the parents to think that they are helping the church to raise and train their children.

Responsibilities Of Parents And Children

The family has important functions to perform for parents and children alike. It should provide safety, warmth and nurture to its members, each of whom has needs for love and belonging. It will promote self-esteem and a sense of worth in Christ.

It is important for parents to recognize that they represent God in the family unit. It is a fact of life that the children's view of God usually is similar to their view of their parents. If the parents are very loving, so usually are the children. If the children have unforgiving parents, they are likely to see God as unforgiving.

Hebrews 12:3-11 emphasizes the value of discipline of children with the purpose of yielding fruits of righteousness. Failure to discipline can even ruin the child's life (Prov. 19:18). Proverbs 3:11-12 also indicates that the purpose of discipline is for correction and for maturing. The aim of parents is not, first of all, to punish the children, which results in emotional scars of fear, guilt, and hostility, but to discipline which results in security and respect (Heb. 9:28). Children should be disciplined, not punished. Punishment is administering retribution for wrongs, while discipline is designed to promote the growth of the disciplined one.

Discipline is not a means of justice, for justice has already been satisfied in Christ. Discipline is God's way of maturing His children. The purpose of discipline for the child is to train for correction and maturity (Prov. 3:11-12). The focus is to avoid future misdeeds (Heb. 12:5-10). The attitude of the parent is one of loving concern (Rev. 3:19). The resulting emotion in the child should be one of security and respect (Heb. 9:28).

To strengthen family ties and reinforce communication, parents need to show love in giving a "no!" by providing an understanding why there is a "no!" in touching the stove or kicking the cat. Confrontation should be dealt with promptly by first being a good listener and hearing without interruption all of what the child says. Only after the parent has heard the full story should the discipline be given, if needed, and make sure that it "fits the crime." If the parent has made a mistake, he or she should be

202

willing to say "I'm sorry" and admit the wrong when one has been made. Things should be talked over especially when there is no problem. Parents must keep their word. Doing things together and sharing causes can provide children a sense of accomplishment and allow them to live out Christian principles in their daily lives.

The key is to love Christ more than any others, so that we are free to love our children and our fellow man. Such love for Christ will bring with it a consistency of treatment and of love for the children. Christian love will insist on clear priorities and respect for authority, carefully selected friendships, learning to take responsibility, and having loving consideration for others. Everyone will be treated as having great worth, because of Christ's redemption of their souls. Because of Jesus' love, they will know that they are wanted, loved, and worthy of respect and care. That will also be the basis of the discipline required of them. Fathers should reflect God's character in what they say and do, even though sometimes dimly.

Being Single Can Also Be God's Gift

Paul spoke openly about being single, and he even made the strong statement, "It's good for men not to get married...I say to those who are not married, especially to widows: It is good for you to stay single like me. However, if you cannot control your desires, you should get married. It is better for you to marry than to burn with sexual desire" (1 Cor. 7:1, 8-9). We must also deal openly with singleness as we do with marriage. Paul advised, "Everyone should live the life that the Lord gave him when God called him" (1 Cor. 7:17). Singleness is a fact of life with a good number of men and an even greater number of women.

Whether being single is a decision or an involuntary act, singles should make their singleness as positive an experience as possible, as they conduct themselves morally on the basis of Christian principles. Paul describes the single condition in very positive terms, giving insights that can help single people live happily and productively.

203

Even though the Bible is strongly weighted in favor of marriage and the family, Paul's teaching must put singles completely at ease. Without requiring us to make comparisons between marriage and singleness, he states that both are good. Indeed, 1 Corinthians 7 refers to both marriage and singleness as gifts from God. Paul himself was glad that he had the gift of singleness, freeing him to serve God with total dedication in a hostile world. He explains the difference of responsibilities and concerns in verses 32 to 35, pointing out the need to have an undivided devotion to the Lord.

Singleness is not the opposite of marriage, but rather an alternative to marriage. It is an honorable status. When singleness is chosen because of devotion to the kingdom of God, it receives the highest approval of Jesus Himself who said "Still others have decided to be celibate because of the kingdom of heaven. If anyone can do what you've suggested, then he should do it" (Mt. 19:12). Thus, the ability to live positively and productively as a single person should also be considered one of the good gifts that God gives.

The single person can and should use the advantages of his or her singleness to the full, including the cultivating of personal relationships. Singles have more flexibility and freedom to socialize with more people and can better discover the fullness of friendship. The church with its family of believers should provide single people with the human relationships and support they need.

Woman's Place In The Church Family

Having learned of the role that man and woman have been given by God, what does this mean for the woman's role in the church? The roles of service of men and women in the local church must be understood and experienced within Biblical principles. Erroneous opinions have created a crisis in definitions and works, causing a scarcity of both men and women in sound, Biblical relationships in some churches. We must avoid taking direction from secular culture and liberal interpretations which interpolate certain Biblical texts and pass over other Scripture passages that do not fit some preconceived notions and conclusions. This quickly leads to a denial of the Scriptural teaching about what being male and female means.

Women, too, were to disciple women, training them to be good wives and develop godly character (Titus 2:3-5). Priscilla and Aquila invited a man, Apollos, to their home and explained to him the way of God more adequately (Acts 18:26). Women ministered to the physical needs of others in acts of charity (Acts 9:36-41) and as servants (Rom. 16:1-2). They nurtured children (2 Tim.1:5), witnessed to the Gospel (Phil. 4:3), participated in the founding of new churches (Acts 16:14-15, 40), and faithfully worked in the church (Rom.16:6, 12).

When Paul said that women are to "conduct themselves quietly" in the church (1 Tim. 2:12; 1 Cor. 14:34), he did not mean that women should not speak whatsoever, because he does allow for many important roles by women (1 Cor. 11:5; 14:26). His caution refers more appropriately to an arrangement and spirit which does not create disturbances and does not lord it spiritually over man. His specific warning against the women's limited teaching activity in the church or in the home refers only to avoid dictating to man or dominating over man or overthrowing God's authority in His chosen leader. God's design for male spiritual leadership is not to be reversed.

Women are to refrain from taking the spiritual headship responsibilities in the family where husbands are involved, and the eldership responsibilities in the church. This does not mean that they cannot speak or that they cannot do many other vital activities in the church. Rather, this recognizes the orderliness in relations with the male spiritual leadership and the importance of playing an effective role in the home and in the church.

Biblical role definitions of women can be restored only in context of responsible, Biblical male spiritual leadership. God's Word tells that the overseer or spiritual leader in the church is to be the husband of one wife, not the wife of one husband — thus indicating male leadership. Not only is this confirmed in 1 Timothy 3:1-7, but this Scripture also indicates other qualities which church elders are to have (Titus 1:5-9; 1 Pet. 5:1-4). This does not mean that men are to be lords in the church, but that both men and women perform their proper roles.

Women in the New Testament were not shut away in their homes without meaningful outlets of service in the body of Christ. They were active at many levels of activity and many were singled out as examples of faith (Rom. 16:1-15; Heb. 11:1-39), which also involved important church tasks.

The New Testament provides the pattern for leadership, relationships, and ministries and activities. Neither distortions evident in sexism nor feminism aid the church in its mission. There will be an aggressive church when men and women play their own God-designed role and work together to bring vitality to congregations, guiding individuals to maturity and helping win the world to Christ.

Living With Our Fellow Man

We have already dealt substantially with relations with our fellow man, but one area needs further study: human relations and race relations. The same Biblical principles that apply to relations in the family and with others should also apply to relations between races. Although the issue has various economic, social and political aspects, the racial problem is primarily a moral and spiritual one.

The Bible contains no specific directives concerning race, but it reveals very important principles which apply to race relations. We do know that God created all nations and all ethnics from one person (Acts 17:26).

Jesus refers to God as "Our Father" numerous times. God shows no partiality to any people (Lk. 10:30-37; Jn. 4:1-30; Acts 11:1ff). Human beings were created in God's image (Gen. 1:27), are of one lineage (Acts 17:26), are equal in God's sight (Rom. 3:23; Col. 3:11), and have equal worth and dignity (Mt. 16:26).

Salvation is for all people, not just for one group or race (Rom. 10:13). The church is one united body of Christ despite various race distinctions among the membership (1 Cor. 12:12).

Living by the Golden Rule has no race distinction (Mt. 7:12). Love for God and neighbor of whatever race is commanded by Christ (Mt. 22:34-40). Christ set an example in His dealings with others, as can be seen with the Samaritans. He made a "Good Samaritan" the hero of one of His parables.

Paul asserted clearly that we are all from the same source and all one family stock related to God, when he said: "From one man he has made every nation of humanity to live all over the earth. He has given them the seasons of the year and the boundaries within which to live. He has done this so that they would look for God, somehow reach for him, and find him. In fact, he is never far from any one of us. Certainly, we live, move, and exist because of him. As some of your poets have said, 'We are God's children'" (Acts 17:26-28).

God gave life and set the rules, and He determined that the entire human race and all its different nations should come from one man, all descended from the same ancestor. We differ in complexion, customs, and culture, but we are brothers and sisters in the human family under God. No one part of the race has a right to enslave or oppress any other part because of differences in race or culture. If there is "one Father," there is but "one family."

Peter reinforced this when he said: "Now I understand that God doesn't play favorites. Rather, whoever respects God and does what is right is acceptable to him in any nation" (Acts 10:34-35). God's attitude toward all people is to be the basis of our human relations. This includes not only people of other races, but also people with disabilities of one kind or another.

Jesus vehemently condemned the injustices of people. There is only one kind of justice in the Bible, and it allows no preferences, color-line, or measurement of physical perfection. It demands that human relations be based by a single divine standard, the holy Ten Commandments. "You mortals, the Lord has told you what is good. This is what the Lord requires from you: to do what is right, to love mercy, and to live humbly with your God" (Mic. 6:8).

God gives special attention to the disabled in His Old Testament message: "Never curse deaf people or put anything in the way of blind people to make them stumble. Instead, fear your God. I am the Lord" (Lev. 19:14). This is also based upon God's creation of all mankind, which provides a foundation for common rights and mutual concern. To insult or to put down any of them is to insult and put down the Maker.

Our relationship with each other means that we are not beings of or for ourselves alone. Bigotry, segregation, prejudice and exclusiveness are seen in God's Word as a denial of faith. Any hostile attitude towards another denies the wholeness of a person, which he has from God. Affirming God's creation of us all, we will affirm our fellow men. Nothing in the Bible, anthropology, or sociology warrants any kind of bigotry or prejudice. Indeed, God commands positive action on our part when we face conditions where others are in distress: "...Seek justice, arrest oppressors. Defend orphans. Plead the case of widows" (Is. 1:17); "...Judge fairly, and do what is right. Rescue those who have been robbed from those who oppress them. Don't mistreat foreigners, orphans, or widows, and don't oppress them. Don't kill innocent people in this place" (Jer. 22:3).

When the Samaritan woman reminded Jesus that He was a Jew and she was a Samaritan, and that Jews do not associate with Samaritans, Jesus showed again that there is to be no segregation or prejudice between races. Jesus blasted the "we-you" attitude which is the root of many racial and human problems. When the Jews tried to claim to be bluebloods as Abraham's descendants (Jn. 8:33), Jesus shattered their pious religious tradition by exposing their bigoted slavery to religious rules against the freedom of the Gospel.

Hear what Paul says about Jesus: "So he is our peace. In his body he has made Jewish and non-Jewish people one by breaking down the wall of hostility that kept them apart. He brought an end to the commandments and demands found in Moses' Teachings so that he could take Jewish and non-Jewish people and create one new humanity in himself. So he made peace. He also brought them back to God in one body by his cross, on which he killed the hostility...So Jewish and non-Jewish people can go to the Father in one Spirit" (Eph. 2:14-16, 18). No person can be right with God while being wrong with his fellow man. Hatred or big-otry toward any fellow man is totally inconsistent with God's love.

Prejudice against another person is always wrong, for it shows feelings of importance and worth by deeming others unworthy. It often uses aggressive power of dominating others' lives, whereas our Christian faith and the Christian community offer the power that comes from opening ourselves to the riches which come from God's creation for our many marvelous fellow creatures.

Prejudice allows people to feel winners by forcing other people down, while the Christian community demonstrates that the categories of winners and losers are an evil result of our culture. Prejudice promotes the feeling of belonging to an "in group" as it isolates others into loneliness, creating artificial separations. Prejudice forces people to cope with a terrifying world by joining small fortresses and self-preservation groups. The Christian community on the other hand shows people that they need not save themselves, for it has already been done.

Christians must see prejudice as a sin, and point to Jesus who loved the sinner as an example for our love. When we show love to prejudiced people, we undermine the security that feeds their prejudice. Our love should make their prejudice unnecessary.

An unknown author provided this short course in human relations: The 6 most important words: "I admit I made a mistake." The 5 most important words: "You did a good job." The 4 most important words: "What is your opinion?" The 3 most important words: "If you please." The 2 most important words: "Thank you!" The 1 most important word: "We." The 1 least important word: "I."

IV.

LIVING WITH
MY RESOURCES

What does the Word teach about stewardship problems and solutions of the First Century disciples to tell 21st Century disciples how to manage their resources in a godly way?

When God made the world, He arranged the universe in all its parts, including its inhabitants, into a unified whole. Man, as crown of God's creation, is commanded to subdue and multiply what God gave him to manage. It started with a perfect Shalom, a beautiful world with peace and unity.

He placed man as His representative to manage all creation. The emphasis was on God's unique relationship to man as one who bore His image and exercised God's rule or dominion over all creation. Creating man from dust (Gen. 2:7), God knew what man could handle physically and emotionally — so He placed man under Him with Himself as the Supplier.

Christians as managers of God's total creation is the world's oldest job description for people (Gen. 1:28-30; 2:15; 3:23). Management is God's call for people to care, nurture and love their home, Earth. This planet, our home, has been entrusted to us for loving care, as all creatures are dependent upon a complex ecological system for clean food, air, water and living space. The assignment to management, dominion and control is part of God's call to righteousness and holy living. We are not just "passing through" on our way to heaven, but we are God's partners and managers of God's earth.

Godly Management Versus Consumerism

God told Adam and Eve that they were to manage everything except one tree, which He reserved for Himself. He left them to manage the earth and its creatures. Then Satan, the "master consumer," focused on the one tree reserved for God's management, and turned Adam and Eve into themselves selfishly to go beyond the management responsibilities which God had given them.

Satan deceived Eve and Adam to believe that God's supply was inadequate or His plan was flawed. What God had reserved for Himself, man claimed for himself, being dissatisfied with the total and adequate supply he was asked to manage. Now as accumulator rather than manager, man through an act of sin abdicated his position as manager to become possessor, and got himself into irreversible trouble. Control is no longer under God but under man. Adam and Eve had fallen for the great lie: Did God really say that they were not consumers and accumulators, but that they were to live as managers? To answer that question today takes us back to Eden, Babylon and many other places.

God initiated a new start as He sent Adam and Eve out of the Garden into the "paradise of consumerism" — the struggle of thistle land, cutthroat economy, competitive industry, and demeaning technology with bruised relationships. Adam and Eve were now God's agents to get creation back in order. The dismal picture has a ray of hope in the promise of the Head-bruiser, a new creation that gives balance to get man back to godly management instead of selfish consumerism.

Materialism (gaining resources as the greatest goal of life while ignoring relationships) and consumerism (man using selfishly himself that which he is to manage for God) is defiance of God as the rule of life. Such selfishness becomes so great that God prepared to sweep away the human race in a judgment of water (Gen. 6 and 7). God selected Noah, a righteous man of great faith, with the command that he should build a ship to preserve a few people and some creatures to start fresh again the divine order under man's proper management. God protected His earth from those who would ravage and corrupt it, and placed it into obedient hands to manage for the Supplier. God always shows Himself to be the Preacher of righteousness, as He told Noah to repopulate the earth (Gen. 9:1). He placed all creatures under man's power (Gen. 9:3). As a Missiologist, He sent Jonah to Nineveh to overthrow the great gods and to redeem the people and gain them again as His managers.

God's promise to Abraham reaffirmed the covenant that God had made with His faithful servant and manager, Adam. Abraham's life is an account of managing by faith and obedience to God — no mere maintenance or consumerism, but moving out to manage in far-off places, a new home and family. Although Abraham was a faithful manager of the promise, "I will supply you and you will be a supplier to many" (Gen. 12:1-3), he took some detours where his faith wavered. Yet he was called "friend of God" (Jas. 2:23) and received the commendation of Hebrews 11 (vv. 8-10). He showed that knowing God meant obeying Him and managing for Him.

King David was responsible to God for governing God's people and protecting their properties, but at one time he allowed lust to sidetrack him from his care of his people, to steal the wife of one of his subjects and to kill her husband. The collapse of his moral values and his undisciplined life brought disaster. Whole-hearted repentance set David on God's stewardship path again, but seeds had been planted which reaped a harvest of that sin, including discontent among his people and throughout the nation.

Solomon's wisdom and wealth with whole-hearted devotion to God were replaced later by a heart filled with pride and a love for foreign wives, even the acceptance of pagan gods. Because of his idolatry and forgetfulness of the covenant and his turn to consumerism, Solomon caused the kingdom to be torn apart. Crushing taxes put a burden on the nation. Rebellion and civil war raged instead of peaceful management of God's resources. The lesson learned from Solomon (1 Kings 1 to 11), especially from his writings — Proverbs, Ecclesiastes, and Song of Solomon — is that a consistent godly life is the only sure investment for a godly future.

At one time, Israel ignored the covenant of obedience to God, returning to the pagan ways of Egypt. People built idols of wood and metal, devising their own system of worship. Pride, stubbornness and disobedience marked the life of Israel at various times. God was patient, but He judged the unrighteous for their selfish wickedness. As Israel was reduced to live under the Assyrian yoke, God still waited for them to turn from false gods to proper management of His world and all its resources (2 Kings 13 to 17). God looked toward dedicated leaders to guide consecrated people. Godly leaders led the people who spurned the Word to relearn that Word to do the work of God. Management course correction under righteous leaders restored the people to return to be wise stewards.

God's people, Israel, frequently perverted God's gracious plan of man's task to care for the earth and its creatures when they abused earth's divine function (Is. 1:2-3, 6, 9, 13, 15, 17). God had set them as His managers for the good of all creation (Jer. 1:10). Their consumer mentality and ways brought God's anger (Hag. 1:3-7, 11). God's believers were there to be His agents to restore Israel to their God-assigned stewardship, and to teach the people not to hoard God's gifts. The only proper concept of using our resources is to dedicate them to the spreading of the Gospel of Jesus Christ in one way or another.

In the New Testament we see the devil approaching Jesus, as he did Adam and Eve, in order to get consumerism to prevail. The devil took Jesus to a high mountain and showed the splendor of all the kingdoms of the world and said that he would give Jesus all this if Jesus would worship him. Earthly awards and attractions are before us as faced Jesus at a destructive spiritual cost. The devil tried to gain Jesus as the king of consumerism of the new era, but Jesus resisted. Have we taken note of this great temptation to consumerism?

As disciples, we must look for guidance to the Word for managing the total universe and all of God's resources for the good of all and for use in Christ's mission. As we come to God daily, bankrupt with empty hands, we can leave with the free resources of grace, enriched in every way for our work. We bring nothing to God but yet receive forgiveness, love and faith. That is God's value system that contradicts man's system of consumerism and piracy.

If all we have accomplished for our earthly life is success, progress, collectibles, leisure, and education, then we have not planned big enough. Our system must be big enough to include the management plan of God where He is owner while we are His administrators.

The Materialistic Consumerism Mentality

Christians are caught between two distinctly opposing ways of life — godly management or human consumerism — to which Jesus alluded in the New Testament: "No one can serve two masters. He will hate the first master and love the second, or he will be devoted to the first and despise the second. You cannot serve God and wealth" (Mt. 6:24). God has made us custodians, not owners. We are managers chosen to serve and be equipped for mission. God's resources are inexhaustible, while our materialistic society has no lasting thing to offer, and is spiritually bankrupt.

There is nothing wrong with being consumers, for God has given us the good things to use and enjoy. But consumerism is the consuming of goods that has gone wild, a turning into ourselves rather than managing materials and resources for the good of all. Consumerism is the illness of a benefit-driven society, not willing to move unless selfish man personally gains special benefit. Materialism and consumerism are a deformed view of property and of the world, as individualism is a deformed view of self, and secularism is a deformed view of God. The god of consumerism tells us in a thousand different ways, "Buy, purchase, own," saying we will feel better if we own more. Its message is: Satisfaction, security, and happiness will be ours if we own this or that. Finally, we are led to believe that our identity is tied up in what we possess.

Consumerism is dangerous because it destroys the spiritual roots of our lives, as we are told, "The love of money is the root of all kinds of evils" (1 Tim. 6:10). The damage is done when all our time, energy and thought are focused on the physical aspects of life and we overlook the evil that affluence does

215

to us. Materialism obscures our grasp of reality and blunts a living faith. Many come to the point that if they cannot see it, taste it, touch it, smell it or measure it, they doubt that it is real. Such people become self-sufficient without God and run things their own way, not thinking of negative effects on relationships or ecology.

There is a great difference between consumerism and Christianity, for consumerism views life only from the now, while Christianity views life from an **eternal** perspective. Consumerism builds life only on material reality for the present world, while Christianity sets life in the hand and providence of God. Consumerism gets for self and sees life for indulging in luxury, while Christianity gives of self and sees life for serving and having loving relationships. Unfortunately, consumerism has become the strongest voice of modern society.

Christianity must challenge those who have bought into materialism and technology as their value system, ones who have a "go for it all now" attitude with consumerism goals. The Christian faith challenges the self-oriented values of the society in which we reside. God calls us to abandon self-centered lives and value systems, as we recognize Him as Lord-Creator of the universe with ourselves as managers of it in complex relationships.

The Bible does not condemn the possession of material things, but recognizes a place in everyone's life for enjoying things. While God tells us that there will always be the rich and the poor, He informs us that luxury and wealth are dangerous because of what they tend to do to a person. So possessions must be handled with care. The Bible recognizes no purpose for abundance other than a means of serving God and fellow men. God always values people more than possessions, and tells people not to covet and not to be greedy, but to be content. He forbids waste and careless destruction of His resources.

James warned people who have more than what they really need for simple living, who are making possessions and money their security and god: "...Cry and moan about the misery that is coming to you. Your riches have decayed, and your clothes have been eaten by moths. Your gold and silver are corroded, and their corrosion will be used as evidence against you. Like fire, it will destroy your body. You have stored up riches in these last days...You have lived in luxury and pleasure here on earth..."(Jas. 5:1-6). God is letting the world know that He is the true and living God, and is warning people against treating material goods as if they are really gods. Instead of their temporary happiness going on forever, they will weep and howl for the miseries that are coming upon them.

These warnings are important because our work and our money are tied to the significance of creation itself and our part of the interrelated scheme of creation and God's providence. Adam's pleasure was to be God's pleasure, and so it is with us. How do we maintain our balance in the outrageous extremes we see in materialism and consumerism? Through these excesses, we turn good into bad, eating into gluttony, sex into adultery, and relationships into misery and competition.

The result of it all is that the rich, and the government, and the system or establishment dole out money, and gain and hold the power. The effects of consumerism and secularization have brought us to a crisis point in search of our own identities — as we have become lords of the universe and are lost in the mass of possession. We have accumulated things but have been alienated from people. We have become slaves of our possessions and technology. Hands that push buttons, throw switches and steer wheels have lost considerably the ability to lovingly touch, care, defend, plant and reap.

So we see the lack of community as the self-centered person walks down the street with earphones attached only to his private world. He hears so much and owns so much, and yet is deaf to and ignorant of the needs and suffering of his fellow man. He is blind to the glory of God all around him which fills the heaven and the earth. There is nothing left to quiet his own thoughts and feelings, except chemicals or alcohol which drug his mind from experiencing reality. Thus he loses contact with the reality of creation and of his fellow man. He has lost his sense of values, as the world becomes a series of external ornaments, status symbols, and games all of which wither and fall as fast as a cut flower. Then he loses reason to live and die, and loses appreciation of himself and his fellow man as the crown of God's creation. He is blinded to his management responsibilities, while consumerism demands his life totally. The result is a painful void inside of ourselves while living in a world which fills life with so many things and fills the air with sound and light diluted with pollution and acid rain, and fills people with diseases such as AIDS.

The consumer world is a very vicious place which makes no sense. The result is that many have escaped inside themselves into a dream world. Outside we are devoured by exploding ideas and massive systems, while inside we can romanticize and deny reality. Everything becomes subjective while we cannot define any values or anchor any relationships. Everyone becomes a law unto himself, ignoring the realities of the world and of God. This results in the choosing of a world of counterfeits.

Throw Money At It

In a consumeristic and materialistic world, which has lost its moorings, money becomes the solution to every problem. "Throw money at it" is the cry from every quarter. It is the plea of all individuals who think they have a problem. It is also the solution of bleeding hearts and of big government to aid people in a humanistic society.

Forgetting about God's system of working, earning, participating in community, providing charity, caring, helping, and loving as individual disciples and as a Christian community, people in a humanistic culture will look at government structures on all levels for money to be sent to the point of need, that is, "to throw money at it!"

The failure of the church to teach Christians properly about the stewardship of money and Biblical giving has resulted in governments taking over the charity which God has required of Christians to perform. As Jesus' ministry demonstrated concern for the poor and needy, so we, too, are to "...do what is good for everyone, especially for the family of believers" (Gal. 6:10).

Hebrews 13:2-3 reminds us that we are to show hospitality to strangers and to remember those who are ill-treated or in prison. John warns that if we close our hearts to needy brothers, the love of God does not abide in us (1 Jn. 3:17). In Jesus' description of the Last Judgment, He equates gifts made to the poor as made to Him (Mt. 25:40). It is the Lord's will to provide opportunity for the servant of Christ to display love. God wants to be glorified through the gifts, and that is done only through Christian giving, for governments do not glorify God through gifts which have been taken through taxing people.

Redistribution of property and income by force in order to give charity to the needy spoils production, which then provides less and less to redistribute. This is dismantling God-given resources, as people will work less, save less, invest less, and produce less. This is making man's supply house the all-in-all and taking glory away from God's Supply House. It finally results in trying to divide poverty in order to gain prosperity to take care of the needy.

The reason why governments get into the "giving to the poor" is because Christians in the church have failed to be faithful to their God-given responsibilities. God has said that neighbors should care for neighbors and others in the community. The Bible tells of distant Christians who gave offerings to help the poor in Jerusalem. That's God's plan. Instead of allowing governments to throw money at the problem, the church should reinstate the divine plan of teaching Christians to give as God has given to them, thus glorifying Christ in the process.

It has also been learned by research that the redistribution policy of taking from one to give to another destroys incentive among the poor to help themselves and hurts human dignity. People come to feel that the government is the giver of gifts and that it owes them a living, while they ignore God's Storehouse from which Christians should receive what they need. Christians and churches have the resources to do the job. If anyone doubts it, they should look at the two fishes and five loaves which Jesus used as a starting point on one occasion.

In the Old Testament, all families were required to have

personal contact with the poor in their communities, insuring that funds for the poor would be given to those who were truly in need. God's Law was generous to the poor: He commended charity toward them from believers, and made various provisions such as gleaning food from the fields on their behalf. However, the poor did not have an unqualified claim on the goodness of others. God's Law sought to teach responsibility to those who had plenty and to those who did not have much. God's method of helping the poor was through regeneration rather than revolution, and production rather than confiscation.

The riches of some are not the cause of the poverty of others. Throwing money at the problems is not the solution. The solution lies in the church being the church, and Christian disciples being the caring force God intended them to be in the world. Churches should be resource centers for gifts to the poor, like maintaining food and clothing banks to meet legitimate needs.

Channels Of God's Grace

The enduring force for the management and stewardship of God's resources is the grace and power of God. Christians are channels of God's grace, as they have unlimited resources to tap to be available in God's Supply House. As we manage these resources, see what is available:

"...Share the same promise that God made in Christ Jesus...He allowed me to explain the way this mystery works...He did this so that now, through the church, he could let the rulers and authorities in heaven know his infinite wisdom...I'm asking God to give you a gift from the wealth of his glory. I pray that he would give you inner strength and power through his Spirit. Then Christ will live in you through faith. I also pray that love may be the ground into which you sink your roots and on which you have your foundation. This way, with all of God's people you will be able to understand how wide, long, high, and deep his love is...Glory belongs to God, whose power is at work in us. By this power he can do infinitely more than we can ask or imagine" (Eph. 3:6-20).

Looking at this divine Source, it is obvious that God has supplied His people with all the spiritual and material resources required to get the saving Gospel of Jesus Christ to all people in the world in our lifetime. With God as our Source, we shall never lack the spiritual or material resources to reach the unregenerate multitudes in all the world, locally and worldwide, in our generation. J. Hudson Taylor knew this. He maintained that churches or missions lack sufficient supply to reach non-Christians effectively when they fail to avail themselves of God's rich supply. Taylor said, "God's work done in God's way will never lack God's supply."

In view of God's great resources available to us, how is it possible that we Christians as a minority in the world enjoy and retain in our own reservoir the constant flow of God's grace, love and mercy in Jesus Christ, while the unbelieving majority do not enjoy the spiritual wealth which God wants to share with them through us?

What other supply house can be commended with so many superlatives and which offers so much? "Besides, God will give you his constantly overflowing kindness. Then, when you always have everything you need, you can do more and more good things" (2 Cor. 9:8). There's no way that we can honestly call ourselves poor, weak, and incapable of taking on the challenges God has placed before us. Our inadequacies come from our own doubts and refusal to allow God's grace to flow through us, and to use us as channels according to His design.

Will we fully comprehend the exciting partnership which God has given us with Him to be channels of His grace? Are we prepared to act on His promises? "God gives seed to the farmer and food to those who need to eat. God will also give you seed and multiply it. In your lives he will increase the things you do that have his approval. God will make you rich enough so that you can always be generous. Your generosity will produce thanksgiving to God because of us. What you do to serve others not only provides for the needs of God's people, but also produces more and more prayers of thanksgiving to God. You will honor God through this genuine act of service because of your commitment to spread the Good News of Christ and because of your generosity in sharing with them and everyone else" (2 Cor. 9:10-13).

Our management and stewardship deeds are called a harvest of righteousness, and God promises to supply and increase the seeds which we are to sow in His world to do His work. God gives us three reasons why He gives: that we may have enough for ourselves; that we may have a way to give to spiritual causes and the needy; and that it should result in many thanksgivings to God from us and those who receive through us.

God could have used angels to do the job, for He has armies of them. Instead, He has provided us with resources which we are to manage and over which we are stewards. But we need to keep our roles straight and not confuse ourselves as owners: "So neither the one who plants nor the one who waters is important because only God makes it grow" (1 Cor. 3:7). Driving the point home even harder, God continues: "...What do you have that wasn't given to you? If you were given what you have, why are you bragging as if it weren't a gift?" (1 Cor. 4:7).

God's message comes off just as strong in Psalm 50:9-12: "But I will not accept another young bull from your household or a single male goat from your pens. Every creature in the forest, even the cattle on a thousand hills, is mine. I know every bird in the mountains. Everything that moves in the fields is mine. If I were hungry, I would not tell you, because the world and all that it contains are mine." Will the manager tell the owner that he will not manage according to the owner's desires? Will the manager ignore the owner's request for sharing, while he hoards the owner's goods and refuses to utilize them for the task the owner embraces?

That God can and will provide all our spiritual and material needs so that we are also able to give away generously from His store house is the assurance of this amazing promise: "My God will richly fill your every need in a glorious way through Christ Jesus" (Phil. 4:19). This is the incredible resource of the Heavenly Banker, Who offers us the Bank of Heaven itself where we cannot overdraw our account, cannot write a check too big, and cannot break the bank. God offers us blank checks signed in the name of Jesus Christ, Who invites us: "Ask, and you will receive...Everyone who asks will receive..." (Mt. 7:7-8); "...So how much more will your Father in heaven give good things to those who ask him?" (Mt. 7:11).

For those who think that God's plan for management should be revised in order to pamper our doubts and fears concerning our own survival, let them learn the wisdom of the divine purpose: "God's riches, wisdom, and knowledge are so deep that it is impossible to explain his decisions or to understand his ways. 'Who know how the Lord thinks? Who can become his adviser?' Who gave the Lord something which the Lord must pay back? Everything is from him and by him and for him. Glory belongs to him forever! Amen!" (Rom. 11:33-36). Note: Who has advised God about His stewardship plan? Who does God have to repay for his offerings?

God's plan of management is clear and simple: "Each of you as a good manager must use the gift that God has given you to serve others. Whoever speaks must speak God's words. Whoever serves must serve with the strength God supplies so that in every way God receives glory through Jesus Christ. Glory and power belong to Jesus Christ forever and ever! Amen" (1 Pet. 4:10-11).

Representatives And Priests Of God

One title for God's chosen people both in the Old and New Testaments is that of priests. In Exodus 19:5-6, God first reminds the believers that all the earth and its resources are His, and that they are "a royal priesthood and a holy nation." He said to us New Testament Christians: "However, you are chosen people, a royal priesthood, a holy nation, people who belong to God. You were chosen to tell about the excellent qualities of God, who called you out of darkness into his marvelous light" (1 Pet. 2:9).

As God's priests, we have the sacred task of going to Him for people and to go to people for Him. People are His most precious resources on earth. As priests living under the heavenly King, we do not abandon our daily work in order to spend all our time to perform sacred rituals, but as God's priests we bring the sacred to the secular, our daily work and life. Our task is to go to God for people, and to go to people for God.

"Going to God for people" means that we pray for ourselves, our family, our neighbors and friends, our community, our nation, and the entire world. We make supplication and intercession that God's saving grace and providence would provide all that is provided for people everywhere to live the abundant life in Christ (Jn. 10:10) as God gives either directly to them or through us as His managers.

"Going to people for God" means that we are God's representatives or priests as part of the community of God to be involved in the human community in meeting spiritual and material needs wherever they may be found. This means that we do not live merely to gain resources, but that we utilize God's resources in order to live profitably as His managers for the good of all. It means that we are to love and serve each other in the entire human family. God has given us abundant resources so that we may be generous as we go to people for God.

Rather than being called out of our work to sit in church, we are called from church to our work in the world.

Most Christians are not called to full-time professional church service, but everyone is called to a full-time job for responsibilities in the home and at work, sharing Christ. God sees our jobs as an important part of His work on earth. Do we see God at work in our lives and in our work?

As God continues to work even now, upholding His creation (Col. 2:16-17; Heb. 1:3), He meets His creatures' many needs (Ps. 104). Working out His purposes in history (Deut. 11:1-7), He created Christians to be His priests and co-workers ever since He placed man in the Garden to "work it and take care of it" (Gen. 2:15). We seed and cultivate, but God gives the increase, thus God gives us great value as His co-workers.

All legitimate work is an extension of God's work: "When I look at your heavens, the creation of your fingers, the moon and the stars that you have set in place — what is a mortal that you remember him or the Son of Man that you take care of him? You have made him a little lower than yourself. You have crowned him with glory and honor. You have made him rule what your hands created. You have put everything under his control: all the sheep and cattle, the wild animals, the birds, the fish, whatever swims in the currents of the seas" (Ps. 8:3-8).

Because of our sin, none of our work completely fulfills God's intentions, but this does not take away from the dignity in the work that God has assigned us. Such work is a means to several purposes: through work we meet our own needs, our family's needs, and the needs of others through providing service or gifts of money. Through our work we show love to God. Christian disciples, priests or co-workers with God are told: "Whatever you do, do it wholeheartedly as though you were working for your real master and not merely for humans. You know that your real master will give you an inheritance as your reward. It is Christ, your real master, whom you are serving" (Col. 3:23-24). Under God's authority as priests and disciples, we exercise our privileges to influence His whole creation through the careful use of His resources.

Living As Servants

Only one stewardship model is fully adequate for proper use of God's resources. Jesus, the very picture of a servant, said, "But I'm among you as a servant" (Lk. 22:27). Only the servant model of Jesus in His life and work can be fully adequate for stewardship: "Those who serve me must follow me. My servants will be with me wherever I will be. If people serve me, the Father will honor them" (Jn. 12:26). Everything Jesus said and did demonstrated an attitude of servant. Servanthood is the basic model for Christian stewardship.

Jesus bestows "servanthood" on those He has cleansed of sin and called by His reconciling Word: "I've given you an example that you should follow...Slaves are not superior to their owners, and messengers are not superior to the people who send them. If you understand all of this, you are blessed whenever you follow my example" (Jn. 13:15-17). Jesus said this just after He had washed the disciples' feet over the objections of Peter, who viewed the situation from a human viewpoint.

Recognize that this was the King of heaven and earth Who from a human viewpoint should be sitting on a throne wearing a crown and a gorgeous robe to exemplify the fact that He had all power, and had come from God and was going back to God. Instead, He stripped Himself to His underclothing and wrapped a towel around His waist and washed their feet: "The Father had put everything in Jesus' control. Jesus knew that. He also knew that he had come from God and was going back to God. So he got up from the table, removed his outer clothes, took a towel, and tied it around his waist. Then he poured water into a basin and began to wash the disciples' feet and dry them with the towel that he had tied around his waist" (Jn. 13:3-5).

Jesus, our example of a servant, said: "So if I, your Lord and teacher, have washed your feet, you must wash each other's feet...I'm giving you a new commandment: Love each other in the same way that I have loved you. Everyone will know that you are my disciples because of your love for each other" (Jn. 13:14, 34-35). Here Jesus showed His disciples what love and stewardship really are.

Such servanthood is unnatural to our self, who considers it an insult to his pride and an intrusion on his freedom. Our old nature wants to dominate and put people under human bondage: "You know that the rulers of nations have absolute power over people and their officials have absolute authority over people" (Mt. 20:25). These words of Jesus came as a rebuke to the mother of Zebedee's sons, who asked Jesus to grant that one of her two sons may sit in a position of honor at his left in His kingdom. She obviously wanted them to be "big shots," but Jesus told her that she did not realize what she was asking. She later was told: "Whoever wants to become great among you will be your servant. Whoever wants to be most important among you will be your slave. It's the same way with the Son of Man. He didn't come so that others could serve him. He came to serve and to give his life as a ransom for many people" (Mt. 20:26-28). Church members need to get this picture very clear — that they as members of the church are not only to be served, but to be servants themselves.

When Jesus' popularity caused great crowds to follow

Him (Mt. 4:25), He taught a great lesson in servanthood to His disciples. He left the crowd and sat His disciples on the mountainside and said, "Blessed are those who recognize they are spiritually helpless...the gentle...the merciful...those who make peace..." (Mt. 5:1-12).

Our lives are to be integrated to meet people's needs in a servant role. This begins with accepting the mentality and example of Christ (Phil. 2:1-11). We are not just to perform acts of service, but to be servants. We are not to be spiritual sponges which absorb teaching and doctrine, but disciples of Christ to offer unselfish service through servanthood. We are not to strive for service positions and recognition with self-serving motives, but to seek a place to serve joyously with our God-given abilities. Service underlies all Christian life and activity. This servanthood is the support system required for those hurting in Christ's body and in the world.

A servant is one who sacrifices self-interest for self-extension in which concern for others is not sacrificed for a concern for oneself. The basis of extending ourselves to others is sacrificial love, which is an essential characteristic of the servant. Christian servants will give of themselves because it is the only way to bring others into the fold, which is the purpose of our lives.

To be faithful servants, God requires us to be humble, not proud: "...All of you must serve each other with humility, because God opposes the arrogant but favors the humble. Be humbled by God's power so that when the right time comes he will honor you" (1 Pet. 5:5-6).

If we are blind and unresponsive to the world's needs, we will pretend that the needy are not really in distress even though we see them bleed; if we see them alone, we may tell ourselves that they like it that way. Jesus alone can correct our sight to be loving servants who see that the neighbors in need are not an interruption in our schedule, but they are there by divine appointment. To take the servant initiative opens us to the risk of all kinds of difficulties, including ridicule and even rejection. It is a risky business to abandon our security blankets in order to penetrate the lives of others as their servants.

227

A Call To Servant Life Style

Christian servants will examine their lifestyles and confront the cultural forces that sap their spiritual strength. Recognizing a need in life for something more than bread, God does not condemn the possession of material things on the part of the Christian servant. Labeling luxury and wealth as dangerous because of what they tend to do to people, God recognizes abundance as a means of greater service. While we enjoy advantages, at the same time, God tells us to be concerned about the disadvantages of others.

The servant is always confronted with the question, "How much is enough?" This is the dilemma faced by the rich farmer in the parable taught by Jesus (Lk. 12:15ff). There is probably no area in which a servant's commitment is tested more severely than in his disposition of surplus. There are few situations that will reveal more clearly what kind of people we are. A serious problem is the exploiting of the resources of God's world.

Jesus has a message to those who turn servanthood related to money into what is termed the "prosperity Gospel." "I can guarantee this truth: Anyone who gave up his home, brothers, sisters, mother, father, children, or fields because of me and the Good News will certainly receive a hundred times as much here in this life. They will certainly receive homes, brothers, sisters, mothers, children and fields, along with persecutions. But in the world to come they will receive eternal life" (Mk. 10:29-30). We do God and ourselves an injustice if we take these words of Jesus to make such a promise as "Invest heavily in God; the returns are staggering, 100 to 1!...Every man who invests in the Gospel has a right to expect a staggering return of one hundred fold." Such free-wheeling advice is inconsistent with Jesus' model of servanthood. That interpretation is wrong because Jesus said that there would be a hundredfold blessing not just on material things but also on brothers, etc., and that this promise is for those who had left everything to follow Him. This teaching immediately follows the lesson which reveals the spiritual danger, not the spiritual benefits, of riches. Someone has said, "God has promised to meet our needs, not our greeds," which means that He does not promise to give us all we desire.

It is dangerous for a servant to think, "Now that I obey, I expect something in return." There is no way that we dare promise or expect such returns or manipulate God to "invest" through our gifts in a way that He owes us anything. There are no instant or guaranteed returns on any specific amount that we give God. It is all under grace, for it is not a deal that God makes with us. God cannot be manipulated that way. God does not make deals. A gift is given without expectation of return or otherwise it is not a gift.

God is not a celestial slot machine for depositing one dollar and getting one hundred in return. Can you imagine the pounding on God by ignorant people who believe such prosperity gospel nonsense when their manipulative approach does not bring returns on their spiritual investments? Can we imagine them reminding God of His responsibility in return for their "faithfulness"?

Does God really want us rich? He did say that He wants us to be "rich in good works." God does give good material gifts, including Cadillacs, to some of His servants, but He told us that we would more likely pass through much tribulation than ride through life in a BMW or Saab. Yet a gracious God is pleased with generosity: "A generous person will be made rich, and whoever satisfies others will himself be satisfied" (Prov. 11:25).

The danger of the "prosperity gospel" is that it makes false promises. These encourage unbiblical desires for material prosperity and give false hopes for perfect physical health. Of course, there is some truth embedded in the gospel of health and wealth, for God does promise good to His servants. But we are not to define that good by our demands, especially in material terms.

Material gifts are a snare as much as a blessing. Pious prayers for prosperity are dangerous if they are not accompanied with the caution about the "deceitfulness of wealth" that can choke the Word of God in our lives (Mt. 13:22). "But people who want to get rich keep falling into temptation. They are trapped by many stupid and harmful desires which drown them in destruction

229

and ruin" (1 Tim. 6:9). Such are the traps that are faced by those who make positive financial confessions or "name it and claim it" deals with God. Prosperity gospel proponents use isolated Biblical texts and try to make universal laws out of them to hold God to a deal that He never made.

The "seed-faith" emphasis seems so logical, but when the message is presented that the seed is guaranteed to become a harvest of dollars and possessions, it reduces God to what someone has called a "sugar-daddy." When you want His blessings, you pay Him off. This emphasizes bartering, not giving to God out of love regardless of the results.

It is also unwarranted to say that we should never pray, "If it is the will of God," when we ask for material things, as though we are praying in doubt. It is wise to leave the decision in God's hands: "We are confident that God listens to us if we ask for anything that has his approval" (1 Jn. 5:14). The fact is that "we do not write our own ticket with God," as some indicate. There are no four simple steps to receive from the Lord what we want: say it, do it, receive it, and tell it. This treats God as a giver only, not as the Lord of our lives.

God does not want us merely to embrace a system of receiving, but rather to enjoy a lifestyle which embodies a totality of God's goodness to us. What we should earnestly seek from God is a contented heart, happy with whatever God gives. "I know how to live in poverty or prosperity. No matter what the situation, I've learned the secret of how to live when I'm full or when I'm hungry, when I have too much or when I have too little. I can do everything through Christ who strengthens me" (Phil. 4:12-13). Let us allow God to decide what harvest He will give in response to the seed we sow.

The "prosperity gospel" makes Christianity just another selfish self-fulfillment program, little different from the "me-generation" culture of this era filled with self-concern and self-aggrandizement.

Our old self tempts us to strive to get what will soon be gone, some of which should never have been sought. That old nature wants us to seek accumulation as our chief goal in life, but possessions can soon pass away as a cloud. Having Christ as the Center and having right Christian goals helps us avoid vanity, defeat, and frustration.

Some people reach all their goals in finances, position, and life achievements, and then sitting at the top they may ask, "Is this all there is?" That question accentuates the important issues of purpose in what we are doing and accumulating in life. Ecclesiastes provides spiritual insights into this matter related to pleasure, wealth, and even work and tells us that there is no real satisfaction in:

1. Pleasure — I tried pleasure and tried to be cheerful through wine, but this also was vanity. I did not deny myself anything my eyes desired and I kept my heart from no pleasure (Eccl. 2:1, 3, 10).

2. Wealth — I built houses, made gardens and parks. I had great possessions of herds and flocks. I gathered silver and gold. Every man to whom God has given wealth and possessions and ability to enjoy them — this is the gift of God (Eccl. 2:4-8; 5:19; 6:2).

3. Work — I made great works. I hated all my work, seeing that I must leave it to the man who comes after me, and he will be master of all for which I toiled. Work is troublesome. All man's work is for his mouth, yet his appetite is not satisfied (Eccl. 2:4, 18, 22, 23; 3:9, 22; 6:7).

4. Money — He who loves money will not be satisfied. What gain has the owner when possessions increase but to look at them with his eyes? Many riches are kept by their owner to his harm. As he came into the world naked, so naked he shall leave and carry nothing away (Eccl. 5:10-11; 11:13).

The writer concludes that "all is vanity": I hated life for what was done, for all is vanity and a striving after the wind. Vanity of vanities; all is vanity. (Eccl. 2:17; 12:18) What is your life? For you are a mist that appears for a little time and then vanishes. (Jas. 4:14)

Some need to redefine what it means to be happy. They find most of their joy over a pay raise or an inheritance that fades and is replaced by a new craving. God does not value things as man does.

Abilities And Gifts For Service

In 1988 a study was completed by the University of Michigan Survey Research Center of 2700 people in the Tecumseh area of Michigan over a 10-year period to determine the impact of social relations on health, especially volunteer work and service to others. Those who performed regular volunteer work had a dramatic increase of life expectancy, whereas people who did not perform volunteer work were 2 1/2 times more likely to die during this time than those who provided some service at least once a week. Research at the University of California, Johns Hopkins, and Yale supports these findings. Those who were turned in to themselves were less healthy than those who looked out from themselves to serve others. Psychologist Joyce Brothers commented on national television that in view of these findings wise doctors will consider a prescription of service and volunteer work to their patients for being healthier.

We human beings are part of a social family planned by God to be dependent upon each other by services we give through our abilities and daily work. Christians have been given special abilities to use for others in the body of Christ. Jesus is our model, who "didn't come so that others could serve him. He came to serve..." (Mt. 20:28). We are to offer service to others on the basis of our gifts, as others provide them to us. Much of what we do is given and received through the market system, but there is also volunteer service for us to provide.

God planned His work on the basis of gifts He has given to believers. Through gifted individuals — each member — God gives to His church all that is needed to accomplish His work. God does not want us to be ignorant or unaware of our gifts (1 Cor. 12:1). He does not want us to neglect our gifts (1 Tim. 4:14). Every gift God has given to us is to be a blessing to others. Truly, we Christians are created for a divine purpose — good works.

Many Christians seem to be bothered by a spiritual inferiority complex, ignorant of their great assets and resources while being too aware of their weaknesses and liabilities. The

232

result is a sense of worthlessness and weakness in living for and serving the Resurrected Christ.

There is no Christian who has not been gifted somehow for God's service. The Holy Spirit will empower Christian disciples to use their abilities and gifts. Unfortunately, many disciples are not conscious of possessing an ability or gift, or what to do with gifts.

Is God asking us too much when He urges in view of His mercy to offer our bodies as living sacrifices (Rom. 12:1)? Is it unrealistic? Not if we understand that our entire life is to be lived for God and that Christ dwells in us. Our physical body wears down through the ravages of time, but our spiritual selves grow stronger under grace the more exercise they get. Physical bodies become consumed, while spiritual bodies as living sacrifices become stronger.

Accountants use an interesting device known as a T. On one side of the T are listed assets — things we own, such as our home, car, etc. On the other side are liabilities or debts — what we owe. Then each column is totaled. If the liabilities exceed the assets, there may be some problems. If the assets are more than the liabilities, the account seems safe.

We will be benefited by doing a periodic T-account of ourselves as we list our assets of abilities, gifts, and other such assets, and then list in the other column how we are using them. How do we balance on each side of the T? Are there too many liabilities such as fear, doubts, poor stewardship habits, negative things about ourselves, and the handicaps that come from such thinking?

We need to be aware of the direction we are going. Through our self-evaluation, we can be led to shed useless baggage that may be weighing us down, and then to re-establish our priorities, and activate any abilities or gifts that are not being used at this time.

Realistic and honest reflection is a useful activity. Let us take the occasion to audit our total self and to study what we are doing with our personal resources — using them for God or for self.

Body Action Through Spiritual Gifts

The renewal of the church is dependent upon the work of the Holy Spirit manifested in the recognition and use of abilities and God-given spiritual gifts as members are equipped for the building up of the body of Christ for all to become mature in the faith (Eph. 4:7, 11-16; 1 Pet. 4:10-11). As renewal efforts lead us to the Biblical understanding of the formation, spiritual organization, power, life, structure, leadership, and living dynamics of the flock, so we also recognize the gifts of the flock.

Even though Paul said (about spiritual gifts), "Brothers and sisters. I don't want there to be any misunderstanding concerning spiritual gifts" (1 Cor. 12:1), many churches until recently knew little or nothing about the subject. The nature of the church demands that God's people understand spiritual gifts since the church is God's people functioning interdependently according to their unique God-given gifts and ministering one to another in love.

Paul's most extensive discussion of spiritual gifts is in 1 Corinthians 12-14, from which we learn: Christians are to be informed about the gifts of the Spirit. There is a great diversity of spiritual gifts, but a unity with members of the same body, serving one another for the common good. The one great unifying factor is the fruit of the Spirit (Gal. 5:22), which is love that must govern the exercise of all spiritual gifts. The purpose of proclaiming the Gospel and salvation to sinners must govern their use. All gifts must be used to edify the body of Christ, and must be used in such a manner that they do not violate or disrupt decency and good order as God demands in the church. God definitely places limitations on the use of certain gifts.

Romans 12:1-11 is a counterpart to Paul's discussion of spiritual gifts in 1 Corinthians 12-14: every Christian is a member of the body of Christ and has certain spiritual gifts with which he or she can make a positive contribution to the healthy functioning of the body. People with gifts must serve modestly and with good judgment. Gifts are to be used for the good of all.

Paul's stress in Ephesians 4:1-16 is on the unity of the

234

Church and spiritual gifts are to be used to foster unity. The ascended Christ who has unsearchable riches and who gives gifts to His people is truly Lord of all and everything. While the emphasis is primarily on persons and offices, the underlying fact is that God gives specific gifts to specific persons for specific offices. These gifts are given to equip or to prepare disciples for their work of service or ministry to build up the body of Christ.

Peter (1 Pet. 4:10-11) summarizes in two verses what we read in Corinthians, Romans, and Ephesians. He states that every Christian has received some spiritual gift, which is not his to use or bury as he pleases. Christians are to exercise their gifts as stewards of God.

Spiritual gifts are God's way of getting His work done in the world through the church. They are a key to His ministry through people. They build up the body, but they are not marks of spirituality by themselves. All authority and direction for their use come from Christ, our Head. There are dangers of pride and counterfeit, and improper use will cause confusion, strife, and jealousy in their use.

Abuses of spiritual gifts include ignoring them, refusing to use them, insisting that all should have a specific gift, insisting that the Holy Spirit give the one who asks a gift like He has given to others, or exalting one gift over another, or failing to realize that gifts come from God.

Some leaders have given hints as to how to discover spiritual gifts through Bible study: **explore** the possibilities by studying the Bible and getting to know gifted people and by discussing Biblical concepts; **experiment** as much as possible with what appears to be a gift and look for opportunities to use it; **examine** one's convictions and inventory one's interests and abilities; **evaluate** one's effectiveness; **expect** confirmation from the Body through the leaders of the church, who should recognize the respective gift.

Great care should be taken to avoid overemphasizing self-discovery of spiritual gifts without Bible study or confirmation from the church, which easily results in self-centered service. The Body is empowered to call members to service, and the Body should be instrumental in aiding its members to identify their gifts. A gifts emphasis should not be individualistic, but rather the church should remind each member: "Each of you as a good manager must use the gift that God has given you to serve others...so that in every way God receives glory through Jesus Christ..." (1 Pet. 4:10-11).

Another area that should receive more careful handling is the **overemphasis** on **human abilities**. This easily becomes an excuse for inactivity on the part of timid individuals. Indeed, all members should be challenged not only to identify their strengths, but also to identify their weaknesses. This leads to proper humility in contrast to references made only to strengths, which encourages one to take credit and thus lose spiritual perspective. In reality, it is through weakness that the power of God is revealed in church work. Paul set the example, "When I came to you, I was weak. I was afraid and very nervous. I didn't speak my message with persuasive intellectual arguments. I spoke my message with a show of spiritual power...Who says that you are any better than other people? What do you have that wasn't given to you? If you were given what you have, why are you bragging as if it weren't a gift?" (1 Cor. 2:3-4; 4:7) Discovering strengths tempered with identifying weaknesses will keep us from mis-identification of gifts, and should lead us to be more effective tools of God through a repentant and faith-filled life.

Too many Christians are confused about the possibility of gaining victory in the Christian life. We can't look only at human and mental strengths to assure victory in our daily battles. Because some are not highly gifted, they may too quickly be rated as not valuable assets in Christ's kingdom. We look at strong men in business and in athletics who will face any situation and take on great challenges but we find sometimes that they are spiritually weak in temptations and fall easily and repeatedly. The fact is that God can do more with one who is weak physically but who is spiritually strong to perform great things for God.

"But God chose what the world considers nonsense to put wise people to shame. God chose what the world considers weak to put what is strong to shame. God chose what the world considers ordinary and what it despises — what it considers to be nothing — in order to destroy what it considers to be something. As a result, no one can brag in God's presence" (1 Cor. 1:27-29). Strong men fall because they depend upon their own ingenuity instead of on God, whereas if they depend totally on God for service and in temptations, God will "do infinitely more than we can ask or imagine" (Eph. 3:20) and will help us "subdue all things" (Phil. 3:21 NKJ).

One of the areas which has caused real divisions and confusion in churches, both charismatic and non-charismatic, is the matter of speaking in tongues. There is no Biblical warrant for claiming that all Christians either may or should speak in tongues, or that any Christian must speak in tongues today. Tongues must be studied and seen from the general perspective of spiritual gifts and their roles in the Body in the apostolic age and today. They must be seen within the scope of the means of grace. Anything that disparages the power of the Word of God is detrimental to the work of the church.

Unlike the discussion of all the other gifts, the subject of tongues is covered in one entire chapter to present the framework in which the gift of tongues is to be practiced. 1 Corinthians 14 was written because there were obviously serious problems concerning the use of tongues in the church. That chapter states many restrictions and warnings: 1 Corinthians 12:31 tells that we are to seek the greater gifts. 1 Corinthians 13 shows that love needs greater consideration.

1 Corinthians 14 shows that the gift of tongues is a lesser gift. We are shown that prophecy (teaching) is much more important (vv. 1, 3-6). Restrictions of purpose are found in verse 2 and 4 (shows the individual nature, and the necessity to edify), 5 (necessity for interpretation), 6 (it is imperative to teach), 7-9 (must be easy to understand or one is speaking into the air), 11 (know the meaning of the language), 12 (seek to excel in edification, not tongues), 13 (must be interpreted),14 (understanding may be unfruitful), 16 (uninformed will not understand without interpretation), 19 (better to speak five understandable words than 10,000 in a tongue), 22 (a sign to unbelievers, not believers), 26 (for edification

237

suggests teaching and reading a Psalm as more important), 27 (more than one must be involved, including one who interprets), 30 (orderly), 40 (decently and orderly). Even though Paul says in verse 39, "Don't keep anyone from speaking in other languages," his warnings and limitations are such that one must ask what profit there might be in tongues today. Acts 2 reveals that the speaking was in known tongues, as each person heard in his own language; this incident showed there was a mission function to speaking in tongues — that people gathered from many places might hear the Gospel.

Managing Our Time

Time use or management is one of the major issues for living as we enter the 21st Century. There are many activities based on interest and rewards that go beyond occupation. Which shall we choose? How shall we choose? What are the real priorities for life in the 21st Century?

True joy as a Christian is not being where you want to be, doing what you want to do, but being what God wants you to be and doing what God wants you to do. The Bible gives sound advice on living and the management of our time, which gives us a good basis for our time management. "So then, be very careful how you live. Don't live like foolish people but like wise people. Make the most of your opportunities because these are evil days" (Eph. 5:15-16). We are reminded to consecrate ourselves totally in our use of time to perform our tasks.

The primary consideration in time use is the will of God, living harmoniously in the plan of God for us. Time decisions are to be based on the deep dimension of God's urge that we "live the kind of life which proves that God has called you" (Eph. 4:1).

Jesus told of the value of time (Lk. 2:49), the limit and brevity of time (Jn. 9:4), the use of time (Jn. 4:34), and the reward of time (Jn. 17:4).

Paul informs us of the seriousness of time, not filling it with domestic cares, sorrows, and worldly affairs (1 Cor. 7:29-31). Romans 13:11-14 asks us to understand the present time and suggests that it is time to wake up...the day is almost here...put aside the deeds of darkness...put on the armor of light...behave decently, and avoid sinful deeds.

Everyone has the same amount of time day by day, but some have long lives and some short lives. Time cannot be saved, stored, stretched or stopped for a future date. Time never takes time off. No one really has enough time. People can usually find ways to save time.

God expects good management of time, and it is possible. We are accountable individually for the use of our time. It is important for us to determine God's timetable for us. We need to distinguish between **God's time** and **our time**. God's time is very exact, which we might term time determined by the clock. Our time can be conditioned by a lack of clear goals or commitment, and by our own procrastination and excuses for not being on time. Those who are consistently late for agreed-on appointments need to recognize that "their time" is infringing on the rights and time of others. So we ask the question whether we are setting our appointments on God's time or our time?

What is time? Time is life! Some say, "Time is money." Some, "Time is love." Some, "Time is talking, working, resting, sleeping."

How can it be said that time is love? What is good about it and what are its dangers? If time is love, then it is something to be shared, to be invested in people for specific purposes. Love has its own speed, different than the speed of technological speed or the speed we walk.

Time can be figured by night and day, by seasons, by years, by the ringing of a bell in the morning or at night. All are measures of time.

Some people count time according to events or activities, or even a year. Event-oriented (occasion-conscious) people are not too concerned with time periods. They will be with people without planning a detailed schedule and will work on an idea or problem until it is resolved regardless of time. Time-oriented (time-conscious) people set time periods for accomplishing tasks, depending upon the intent or purpose of that task, and they set goals and plan ahead accordingly with checking the clock. They maintain the idea of accountability, for when time is not well used, productivity and money are lost.

Time is a valuable resource. Because there is meaning and purpose to life, it does make a difference how we act and what we do. The use of our time should fit God's time schedule. "The day of the Lord will come like a thief. On that day heaven will pass away with a roaring sound. Everything that makes up the universe will burn and be destroyed. The earth and everything that people have done on it will be exposed. All these things will be destroyed in this way. So think of the kind of holy and godly life you must live" (2 Pet. 3:10-11).

The Bible gives us an understanding of time as we study the Greek terms used for time in the Bible with their meanings:

1. **"Chronos"** — a certain period of time. Time measured by the sun, clocks with seconds, minutes and hours, and calendars with months and years (Lk. 1:57; 1 Pet. 1:17). The word "chronological" is used in this sense. Some people are slaves of time, while others have no sense of time.

2. **"Kairos"** — point of time filled with a specific content, an opportunity, like harvest time or God's time, the right time. (Mk. 1:15; Acts 17:26; Eph. 1:9-10; Mk. 13:33)

3. **"Aion"** — length of time either limited or not limited. Endless time, eternity.

Managing our time implies that we understand God's time (kairos) while we are living in and making decisions about our time (chronos). We should not only fill hours and days by personal desires but recognize the spiritual dimension of time, the wise use of time (kairos). We can miss an opportunity for service if we act as though we have all kinds of clock time (chronos) for doing God's work because the time for service (kairos) comes only at God-given opportunities. We use clock/calendar time (chronos) to accomplish God's work in the time He gives us to do it (kairos). Time used in work, visiting, play and church tasks is to be evaluated within the full meaning of God's time.

General principles for using our time may be developed

from values and the purpose determined for our lives. Consider the following:

1. Decide what we want to do with our life. Why are we here? What are we good for? What is our purpose? The gifts and abilities God has given us will help us determine how we should use our time.

We will want to be willing to grow. We will want to give priority to the study of God's Word. His Word will direct our thinking and our attitudes, which will influence our decisions in the use of our time.

2. The purpose of our life and the planning of our time can be divided into the following areas:

Spiritual — This must always be our first priority. As there is a great need for physical breathing every moment, so there is a similar need for spiritual breathing every day (study of God's Word and prayer).

Family — God built the basic social unit to be the family, consisting of the father as the spiritual head, and the mother to bear children and to raise them in the fear of the Lord. Our family is a primary responsibility.

Social — We are created to desire and need relationships within our immediate family, extended family, co-workers and friends. What will build positive social relations that will meet our emotional and psychological needs, and that will edify others?

Financial — How much money (or goods) is needed to accomplish our goals and to fulfill our purpose in life? How much time is required to meet reasonable financial goals?

Job and Occupation — Are we spending all the time necessary to do a good job, or do we achieve less work than we should be doing? Are we underworking or overworking?

Mental - What realistic plans should we make in our circumstances for reading and learning, and in what way?

Physical - How much work or money for food is required for a proper diet and for nutrition to keep us healthy? How much time need we take for proper exercise?

We should evaluate demands on our time from relatives and friends to learn whether they are necessary and to determine what can be eliminated. There will always be tensions between what our customs and cultures expect and what God wants us to do. God will give direction as we pray so that we do His will, not our will also in respect to the use of our time.

In order to manage our time effectively, we have to realize time robbers that stop us from being good managers of time. A time robber is anything that hinders a person from achieving effectively God's purpose for his life. **Internal time robbers** are lack of goals or of being organized, a problem of indecision, inability to discipline oneself or to say "no," responding only to the urgent or problems, daydreaming, attempting too much and failing to delegate, and/or failing to have leisure or relaxation time. **External time robbers** are TV and VCR's, overindulgence in socializing and spectator sports, interruptions, and unproductive or unnecessary meetings. These involve misplaced priorities.

TV is one of the cruel masters of our day, as it steals precious time from such positive things as spiritual feeding, personal interaction and conversation, reading of good books, exercise, etc. People arrange and re-arrange their schedules in order to view the favorite shows on which we are hooked. Devotion times, Bible study, conversations, family life are harmed as prime time is given to TV instead of the real productive priorities of life. Rather than positive influences, TV often glamorizes sinful lifestyles which are portrayed as the norm while virtues are seen as dull, contradicting every Christian value. The result is that TV viewing often causes some to grow dissatisfied with their spouse, their family, and even themselves. Their own simple pleasures look old-fashioned and dull, which is another subtle tactic of the enemy who offers us the TV "apple."

Television teaches an instant gratification which is destructive of the Christian faith and life style. The incessant carnal images have desensitized us to what is important now and eternally. It promotes an individualism which is harmful to a care-giving community. It portrays a well of materialism that poisons the Christian value system.

Time can be used wisely in church work and meetings by: 1) identifying the problem; 2) naming the alternatives and comparing them; 3) selecting the best alternative; 4) starting and ending on time. Ask: why, when, where, who regarding use of time at church meetings.

Church leaders must delegate some tasks to others. Learn what to delegate and what not to delegate. Give clear instructions. Train them when necessary. Ask them to report back as to successes and failures in the tasks delegated.

Christian motivation is the key to the proper use of time. This will lead to proper planning of the use of time for ourselves, for our immediate family, for our extended family, for our work, and for doing God's work in the church.

Priorities for the use of time are:
1) Time with God for meditation and Bible study
2) Time with your family
3) Time for yourself for quiet
4) Time with the body of Christ
5) Time for your work
6) Time with other people
7) Time to plan
8) Time for recreation
9) Time for rest and relaxation

It is wise to make a list of our goals for success and happiness — our dreams. Then we should arrange these goals in the order of priority we give them.

Let us consider suggestions for managing our time: Decide what it is that you want to do with your life, and set your goals accordingly. Establish priorities for using your time based on that plan. Change whatever habits need changing to achieve your goals. Have a desire to use your time according to God's will. Pray that God will help you to overcome bad time management habits (Ps. 50:15; Heb. 4:14-16). After assessing your needs and expectations in your life, set a half dozen personal goals for the next six months. Then write a tentative job description that will attempt to meet those needs and expectations. The key to setting a monthly, weekly, and daily work schedule is to have a clear set of values and goals, and to determine your priorities.

Use "to do" lists which include "what to do short range," "what to do long range," and "what to delegate."

Consider other hints in ways to save time:

1. Work on tasks requiring concentration when you are most alert. Do not get trapped by the tyranny of last minute hurriedness.

2. When doing paperwork, try to handle each piece of paper once, rather than giving it a temporary parking place.

3. At meetings with others, stick to an agenda, setting specific starting and finishing times.

4. Organize your work area with needed tools close at hand.

5. Do not feel obliged to accept every invitation that comes your way, and learn to say no tactfully.

6. Get sufficient rest and relaxation so that you can work effectively. Always plan a period of rest to follow a time of high demand or activity.

7. Set deadlines.

8. Do not procrastinate.

9. Break big tasks and assignments into smaller ones. Don't waste energy on petty things.

10. Do not be a perfectionist. Concentrate on what is most important.

11. Make good use of waiting time. Carry with you reading material or take time to write letters.

12. Know that there will be occasions when you will need to spend time on activities you would not choose, and do not waste time fretting about it.

13. Maintain devotional and prayer time to stay in tune and to keep proper balance.

Gordon McDonald provides sound advice in capturing or recapturing our time in what he names, "**McDonald's Laws of Unseized Time**" (unplanned time):

#1: UNSEIZED TIME FLOWS TOWARDS MY WEAKNESSES.

#2: UNSEIZED TIME COMES UNDER THE INFLUENCE OF DOMINANT PEOPLE IN MY WORLD.

#3: UNSEIZED TIME SURRENDERS TO THE DEMANDS OF ALL EMERGENCIES.

#4: UNSEIZED TIME GETS INVESTED IN THINGS THAT GAIN PUBLIC ACCLAMATION. 10

The solution to this problem is to plan ahead and plan carefully. Never enter a day aimlessly. Without such plans, non-essentials will crowd into our schedules before necessities do. The next time someone asks, "What time is it?", don't look at your watch, but look deeper to your mind and heart.

We will be wise to heed this Word of God: "Whatever presents itself for you to do, do it with all your might, because there is no work, planning, knowledge, or skill in the grave where you're going" (Eccl. 9:10). When we are wise time managers, it will be because we have determined that every day will be a day of growth in knowledge and wisdom, growing stronger in our Christian faith.

The Human Body — A Precious Resource For Productivity And Enjoyment

Christian living includes control over our physical bodies and appetites. Our bodies are temples of the Holy Spirit with which we are to glorify God. As we recognize the human body as a precious resource for productivity and enjoyment in life, we will establish priorities and balance for maintaining health and strength to serve God and man. The Bible presents the high view God has of the body.

Many Scripture passages encourage us to give good care to our bodies: "Brothers and sisters, because of God's compassion toward us, I encourage you to offer your bodies as living sacrifices, dedicated to God and pleasing to him..." (Rom. 12:1); "Food is for the stomach, and the stomach is for food, but God will put an end to both of them. However, the body is not for sexual sin but for the Lord, and the Lord is for the body...Don't you know that your body is a temple that belongs to the Holy Spirit? The Holy Spirit, whom you received from God, lives in you" (1

245

Cor. 6:13, 19); "Rather, I toughen my body with punches and make it my slave so that I will not be disqualified after I have spread the Good News to others" (1 Cor. 9:27); "Training the body helps a little, but godly living helps in every way..." (1 Tim. 4:8); "Each of you should know that finding a husband or wife for yourself is to be done in a holy and honorable way, not in the passionate, lustful way of people who don't know God" (1 Thes. 4:4-5); "So, whether you eat or drink, or whatever you do, do everything to the glory of God" (1 Cor. 10:31).

Proper care of the body is one facet of a broader health concept known as "wellness." There are five dimensions that are the foundation for wellness: physical fitness, nutritional awareness, stress management, environmental sensitivity, and self-responsibility.

Wellness means taking responsibility for one's own health by learning how to be healthy, practicing good health habits and giving up harmful ones, and responding to the body's warning signs before something serious happens. Wellness involves the health of the whole person — body, mind and spirit. When our body is kept strong and well-nourished to be able to resist disease, we have more energy and endurance, and spend less time feeling tired or being ill.

Our physical bodies and natural appetites were created by God and are not sinful in themselves. With Christian motivations, we can have our bodies and appetites under control. If left uncontrolled, our bodies will become "instruments of wickedness" rather than "instruments of righteousness" (Rom. 6:13).

Of all people, Christians should treat their bodies as God's temples. They are responsible for development and proper treatment and use of their bodies, following basic health principles, good nutrition and exercise.

Right Values Undergird Good Health

Our attitudes and beliefs determine our actions. We are of great worth to God, so we should treat ourselves as having great worth. Those who believe themselves worthless will treat themselves as worthless. Our sense of self-worth is based on the reality of our redemption in Christ, which should give us a high self-value system.

When our value system is tied to beauty, physical prowess, and intelligence, we tend to accept beautiful, strong and brilliant people, while rejecting those who do not qualify in these human categories. When our joy is gained only through outside factors instead of what's inside — our Christian faith — our values will be attached to quantity instead of quality. It is easy then also to reduce our value to possession of things, and accordingly reduce people likewise and exploit them. This greatly increases stress, frustration, and crises which then lead to the abuse of the mind and body.

Man's well-being is inseparable from his value system, spiritual health, Bible study and worship. The battle over health problems is won or lost in the mind and in the spirit, where psychological bondage can afflict the compulsive person who sets his thoughts on earth instead of on spiritual matters. The "battle of the bulge" or "of the bottle" can be settled when we discover that applying the Word can help our minds and lives dramatically and spiritually.

Basic Health Principles

Someone has said, "You are what you eat" and "Some dig their graves with their teeth." Good nutrition with isolated exceptions determines good health. We need to care also for our bodies through exercise and rest. Ordinarily, we can choose health as we choose food. Refined, processed, fatty foods, stimulants, intoxicants, and additives, which are deficient in essential vitamins, provide poor nutritional balance. Contributing to ill health, physical weaknesses, and cardiac problems are caffeine, alcohol, and smoking.

When we overeat, overdrink, overwork, smoke tobacco and use dangerous substances, underexercise and wrongly use

God's gift of sex, we can expect physical illnesses of many sorts and of varying severity. We can and do cause many illnesses by not living responsibly and by not regarding our body as the dwelling place of the Holy Spirit.

In our culture we tend both to eat too much and eat the wrong foods. We tend to choose food on the basis of taste rather than nutritional value. Chronic overeating can lead to serious health problems. Both the problems of being overweight and being obese are to be avoided. Overeating has come to be a cultural pastime because of our social life style.

Discipline and moderation are the key. A permanent change in attitude toward eating will lead to a permanent change in lifestyle.

Good health habits promote the quality and length of life or the abundant life which God intends for us. Our bodies and minds function better with good and moderate habits of eating, drinking, exercise, rest, work, good hygiene and posture. Poor health and nutrition habits and over-indulgence harm the proper functioning of our bodies.

Plans for a healthy heart and life include eating right with a balanced diet, keeping our weight at the right level, a regular program of exercise, adequate sleep and rest, a positive outlook on life, and a good lifestyle.

Some who start a fitness program quit without giving it a chance. Start exercise, do it sensibly, and stick with it. Combine it with good nutrition and a good diet. If you want to live longer, exercise. It's that simple. Make the decision, then pick the exercise or activity (walking is the simplest), and then decide how much time to spend each week. Choose the times and place, and try to find a partner for support. Set your own goals and reward yourself periodically.

Smoking — A Worldwide Health Hazard

When the health directors of major countries of the world declare that smoking is hazardous to health and provide many other warnings, Christians should take note. Television and radio advertisements which come from the secular world present harsh and almost cruel reminders of the harmful habit of smoking, as they announce, "Stop smoking and losing, smokers are losers." This is the message from the world, not the church.

A research company stated, "All cigarette smoking causes lung damage — when symptoms appear, it is too late." Problems that have arisen are cancer, circulatory diseases, emphysema, harmful results to unborn children, and illness that results in work loss. It has also been learned that smoking is addictive. It retards natural processes by slowing blood circulation, affecting taste and smell considerably, and depressing the sympathetic and central nervous systems of the body. It shortens life by an average of five years. It is the chief preventable cause of death in our society.

One church has announced: "In view of the facts and Biblical principles, it seems that the following would be a Christian's appropriate action: 1. Refrain from smoking cigarettes yourself. It is not the abuse but the use of cigarettes which is harmful. 2. Warn others about the harmful effects and encourage them to quit. 3. Refrain from leading others into this harmful habit by irresponsible remarks or example. This would apply with special force to parents, teachers, and ministers whose examples children and youth often imitate. 4. Be patient, understanding, and helpful to those who have developed the habit of smoking cigarettes and find it difficult to break this harmful habit."

Those who smoke can seek assistance from various support groups, which provide sensible step-by-step processes to help them quit. Stages of quitting involve: 1) Think about quitting and seek information; 2) Modify your habit immediately; 3) Make a decision to quit; 4) Set a date for quitting; 5) Stop smoking for 24 hours. Work at it one day at a time; 6) Complete your first week, then your first month, your first three months, then your first year. Celebrate appropriately at specific times. Depend on God for strength.

Alcohol Abuse

Drunkenness is a great health hazard, and has proven also to be very dangerous to others because of drunk drivers. It is expressly condemned in the Bible (Eph. 5:18; Rom. 13:13; Gal. 5:19). It is socially disruptive (Prov. 20:1), physically damaging (Prov. 23:30, 32), morally corrupting (Gal. 5:19-32), spiritually deadening (Is. 5:11-12), and spiritually harmful (1 Tim. 3:2-3, 8; Titus 2:3). Jesus allowed drinking of wine (Lk. 7:33-35), but spoke out strongly against drunkenness (Mt. 24:29; Lk. 12:45; 21:34).

Drunkenness and alcohol abuse are strongly condemned (Rom. 13:13; 1 Cor. 6:10). The ideal of abstinence is presented in the Bible (Num. 6:1-4; Lk. 1:13-15), and Christian disciples are to have a concern for the weaker brother (Rom. 14:21). Consideration of alcohol's devastating personal and social effects on society should cause people to consider abstinence. The Twelve Step program has been reproduced in this book in order to suggest a way of recovery for an alcoholic.

Physical Fitness

Paul Harvey stated, "Most of what ails Americans is self-inflicted...Most of what ails us can be avoided."

Self-discipline is necessary in reference to the intake of food at all times because much food and many delicacies are so appealing. "Put a knife to your throat if you have a big appetite. Do not crave his delicacies, because this is food that deceives you" (Prov. 23:2-3). Is God taking satisfaction and fun out of living because of these warnings? No, because our lives are happier when the flesh or body is kept under control. The uncontrolled body becomes lazy and spoiled, which leads to unhappiness. The key to happiness is discipline. We are to control our physical appetites in the same way we control the devil — resist!

Some years ago a denomination made this announcement concerning care for the body: "Since God is the Giver of life and health, the Christian will earnestly seek to avoid doing whatever needlessly destroys, harms, shortens, or endangers life and health. Since God in love created, redeemed, and regenerated us in order that we might live for Him and our fellow man, the Christian will earnestly endeavor to avoid whatever hinders him in service or shortens his time of service to God on earth. Since the Christian is concerned not only with the eternal salvation of his fellow men, but also with their full life of service to Christ while here on earth, the Christian will strive to avoid setting a bad example which might lead others into harmful habits whereby their service to God could be hindered or shortened."

Physical fitness includes the interrelationship of body and soul, development of purpose for life, sharpening of religious values to motivate behavior modification, and the quest for maximum fitness in every area of life.

Disciples should establish good eating habits, exercise regularly, avoid unnecessary stimulants, get enough sleep and let their Christian faith give them strong and healthy emotions which help them avoid fear and worry and improper lifestyles filled with all kinds of harm and risk.

Healing For The Body

There are various examples of healing by Jesus and the Apostles, even healing through handkerchiefs and aprons that Jesus had touched. However, from all that we learn from the Scriptures and from experience in life, "it is appointed for everyone once to die." Healing when it occurs is always temporary.

The Bible gives Christians reasons to believe in "healing," but that must be carefully defined. In its broadest sense, healing is what Christianity is all about. Sin has invaded the human heart and race and has battered every one of us. Helping to put together what is torn and broken is the very essence of the Gospel and of God's kingdom. So in the broad sense we are either healers or destroyers.

In the narrow sense, healing of the body requires careful Biblical attention to learn of its true nature. For reasons of Biblical revelation and common sense, Christians should not spurn or neglect any appropriate channels of good health or healing. "If you are sick, call for the church leaders. Have them pray for you and anoint you with olive oil in the name of the Lord. (Prayers offered in faith will save those who are sick, and the Lord will cure them.) If you have sinned, you will be forgiven. So admit your sins to each other, and pray for each other so that you will be healed. Prayers offered by those who have God's approval are effective" (Jas. 5:14-16). This together with other Scriptures on healing urge intense prayer in the name of Jesus, but it does not guarantee healing on any particular occasion. Sometimes the remedies for physical infirmities are physical (1 Tim. 5:23).

But what about instantaneous divine healing? We will affirm that God's will for His creation is health and wholeness, despite the seeds of disease and sin which we bear in our human bodies. Sickness, like all of the world's brokenness is an ultimate result of human sin. However, specific sickness or trouble is not necessarily or always related to any specific wrong, or to the sin of any particular individual. When the disciples tried to determine whether a man was blind because of his own sin or that of his parents, Jesus said, "Neither this man nor his parents sinned. Instead, he was born blind so that God could show what he can do for him" (Jn. 9:3).

Death and disease came through the sin of Adam (Rom. 5:12). We also see this from Romans 8:20-22, "Creation was subjected to frustration but not by its own choice. The one who subjected it to frustration did so in the hope that it would also be set free from slavery to decay in order to share the glorious freedom that the children of God will have."

Paul prayed fervently for the removal of his "thorn in the flesh," but God did not remove it. God said, "My kindness is all you need. My power is strongest when you are weak" (2 Cor. 12:9). Christ's suffering and crucifixion is not a guarantee that every one of our physical wounds will be healed, but that God's love which permeates our life for forgiveness and salvation will be manifested in our illness. By Christ's redemptive work, our bodies and whole selves will be finally restored to their intended wholeness. God is interested in body, soul and spirit.

Full healing will be experienced through the resurrection at the Last Day. Until then, even God's people continue to share in the consequences of the Fall, including sickness and death. Even mature Christians cannot always expect perfect health and wholeness now or that their sicknesses necessarily reflect any personal fault or lack of faith (1 Cor. 15:42-49; 2 Cor. 4:16-5:4).

252

Because of Christ's resurrection, we may begin even now to share in God's victory over sin and its consequences manifested in the healing of the body, mind and relationships in ways that exceed human expectation, understanding or ability to produce. God does sometimes heal quickly, but in His own way and at His own time. All healing is God's gift regardless of the means by which it comes or the speed with which it occurs.

The natural process of healing through medicine and surgery is no less the work of God than healing which may come unexpectedly against all human prediction. In times of illness, therefore, we should gratefully apply all appropriate remedial means at our disposal, asking God to heal according to our needs and His glory.

What About Fasting?

God never specifically commanded fasting, but there are various examples of fasting. The Old Testament uses the Hebrew word for "fast" and its derivatives about 45 times. In practically all cases, it is accompanied with expressions of deep sorrow or grief, such as weeping, tearing clothes, putting on sackcloth, throwing ashes or dust on the head. In the New Testament, the Greek word for "fast" and its derivatives are used about 30 times. Jesus totally rejected the outward accompaniments of fasting found in the Old Testament as well as external things the Pharisees did to draw attention to themselves when they fasted.

In the Old Testament, fasting was undertaken voluntarily or by requirement, but the only fast ordained by Old Testament Law was that of the Day of Atonement (Lev. 16:29). It was an indication that a person was trying to suppress the sinful flesh. Fasting expressed grief over death (1 Sam. 31:13). The people confessed their sins and fasted when the Philistines came against them (1 Sam. 7:6). King Ahab fasted and humbled himself after Elijah rebuked him (1 Kings 21:27). Joel called for a holy fast for the people to show repentance (Joel 1:14).

In most cases when the New Testament mentions fasting with approval, it has to do with worship, especially prayer (Lk.

2:37; Mt. 17:21). The church at Antioch was worshiping the Lord and fasting when the Holy Spirit spoke to them to send out Paul and Barnabas (Acts 13:2-3). After conducting an election for elders, Paul and Barnabas with prayer and fasting committed the believers to the Lord (Acts 14:23). Fasting was a normal prelude to seeking God's guidance in the choice of elders and missionaries and in commissioning them to begin their new work. There was obviously a right and a wrong way to fast, and motives were important.

Fasting presents some dangers, too. God told Jeremiah that though they fasted, He would not hear, for they were following the deceit of their own hearts, the delusion of their own minds (Jer. 14:12-14). The Jews added voluntary fasts. The Pharisees fasted on Mondays and Thursdays (Lk. 18:12). Jesus taught that fasting should be done without hypocrisy (Mt. 6:16-18). Jesus speaks of personal discipline in one's spiritual life, especially in terms of fasting. As noble as fasting might be, it involved certain inevitable dangers, the greatest being that religious leaders desired to be seen and praised by men. The fasting of the Scribes and Pharisees seemed to be more a demonstration to men, rather than to God, to show what devoted people they were.

Fasting is useful for keeping the flesh in check. Fasting is a fruit of repentance and faith even as right praying and right almsgiving. It is also a fine external training in preparation for receiving Holy Communion.

When Christians are made unsure of their salvation and their relationship to God by the requirement of anything more than the righteousness of Christ by faith, then fasting should be discontinued. Fasting does not merit salvation, for God is approached only through Christ and His promises. Faith comes only through the Word.

The benefits of fasting are that it can intensify our awareness of God's presence and give evidence of mastery over our bodies. It dramatizes our confession of faith. It helps focus our lives upon ultimate issues.

Personal Money Management

Money is an exchange for work or goods to help create

the kind of life we want. God gives us time and abilities, which can be exchanged for money. Goods exchange and money exchange are important for human survival. The choice is between effective and ineffective management of our goods and money. Following proper principles of money management may encourage responsible choices and make a person free to enjoy more goods.

"A person cannot live on bread alone but on every word that God speaks" (Mt. 4:4). Without God's Word and grace, food and money lose their value. Only when we receive the word of Christ, "Your sins are forgiven," does life have real value and worth.

"But remember the Lord your God is the one who makes you wealthy" (Deut. 8:18). "Whoever loves pleasure will become poor. Whoever loves wine and expensive food will not become rich" (Prov. 21:17). "It is a gift from God when God gives some people wealth and possessions, the power to enjoy them, the ability to accept their lot in life, and the ability to rejoice in their own hard work" (Eccl. 5:19).

If a person believes that he is the owner of even a single possession, that will have a negative effect on his attitude. If he makes a total transfer of everything to God, he will find God's purpose for all he gains. How do we let God's Word direct the use of our goods and money?

Benjamin Franklin said, "Money has never made man happy yet, nor will it. There is nothing in its nature to produce happiness. The more a man has, the more he wants. Instead of filling a vacuum, it makes one. If it satisfies one want, it doubles and triples that want in other ways."

A **definition** of financial planning: A plan for developing step-by-step, where you are financially, what you have, what you need, and what you will have to do to get to wherever you want to go financially.

Basic purposes of financial planning: Conserve the property and income you have; put yourself in control of your finances; identify your financial problems; give you confidence in having your own money.

The **objectives**: Enable Christians to live more meaningfully and joyfully by Christian motivation in managing their goods and incomes; make financial adjustments whenever and wherever necessary; creating awareness that the family income and spending requires careful and prayerful attention; families adopt a wise program involving saving, spending, investing and giving.

We should not cling to our possessions for security, but raise empty hands to God to be filled; God cannot pour His riches into hands already full, sometimes with earthly trash. Money should be our obedient servant, or it will be a cruel master. It seems that the more money we have, the less secure we feel. Oddly, when some people have considerable money, they worry just as much because they have so much to lose.

The love of money increases our concern and anxiety about worldly affairs since it puts our desires and aspirations in the wrong place. It is a big source of entrapment.

God warns against the temptations to use money wrongly: "Be careful that you don't forget the Lord your God...You will eat all you want. You will build nice houses and live in them. Your herds and flocks, silver and gold, and everything else you have will increase. When this happens, be careful that you don't become arrogant and forget the Lord your God, who brought you out of slavery in Egypt...You may say to yourselves, 'I became wealthy because of my own ability and strength'" (Deut. 8:11-14, 17). "Make sure that you don't become...worried about life" (Luke: 21:34). "...When riches increase, do not depend on them" (Ps. 62:10).

Money can kill as well as heal; it can hurt as well as help; it can destroy as well as build; it can poison as well as nourish; it can curse as well as bless. "I have often told you, and now tell you with tears in my eyes, that many live as the enemies of the cross of Christ. In the end they will be destroyed. Their own emotions are their god, and they take pride in the shameful things they do. Their minds are set on worldly things" (Phil. 3:18-19). "Some people who have set their hearts on getting rich have wandered away from the Christian faith and have caused themselves a lot of grief" (1 Tim.6:10).

"What good does it do for people to win the whole world yet lose their lives? Or what should a person give in exchange for life?" (Mk. 8:36-37). "Don't love money. Be happy with what you have because God has said, 'I will never abandon you or leave you.' So we can confidently say, 'The Lord is my helper. I will not be afraid. What can mortals do to me?' " (Heb. 13:5-6). "Don't ever worry and say, 'What are we going to eat?' or 'What are we going to drink?' or 'What are we going to wear?' Everyone is concerned about these things, and your heavenly Father certainly knows you need all of them" (Mt. 6:31-32).

Money can be dangerous and lead to deceit (Mk. 4:19), hinder a person's relationship with God, lead to pride, lead to greed, lead to self-indulgence, and lead to bondage through debt.

The **rich** fool (Lk. 12:16-21) had a small god — himself — which resulted in bad stewardship and ultimate failure, even though as a neighbor he may have looked like a very successful farmer. There are five points to consider in evaluating his management of his possessions:

1. How he received them:

    > He did not receive them as from God or with thanksgiving, but acted as though they were all a product of his own wisdom and strength. He failed as a receiver.

2. How he used (spent) them:

    > When he spent, he chose selfish and unproductive ways to use his resources: eat, drink and be merry. He failed as a user.

3. How he **invested** (saved):

    > First, he invested for greater growth, but then he spent his savings selfishly instead of assigning them to productive investment. Though he began correctly, he ended up as a failure as an investor.

4. How he gave:

    > Being strictly a taker, he had no notion about his role as a giver. He failed miserably as a giver.

5. How he **left it** behind at the end of his life:

>   He left it all, as everyone does. In fact, God took it from him suddenly before he could waste it on himself. God condemns the person who "stores up goods for himself, and is not rich toward God" (v. 20). It should have been left behind as a trust from God. Again, he failed as a manager at the time of death.

Jesus introduced this parable by saying: "Be careful to guard yourselves from every kind of greed. Life is not about having a lot of material possessions" (Lk. 12:15). The rich man had caught the "mania of materialism," which is the danger of measuring life by means of the material. Inflicted with this disease, he mistook time for eternity, his body for his soul, and what was God's for what was his. At the heart of his error was the confusion between ownership and management. Life is not to be valued by the resources of one's possessions, but by the richness of the relationship one has with God.

Each Christian is God's manager of his possessions in these five ares. Are you a wise manager and are you rich toward God? How do you rate yourself on a scale from 1 to 5 (5 being highest) in these important parts of stewardship:

1. Receiving — 1   2   3   4   5
2. Using (spending) — 1   2   3   4   5
3. Investing (saving) — 1   2   3   4   5
4. Giving — 1   2   3   4   5
5. Leaving — 1   2   3   4   5

What areas need most attention? What new plans will you make to be certain that you are faithful in all five areas?

It's a serious matter when God says, "Fool." Jesus did not fault the man for prospering, but for piling up riches and wanting to squander them on himself.

Evaluate the worksheet below and rate the items with the following thoughts in mind: It is important to show hospitality, but not to be extravagant because some are hospitable to a fault and harm their family. We need to avoid throwing a big feast to display wealth. A large landowner must be careful that his only goal is not to get more land and houses. Our giving to the Lord should not only be a response to a stated need, but we should give systematically from what God gives. Some people spend as they get, and do not save for future needs. Do some of the below items show an attitude of pride, "big shot," and self-satisfaction?

CHECKING ON OUR FINANCIAL HABITS

ACTION	GOOD	EXCESSIVE OR BAD	CAN BE EITHER GOOD/BAD
1. Big and expensive meals			
2. Beer and drinks daily			
3. Do not save or invest, but use as get			
4. Gambling			
5. Give firstfruits to God and spend income wisely			
6. Festive occasions for fellowship and love, watching expenses carefully			
7. Expensive clothes			
8. Dollar bills to the church — give leftovers			
9. Tobacco			

Steps To Financial Freedom

There are Biblical principles which will give us financial freedom. The first is to transfer ownership of all our possessions to God. This is a step of surrendering our will to God in the use of our property. This also means trusting God for all our needs while avoiding gambling or trying to get something for nothing. Lotteries, too, are nothing more than legalized covetousness and encouragement of the driving force of greed. Lotteries feed the "something-for-nothing" notion. Legality does not define what is moral, but the Bible does.

The second step is to be free from debt, which should be one of the top financial goals in our lives. A very serious debt exists when the total value of unsecured liabilities exceeds our total assets or when anxiety is produced over the financial responsibility of paying the debt.

The Bible reveals that lending and borrowing are proper under certain conditions. A surplus for lending may be a sign of God's blessing (Deut. 28:12; Ps. 37:21, 26). Commercial lending for profit shows good stewardship (Deut. 15:3, 6; 13:20; 28:12). Lending for individual assistance is approved and sometimes no interest is encouraged, while too much interest is forbidden (Ex. 22:25-27; Lev. 25:37-38; Deut. 15:7-8; Luke 6:34). Debt is sometimes impossible to avoid (Neh. 5:4-5). The lender is in a position of power while the borrower is in servitude (Deut. 15:6; Matt. 18:23-30) or can be harmful. The lender accepts a risk of personal loss, even though there is collateral, and must forgive unpaid debts (Neh. 10:31; Matt. 5:42; Lk. 6:34-35). It is better to be a lender than a debtor.

No financial problem has so dominated or influenced our society in the last fifty years as debts — consumer and government debt. Costly indulging in unnecessary purchases and debt rather than moderation have plunged both consumers and governments into disastrous debts. Many are paying $284,000 through long-term loan interest for a $90,000 home and pay double for a car. This is like paying $94 for a $30 pair of pants, and $315 for a cart full of groceries worth $100. Do we care enough to give up our selfish interests and to stop public officials from running up debts for pork barrel projects in order not to overtax our future? We should never buy or borrow beyond our ability to pay without pressure.

The deception of debt is that many do not look at the whole picture, and so it does not look like debt. We easily assure ourselves that we will have more money soon, which often is a fantasy. The danger of debt is that it makes you a servant to someone else other than God, putting the lender in the place of God. Going into debt prejudices or presumes on the future.

Deliverance from debt involves not taking on any more debt and being content with what we have. Begin immediately to trust God, and set a date for being completely out of debt. Begin systematically to pay all debts, and adjust your lifestyle. Increase the percentage of your income you give to God. Make a commitment that you will stay out of financial bondage.

The next step is to have a written plan for spending and saving. This includes accepting God's promise of provision, setting priorities for living essentials, discontinuing of credit buying, saving on a regular basis, avoiding leverage (the ability to control a large asset with a relatively small amount of invested capital or borrowing money to invest), avoiding indulgence, seeking extra income only after correcting buying habits, and putting God first in giving.

The last step to financial freedom is to know the difference between needs and wants. There are two ways to be wealthy — one is in the abundance of possessions, and the other is in the fewness of wants. We should keep our needs down to needs, and not luxuries disguised as needs, and then settle the level of need in the full light of the needs of others, of our enlightened consciences, and of the standards of God's Word. Financial freedom is then assured when we give a tithe of all we earn while we are lifting our economic level of need. After we have reached that level, we should seek God's grace to increase the percentage we are giving to God.

GOAL SETTING PLAN

Face squarely the fact that you can control your spending habits. Plan in advance rather than trust the impulse of the moment. Realize the consequences of your spending habits. Using the following chart, write out a major goal (what you would like to accomplish) and then the method that you will use to achieve it in your spending plan:

FINANCIAL AREA	GOAL	METHOD
	What I want to Accomplish	How I hope to Achieve it
1. Giving to God and church (generous percentage)		
2. Careful in buying and spending		
3. Saving and investing		
4. Getting out of debt		
5. Protecting my property and income (insurance)		
6. Others (Name)		
7. Increasing income		

Christian giving is an expression of our faith and our recognition that all we have been given has been made possible by God's love and His blessing. Giving is an act of worship: "Give to the Lord the glory he deserves. Bring an offering, and come into his courtyards" (Ps. 96:8). "Brothers and sisters, we want you to know how God showed his kindness to the churches in the province of Macedonia. While they were being severely tested by suffering, their overflowing joy, along with their extreme poverty, has made them even more generous" (2 Cor. 8:1-2).

Many Christians either ignore or are ignorant of the critical economic nature of faith in the handling of their money. Thus they act foolishly in ways that result in wages of sin rather than in wages of righteousness by grace. Therefore, money talks very loudly in their daily lives, while the truth of God's management principles is silenced.

We need to note some of the warning signals or greatest mistakes people make in money management: No specific goals, no savings, not enough protection through insurance or too much insurance, relying heavily on overtime pay or from a second job, paying minimum on charge accounts and juggling their bills, giving leftovers to God, and not taking advantage of avoiding taxes through estate planning.

Debts are deadly to many people today, including Christians. A Christian should get out of debt altogether and be free from debt. Here are some steps to become free from debt:

1. A written plan of all expenditures and their importance is a necessity. Divide between needs and wants in your record.

2. Stop any expenditures which are not absolutely essential for living (Prov. 21:17).

3. Think before you buy, and evaluate every purchase. Ask such questions as: Is it essential? Will it make me anxious? Can I be content without it? Can I afford it? Is the price reasonable? Is this the best time to buy it? Am I being hasty? Have I checked and researched the item? Have I sought advice? Is it a quality product? What upkeep expense does it require? Do I have all the facts? Will it contribute to family unity and harmony? If I am borrowing, is it a necessary debt? Does it increase my effectiveness in serving God? Will I still be able to be generous in my giving? Have I prayed about it? Will it honor God?

4. Stop credit buying unless you have proven that you can keep your desires in control.

5. Practice saving and pay yourself first.

6. Accept God's provision for you and give to Him first.

7. Avoid all indulgences.

8. Never gamble; stay out of lotteries. God's universe is one of order, not of chance, as financial advancement is based upon work. Money is a trust and is to be handled wisely. Covetousness is to be avoided. Biblical examples of casting lots were a search for divine direction, not gambling.

Adopt a sensible life-style and always recognize God as the source of supply (Ps. 50:12-15). Trust God to provide whatever you need and to protect you in the future. Keep your priorities right (Rom. 12:1-2).

Methods to Budget:

1. Determine your goal.

2. Estimate your expected income.

3. Estimate your fixed expenses.

4. Estimate your flexible expenses.

5. Compare your income and expenses. Spend with a purpose.

6. Watch your waste.

If your income would be 10 percent less than it is, what difference would it make in your standard of living? What would happen if you started giving 10 percent of your income to the Lord starting now? Act on your discovery as God gives grace.

A Family Covenant

Realizing that the use we make of our money is an accurate reflection of what we believe about ourselves, about our world, about our God, and about our church, and that it is God that gives us power to make money (Deut. 8:18), and that it is God that gives life, and breath and everything,

WE, THEREFORE, DECLARE THAT, in the further use of all our resources, we will bear witness to our faith in Jesus Christ.

SIGNED

God's Way Of Giving

A major issue in the matter of Christian giving is whether we are giving to the church as an institution or giving to God through the church, whether we are giving to budgets or whether we are giving by Biblical principles. The traditional approach of maintenance or survival giving, which seeks to establish our part in church work by budgets and perceived needs, should be recognized as unsuccessful and be avoided.

While some churches are reaching pygmy budgets or failing to meet minimum financial goals, the real spiritual needs of discipling the world are not being met as there are over three billion people without Christ. This is happening while Christians are giving an average of two and a half percent of their income for God, and keeping 97 1/2 percent for themselves.

The focus on the functioning of church institutions and the attempt to nurture spirituality through programs with dollar goals has created a crisis in church funding. It has also taken away the joy of giving on the part of many Christians. This does not mean that church institutions and programs are not important, but they must be secondary to teaching the basic principles of Christian giving from which will flow the full funding of all Christian ministries.

The result of this confused focus is evident as we look at what has happened in the maintenance approach and what should be happening by teaching Biblical principles:

Maintenance Funding	Teach Biblical Principles
Beg	Teach
Man's way	God's way
Leftovers	Firstfruits
Budgets used as collection or giving guides	Budgets used as spending guides
Reaction to situations (crises)	Acting on God's Word, Biblical principles

"We-they" mentality	"One group" mentality (Body of Christ)
Biblical message is for information	Biblical message is for spiritual formation and transformation
Human (tunnel) vision	Spiritual vision (world vision) based on Biblical goals
Coasting or driven with idealistic hopes	Driven by divine purpose and power
Stagnant and immobile	Great mobility with Biblical direction and purpose
General disregard or disobedience to the Great Commission	Obedience to the Great Commission

The fact is that Christian fund-raising is not just for budgets, buildings or inanimate objects, but it is for the Lord, His work, for all His ministries — nor just for those that we think we can afford. Our giving should not be motivated by sympathy for people or by situations, but by Christian love.

The fact is that God supplies funds for His work as the Provider. Our Father owns it all, and He has authorized us to be His wealth distributors. Our giving is to reflect our adoption as His children and inheritors. Therefore, we do not talk or act as if our Father is poor. It is only when our old nature prevails that we act out of a poverty mentality. God's principles are based on giving (Lk. 6:38).

A Christian businessman who strongly believed that God created us for good works asked one of his staff to remain after work to discuss the stewardship of life. The employer told him, "Don't be a taker. Takers are losers. Be a giver." Jesus said, "Giving gifts is more satisfying than receiving them" (Acts 20:35). This changed the whole course of this worker's life, as he became a generous giver.

A person does not have one ability or own a thing he did not first receive from God. Yet some are little more than takers and hoarders, abusing their stewardship privilege. Givers are winners. Takers are losers.

Do you consider yourself a taker or a giver? Please rate yourself on this scale:

Taker   **Giver**
-5 -4 -3 -2 -1   0   +1 +2 +3 +4 +5

As a giver, you make things happen every day as you share the Gospel, your life, your possessions. God gives so that you might give. God's Supply House offers an endless resource for meeting all of the spiritual opportunities in the world today.

The ability to receive God's gifts is our first need. Giving and receiving are not two separate transactions; each is part of the other. As we give love away, we are able to receive more love. When we give, God refills.

Lessons From 2 Corinthians 8 And 9

Have you heard such statements as these: "I try to do my share...I give as much as others...I try to give more than the average...I do not have much left, so there is not much to give...If I had more money, I would give more...What are the needs?...The cost of living is going up, and it is difficult to give more." There is no Biblical basis for these statements. They reveal a lack of under-standing of the grace of giving.

That giving is an expression of our Christian love and faith is evident as we study 2 Corinthians 8 and 9.

Chapter 8, verses 1-2: "We want you to know how God showed his kindness to the churches in the province of Macedonia. While they were being severely tested by suffering, their over-flowing joy, along with their extreme poverty, has made them even more generous." Giving is a grace or gift from God, for which we are to pray. It is not something which we have any natural inclination to do. It is connected intimately with the condition of our spiritual life, and is evidence of how God's gracious work is accepted in our heart. Poverty should be no barrier and affliction,

267

no obstacle to generous giving. Poor people become rich in giving because of God's grace and power, which the Macedonians exemplified.

Verse 3: "I assure you that by their own free will they have given all they could, even more than they could afford." They gave liberally, generously, lavishly, sacrificially, all flowing out of God's grace.

Verse 4: "They made an appeal to us, begging us to let them participate in the ministry of God's kindness to his holy people in Jerusalem." They recognized that giving was a privilege, not merely a responsibility. It was they that did the begging, not Paul, because they wanted to share in the work of God.

Verse 5: "They did more than we had expected. First, they gave themselves to the Lord and to us, since this was God's will." Giving ourselves must precede the offering of money, which is the most fundamental principle of Christian giving. God first wants the giver, then the gift.

Verse 6: "This led us to urge Titus to finish his work of God's kindness among you in the same way as he had already started it." Titus was God's messenger who had first spoken to the Macedonians about giving. Now Paul reminds them that the act of grace is to be completed in the act of giving according to their original intention.

Verse 7: "Indeed, the more your faith, your ability to speak, your knowledge, your dedication, and your love for us increase, the more we want you to participate in this work of God's kindness." Giving is not an isolated Christian act. It is part of Christian action to have a complete, well-balanced, well-rounded Christian life. Our behavior in giving is a great test of our faith.

Verse 8: "I'm not commanding you, but I'm testing how genuine your love is by pointing out the dedication of others." By our gifts, we prove the sincerity of our love, which is a spiritual test of our sincerity. We cannot love without giving.

Verse 9: "You know about the kindness of our Lord Jesus Christ. He was rich, yet for your sake he became poor in order to make you rich through his poverty." This is the great exchange — Christ's richness for our poverty, His strength for our weakness. Now we have the vitality to give generously as He did. The power of Christ's giving of Himself to us is the source of our gifts. God's enriching grace to us through Christ is the reason we can and should give sacrificially. Here is the supreme motivation.

Verse 10-11: "I'm giving you my opinion because it will be helpful to you. Last year you were not only willing to take a collection but had already started to do it. So finish what you began to do. Then your willingness will be matched by what you accomplish with whatever contributions you have." Desire and good intentions, though praiseworthy, are not enough. We should not only think and talk about offerings, but should take definite action by giving regular and generous gifts.

Verse 12: "Since you are willing to do this, remember that people are accepted if they give what they are able to give. God doesn't ask for what they don't have." People sometimes say that they would give a large offering if only they had more money. God is not asking us to give from what we do not have, but from what we do have. We are to give from what we have and what we earn, not from what we wish we had. The big question is whether we have a willing mind and heart to give generously.

Verses 13-14: "I don't mean that others should have relief while you have hardship. Rather, it's a matter of striking a balance. At the present time, your surplus fills their need so that their surplus may fill your need. In this way things 'balance out.' " This indicates a community that cares for others and will share voluntarily to others in need.

Verse 24: "So give these men a demonstration of your love. Show their congregations that we were right to be proud of you." Our good works performed in faith prove our love, which should be an encouragement to others. This fruit reveals God's grace at work in us.

Chapter 9:5: "So I thought that I should encourage our coworkers to visit you before I do and make arrangements for this gift that you had already promised to give. Then it will be the blessing it was intended to be, and it won't be something you're forced to do." Teachers and messengers to tell and exhort believers about God's principles and the needs are important, so that the gifts are brought willingly. God wants generosity, not complaining.

Verse 6: ..."The farmer who plants a few seeds will have a very small harvest. But the farmer who plants because he has received God's blessings will receive a harvest of God's blessings in return." This is God's law of spiritual action and reaction. God does not urge giving on grounds of reward, but generous giving does bring its own rich reward by grace. No giving of ours can be an adequate return for the wonderful gifts of God. This is not the same as the "prosperity gospel" or making a deal with God, but it is giving without expectation of return. God does promise to give generously in His own way and in His own time.

Verse 7: "Each of you should give whatever you have decided. You shouldn't be sorry that you gave or feel forced to give, since God loves a cheerful giver." The complaint, "The church is always asking for money," does not come from a knowledgeable and faithful Christian who understands God's grace to him and God's principles for giving cheerfully.

Verse 8: "Besides, God will give you his constantly overflowing kindness. Then, when you always have everything you need, you can do more and more good things." Our giving reflects the divine ability working through us. God's goodness should cause Christians to give a generous percentage of their income, and enable them to live adequately, too. God is able to make this grace abound to us, but do we believe it and expect it? Will we allow Him to make all grace abound toward us?

Verses 10-11: "God gives seed to the farmer and food to those who need to eat. God will also give you seed and multiply it. In your lives he will increase the things you do that have his approval. God will make you rich enough so that you can always be generous. Your generosity will produce thanksgiving to God because of us." God has announced His plan to provide our food and to multiply our gifts. He calls our giving a harvest of righteousness. He promises sufficient resources so that we can be generous on every occasion, and that our generous giving will result in people thanking God. This is a statement of pure grace, showing us to be channels of God's grace. Our own doubts can clog those channels.

Verse 12: "What you do to serve others not only provides for the needs of God's people, but also produces more and more prayers of thanksgiving to God." God's reason for requesting us to give has a purpose: to meet the spiritual and material needs of others, and to prompt thanksgiving so that God will be praised. Miserly giving dishonors God.

Verse 13: "You will honor God through this genuine act of service because of your commitment to spread the Good News of Christ and because of your generosity in sharing with them and everyone else." Here we are told that our giving actually will cause people to praise God for our obedience that accompanies our confession of the Gospel of Christ. The Gospel is tied intimately to our giving, and lack of giving appears to be a denial of the Gospel, and a lack of confession of Christ. We confess Christ through our giving.

Verse 14: "With deep affection they will pray for you because of the extreme kindness that God has shown you." This surpassing grace of God is the cause of our generous giving. How is the surpassing grace of God evident in our lives on the basis of our giving?

Verse 15: "I thank God for his gift that words cannot describe." Those who fail to show the unsearchable riches of Christ in their lives and their giving may be materially wealthy, but spiritually impoverished. Christian giving as our grateful response to God's grace defies description. Giving to God is never a loss, but always a gain. The Gospel, the indescribable gift of God, is the center of it all, and the force of it all.

Lessons that can be learned from 2 Corinthians 8 and 9 are: 1. All we have is given; 2. All we need is promised; 3. All we give enriches us and causes thanksgiving to God; 4. All we do is accountable. These are part of giving under grace.

Some Giving Principles Flowing From Grace

An old gravestone records: "What I spent, I had; what I saved, I lost; what I gave, I have." Everything will be lost at death except what we return to God.

271

Because of our old nature, giving money to God does not come naturally to us. In fact, it appears natural to complain that God wants our gifts of financial resources. God's people in the Old Testament grumbled about offerings at times: "From the nations where the sun rises to the nations where the sun sets, my name will be great...But you dishonor it when you say that the Lord's table may be contaminated and that its food may be despised. You say, 'Oh what a nuisance it is,' and you sniff at it in disgust..." (Mal. 1:11-13).

Offerings and gifts do not take the place of a repentant heart. God is concerned about the spiritual attitude and condition of the Christian steward, for whatever is not right in one's life needs correction as one gives a gift. "'You did not want sacrifices, offerings, burnt offerings, and sacrifices for sin. You did not approve of them.' These are the sacrifices that Moses' Teachings require people to offer" (Heb. 10:8); "I want your loyalty, not your sacrifices. I want you to know me, not to give me burnt offerings" (Hos. 6:6). Some people have the mistaken impression that God wants gifts for the church while He is not concerned with what they do with the rest of their possessions or their lives.

"...We must get rid of everything that slows us down, especially sin that distracts us. We must run the race that lies ahead of us and never give up" (Heb. 12:1). Christian living and stewardship demand discipline which is important in order that bad habits do not cause us to be slaves to sin. Such "crucifying of the flesh" is not easy to take, for it causes anger, resentment and hostility on the part of the old nature. Have you identified any things you need to sacrifice or denounce as you have Christ as Master? Do any of these trouble you: pride, temper, hatred, gossip, cursing, greed, slavery to eating or drinking or smoking? God is greatly concerned that we do not substitute church gifts for general obedience to His will. There is a prior condition to bringing a gift to God — the giving of one's self, giving up one's sinful habits and slavery to anything.

"So if you are offering your gift at the altar and remember there that another believer has something against you, leave your gift at the altar. First go away and make peace with that person.

Then come back and offer your gift" (Mt. 5:23-24). Here Jesus offers a stewardship formula for anyone who is unreconciled: **Stop**, don't give your offering now...**Go**, reconcile with your fellow man or stop a sinful habit...**Return**, present your offering. The pardoning love of Jesus produces the deepest motives for good conduct. The forgiving love of Christ will give you strength to repent and to do the works that show you have repented and are no longer a slave of a sinful habit.

God has given His plan for our giving habits in the Word, where His total will for our lives is revealed. This plan includes:

1. **Give to God first**. "But seek first His kingdom and His righteousness, and all these things will be given to you as well" (Mt. 6:33 NIV). This answers the question, "Who comes first in our giving?" The main lesson in Matthew 6:19-34 is not that we should not worry, but that we should put God first and then we will have nothing to worry about. The priority for giving is higher than personal and family needs of food and clothes, for these are promised when we give to God first. God did not say that we should first purchase food, clothes, cars, homes and all other necessities, but we are to seek Him first, and all these things will be ours as well. The "God first" principle has God's promise that He will provide all our needs, and is the key to happiness and security in life. Putting God first is an act of faith by the Holy Spirit's power.

"Leftover giving" hurts the person and is an offense, grieves the Holy Spirit, hinders kingdom work, and dishonors God. God could not get the attention of His people through His Word proclaimed by the spiritual leaders in Haggai's day, so He took drastic steps and asked, "Is it time for you to live in your paneled houses while this house lies in ruins? Now, this is what the Lord of Armies says: Carefully consider your ways! You planted a lot, but you harvested little...You spend money as fast as you earn it...You expected a lot, but you received a little. When you bring something home, I blow it away. Why?...It's because my house lies in ruins while each of you is busy working on your own house. It is because of you that the sky has withheld its dew and the earth has withheld its produce. I called for a drought on

273

the land, the hills, and on the grain, the new wine, the olive oil, and whatever the ground produces, on humans and animals, and on all your hard work" (Hag. 1:3-11).

God took away the income of His people by drought and inflation (holes in their purses). That apparently caught their attention and they sought God's mercy. When they laid the foundation for His house (Hag. 2:18-19), and showed they had repented and accepted His forgiveness and guidance, they were blessed. God is displeased when His people give priority to their own homes and work instead of His house and work. Even more, many Christians today put their desires, luxuries, and discretionary expenses before their gifts to God. Christians in the United States on the average give less than 2 1/2% to God while spending more than 97 1/2% for themselves. It has been said that Christians are over 30% of the world's population, receive over 60% of the world's income, and spend 97 1/2% of it on themselves.

Paul wrote that we are to set aside a portion for God on the first day of the week (1 Cor. 16:2). Spending for physical needs does not come before giving for spiritual responsibilities.

Henry Drummond said, "Above all else, do not touch Christianity unless you are willing to seek God first. I promise you a miserable existence if you seek Him second." Luther stressed the promise of Matthew 6:33 as he recognized that some people may have a very difficult situation but God knows all about it: "God will not let your situation make a liar out of Him. Just believe!"

2. **Give a planned percentage or portion of your income**. Both the Old and New Testaments emphasize a portion or part to be set aside for God's work — sacred or separated for kingdom tasks. Proportionate giving is the basis for the Old Testament tithing system and the key principle for New Testament giving. Proportionate giving means giving in proportion to the income we receive, whether large or small.

Proportionate giving places the emphasis where it belongs — on giving **from** our income, not **to** budgets.

Does one figure from gross or net income? Our **attitude** is the starting place. Matthew 6:33 provides the principle of giving first before we spend for anything else, which in our modern economy would mean an adjusted gross income. It means a gross income for wage earners and adjusted gross income for businessmen and farmers. Farmers and business people deduct operational costs, not capital expenditures, which become future investments. Suppose that a relative promised a bonus of one tenth of our income at the end of each year. How would we figure our income? We would add everything we could find as income. A sincere and willing heart will treat God the same.

3. **Give a generous part or percentage to God.** As New Testament believers, we will prayerfully consider whether we will give more or less than God's people in the Old Testament — ten cents out of each dollar. To give a small portion is contrary to the new nature in Christ. To give a generous part, 10% and more, is a true expression of the "Christ in us."

Love does not have mathematical standards, nor does it fix certain rates or limits. Grace gives faith and strength not only to give 10% of our income to God, but also to grow beyond the tithe.

4. **Faith sets the percentage.** God tells us: "Managers are required to be trustworthy" (2 Cor. 4:2) — full of faith. The weaker the faith, the lower the percentage. The stronger the faith, the higher the percentage.

Some are possibly giving three cents or less out of every dollar of income. Others are giving five or seven cents, and some 10 to 15 cents of every dollar. Whatever portion or percentage, we will ask ourselves whether this part is the true measure of our faith and love. As we grow in faith, we will give a larger percentage. So we pray, "Lord, increase our faith."

5. **Generous percentage giving is a grace or gift from God.** Paul said, "We want you to know how God showed his kindness to the churches in the province of Macedonia" (2 Cor. 8:1). Although these Christians were very poor, they were very rich in giving. That was a result of God's grace. Generous proportionate giving is a grace or gift from God for which each of us

is to pray. God's grace will cause us to give generously in a way that we personally do not have the natural inclination or strength to do.

Who comes first — the gift or the Giver? What comes first in our spending is a great test of faith. Financial responsibility is learned only as we learn to put God first and spend all our money to the glory of God. God's grace and Gospel power will make it possible.

Now For Our Commitment

Will you take a close look at what you are giving and take a new step of faith by God's grace as you go through this exercise:

My estimated annual income is: $_____
Tithe (10%) of this would be: $_____
My present annual offerings are: $_____
This amounts to an annual percentage of: _____%
I plan my percentage offering for next year to be: _____%
This will approximately amount to an annual total: $_____
This will represent a weekly offering of about: $_____

When we have proper relations with God in Christ, our giving will reflect it. With God as our Senior Partner, why will we keep 98% or 97% for ourselves and give leftovers to Him? What partnership can flourish in a healthy manner if the junior partner withholds much from the senior partner? Our Heavenly Father, our Senior Partner, is fully able to make 90% of our income kept for ourselves go much farther than if we fearfully keep 97% for ourselves. Let us abound in the grace of giving also.

Sharing Christ — Evangelism and Missions

All Christians have a spiritual aroma which makes a fragrance to individuals and groups with whom they come in contact: "To God we are the aroma of Christ among those who are saved and among those who are dying. To some people we are a

276

deadly fragrance, while to others we are a life-giving fragrance..."
(2 Cor. 2:15-16). To those who receive Christ, we should be an
irresistible influence for the Gospel. To those who reject Christ,
we will be a threat, as their anger will sometimes be aroused
against us. It is our nature as Christians to influence others through
that scent. This aroma is one of our basic resources in living for
God.

Jesus told of our evangelistic influence by use of several
analogies — salt and light: "You are salt for the earth. But if salt
loses its taste, how will it be made salty again? It is no longer
good for anything except to be thrown out and trampled on by
people" (Mt. 5:13). The nature and value of salt is found in several of its functions:

1. It can be used as a preservative when refrigeration is
not available, thus stopping spoilage of food. Likewise, we
Christians are to retard and halt the decaying ways in unregenerate society. Ours is a preservative role in the world.

2. The basic purpose of salt is as a seasoning for foods, to
enhance or draw out the flavor. In like manner, we Christians
will affect people around us positively through the Gospel.
Christians should have a positive flavoring effect upon society.

3. Salt can create thirst. This, too, is the function of Christians. We should live in such a manner that unbelievers will desire
to know why there is hope in a hopeless world.

Jesus also said that Christians are lights: "You are light for
the world. A city cannot be hidden when it is located on a hill.
No one lights a lamp and puts it under a basket. Instead, everyone who lights a lamp puts it on a lamp stand. Then its light
shines on everyone in the house. In the same way let your light
shine in front of all people. Then they will see the good that you
do and praise your Father in heaven" (Mt. 5:13-16).

Light provides visibility on the paths we walk and the ways
we go. Living in a spiritually dark world, Jesus commanded us to
be lights so that people may have light for their way, seeing our
good works and glorifying our Father.

Being a light does not mean just to go to church or to be
busy at church activities. Being a light means to share the good

news of the Gospel so that our neighbor might know Christ as the Way, the Truth, and the Life. That light will be seen as we demonstrate godliness, holiness, and kindness in our lives while proclaiming Jesus Christ to be Savior and Lord. In every way, we are to reflect the true Light — Jesus Christ.

We must seek to expose our faith in Jesus, not impose it on others. We cannot cause others to be Christians, but only God can do that through our witness of Christ by the Holy Spirit. Avoiding cliches about God, we should learn to speak and witness in plain language about what Jesus means to us.

At the same time, we need to help non-Christians to see that their own current view of life and of God has weaknesses. Many people cannot articulate their own world view or beliefs for any time without becoming inconsistent. They do not know why their beliefs are not true. We can encourage them to clarify their ideas so that they find out how unsupported these views are by Biblical facts. They should be led to discover the inadequacy of their spiritual views and that the Word of God and the Gospel does make a great difference.

Evangelism is not merely sharing doctrines about God, but the person of God and our Savior Jesus Christ. As witnessing disciples, we reflect a firsthand experience with Christ, which is the basis for our evangelism. As we witness, we have confidence in the guidance of the Holy Spirit to give us the right words. With great compassion for the lost, we will be active in witnessing and evangelism. Our words will then be relevant to the people.

Going to church is an outgrowth of knowing Jesus in order to worship Him. Often, the worship service or the particular sermon is not the type of message which is effective to influence individuals. The best evangelistic approach is a personal face-to-face sharing of Christ on the level that is required at that time. Then this is to be followed by worship.

There's a need for more than our presence through which the non-Christians can watch our conduct. True, they may be attracted by the quality of our lives, but they need to hear the Gospel verbalized in a way that they can understand the message.

In witnessing and evangelizing, the Christian should seek to relate to the unbeliever's human situation in order to help him solve specific misunderstandings and problems. The witness should discover the person's problems and needs for which the Gospel provides the solution. He should help him see the commitment which will make the Gospel solution work in his life by the power of the Holy Spirit. He should provide support for his thoughts as he considers the full ramifications of the Gospel for his life. In doing this, the disciple will show the benefits of Biblical truths. Throughout he will ask questions and listen carefully, showing humility and gentleness.

The disciple will seek to have his witness Biblically accurate and balanced, being logical in the development of his presentation of Law and Gospel. The witnessing disciple will want to avoid churchly and unfamiliar language, being clear about what the Gospel means in the person's situation. Throughout, the message should be simple, not complex, and positive to reflect the reality that the Gospel is indeed Good News.

We need the great urgency of evangelism which Jesus displayed throughout His entire ministry. Jesus had to go through Samaria for the purpose of winning one person, and He had to leave the crowds in Jericho to go after one person — Zacchaeus. He pictured Himself as the Good Shepherd, telling of concern in parables about leaving 99 to seek one lost sheep and searching for the one lost coin (Lk. 15).

The Book of Acts tells of many instances about the urgency of the Gospel preachers and teachers who reach out to new places and to different people, going as the Great Commission commanded. Paul talked about necessity being placed upon him to tell others. We should be obedient to the command: "Go home to your family, and tell them how much the Lord has done for you and how merciful he has been to you" (Mk. 5:19). Paul tells: "So never be ashamed to tell others about our Lord or be ashamed of me, his prisoner..." (2 Tim. 1:8). The urgency was seen in Acts 4:20: "We cannot stop talking about what we've seen and heard." The Lord spoke to Paul in a vision: "Don't be afraid to speak out! Don't be silent!" (Acts 18:9).

Our response should be to name the steps now that we will take to share the love of Jesus with our non-Christian friends. Then we will want to list the names of our non-Christian friends to whom we will witness.

Tell The World: Jesus Is Coming Again

The summons to repentance in view of the coming of Christ and the kingdom of eternal glory is a serious call to all Christians of all times. On the Last Day, we "will see the Son of Man coming in clouds with great power and glory" (Mk 13:26). "Be ready, because the Son of Man will return when you least expect him" (Lk. 12:40). "The Son of Man will come with his angels in his Father's glory. Then he will pay back each person based on what that person has done...The people of every nation will be gathered in front of him. He will separate them as a shepherd separates the sheep from the goats" (Mt. 16:27; 25:32).

"Therefore, don't judge anything before the appointed time. Wait until the Lord comes. He will also bring to light what is hidden in the dark and reveal people's motives. Then each person will receive praise from God" (1 Cor. 4:5).

The Gospels seriously depict the life of repentance and forgiveness which Christians are to live at all times. Jesus shows in the Sermon on the Mount that it is better to be maimed and crippled in this life than to be physically whole and cast into hell (Mt. 5:29-30). Likewise, treasures are to be laid up in heaven as eternal investments rather than trying to store it up here on earth (Mt. 6:19-20). Those who refuse forgiveness to others now will be denied divine forgiveness at the coming of Christ (Mt. 6:15).

Jim Elliot, who died at the hands of the Auca Indians in 1956, made a classical eschatological statement: "He is no fool who gives what he cannot keep, to gain what he cannot lose." Repentance is a giving up of something that harms us — that we should not keep.

The disciples were not to fear what people around them would do to them, but rather to fear only Him who would be able to destroy both body and soul in hell (Mt. 10:28). The entire New

Testament is filled with the idea of our lives and ethics being conditioned by the thought of the last times or eschatology.

The eschatological or last times theme of repentance and the new life is filled with urgency from the fact that it is depicted as somehow already underway with the first coming of Christ. Life does not carry its value in itself, but in the expectations of the future life. The road on which we travel has its sure goal in Christ, and the road and the goal are inseparably interrelated, for life here and life hereafter cannot be separated.

The "last times" message maintains the present life and the future life to be a living relationship, for life does not end at death. Therefore, all hopelessness is gone. The "Let's eat and drink because tomorrow we're going to die!" (1 Cor. 15:32) theme is a fraud. In Christ our lives will be consummated in glory. This places our lives and actions within a purposeful movement of history in which our actions are directly related to an eternal spiritual realm. Thus heaven and our present ethics are inseparable.

The Last Times also raise the issue of our own death, which is a universal fact of life. The Christian has no reason to fear death because it has no power over them who will be raised with Christ (1 Cor. 15:54-57). Unbelievers will be sentenced to eternal punishment in both body and soul (Mt. 10:28).

The signs of the Second Coming of Christ are false christs and false prophets who deceive many, wars, famines, earthquakes, persecution, increase in wickedness, love of many growing old, and the Gospel preached in all the world (Mt. 24:4-14).

Christ will return to resurrect all people (believers to glory and unbelievers to hell). Jesus' Coming will end the world. The universe will be destroyed, and God will create a new heaven and a new earth (2 Pet. 3:12-13).

In heaven we will be with Christ and know Him face to face (1 Cor. 13:12) and be like Him with perfect joy (1 Jn. 3:2; Rev. 21:4). We will be able to worship and serve God perfectly (Rev. 7:15).

When we talk about the church on earth and the church in heaven, we are voicing the conviction that the fellowship of believers in Christ is an eternal relationship. Everything and every action is charged with eternal significance.

V.

LIVING IN THE BODY OF CHRIST AND IN THE CHURCH

All those everywhere who believe in Jesus as Savior are part of the body of Christ or the Holy Christian Church. The Holy Spirit calls, gathers, enlightens, sanctifies, and keeps the Holy Christian Church by the Gospel. The church is found only where the Gospel is preached and the Sacraments are used. This spiritual family of faith is not visible, and it is called the Invisible Church. When Christians gather together in a congregation, that is the visible church.

The church is both visible and invisible. The invisible church denotes all true believers in Jesus Christ, while the visible church or congregation contains believers and hypocrites. The church seems to be a paradox: it is divine, a Body in which the Spirit of God Himself lives and acts; yet it is human, made up of people who are faulty. The Church is spiritual, yet earthly. It is holy, yet is composed of sinful people. It experiences the same kind of dichotomy as the Christian himself, who is both sinner and saint.

A. The Body Of Christ, The Invisible Church

God has called Christians to a living, loving community, which is Christ's body, whose Head is Christ Himself. Bonding together into Christ's body is not an escape from the reality of life, but an entrance into reality.

Jesus is the Head and Lord of the body, and the Holy Spirit is its life and power. It is divine in human forms, heavenly in earthly structures, and perfect in imperfect embodiment. It is an organism, not an unchanging institution. It exists to fulfill the purposes of God in Christ on earth.

The reality of the body of Christ is key to understanding not only the believer's relationship to God through Christ, but also his relationship to every other believer in the world. The body of Christ refers to the universal church — all true believers. This is the Invisible Church, where true believers are known only by God.

Metaphors (figures of speech, analogies or parallels) that are used both in the Old and New Testament to describe the Church are: a bride (Hos.; Eph. 5:25-32); a vine or vineyard (Is. 5; Jn. 15:1-8); a flock (Is. 40:11-12; Jn. 10:1-16).

Those in the New Testament are: a household or family (Rom. 8:16); a kingdom (Col. 1:3-13; Rom. 14:17). One that is very meaningful and useful, named both in 1 Corinthians 12 and Ephesians 4, is "a body." The body of Christ is the unique fellowship of Christians in one body. Christianity involves Christ living in and through the believer. The church as a body is a "unit" with Christ as Head, the Source of life and of all resources. The believers are members of the body.

"For example, the body is one unit and yet has many parts. As all the parts form one body, so it is with Christ. By one Spirit we were all baptized into one body. Whether we are Jewish or Greek, slave or free, God gave all of us one spirit to drink. As you know, the human body is not made up of only one part, but of many parts...You are Christ's body and each of you is an individual part of it" (1 Cor. 12:12-14, 27.) "...We will grow up completely in our relationship to Christ, who is the head. He makes the whole body fit together and unites it through the support of every joint. As each and every part does its job, he makes the body grow so that it builds itself up in love" (Eph. 4:15-16).

God's plan for a functioning, growing, witnessing, love-manifesting and powerful Church is that every member be a vital organ of the body of Christ and be actively involved in the God-given functions so that the whole body can be healthy and nurtured for service and witness.

Life and gifts in the Body are revealed in Ephesians

4:7, 12-16. Here we learn how believers are fit and held together for God's service. The focus is on individual members, identifying their personal abilities and giving from what God has given them. We learn that we have not chosen for ourselves what gifts we should have, but this was decided by the Ascended Lord: "God's favor has been given to each of us. It was measured out to us by Christ who gave it" (Eph. 4:7). Our responsibility individually is to discover what gifts Christ has given us.

The amazing thing is that God has made His work in the Body dependent upon the activity of every member: "He makes the whole body fit together and unites it through the support of every joint. As each and every part does its job, he makes the body grow so that it builds itself up in love" (Eph. 4:16). Just think of it, we are made fit and held together by what every member supplies. Little wonder that 1 Corinthians 12 talks about individual members of the human body to remind us of their importance individually, and then that we are taught the spiritual lesson about our part in the body of Christ.

What we supply by God's grace contributes to the Body growing and building itself up in love, as each part does its work. God has chosen us as His instruments of service to each other in the effective functioning of the Body. When believers function in the capacity for which God has prepared them, there is a flow of divine energy between us that is unique.

The church as the body of Christ is an organism, a living system. The church as an organization is a structured system. The Corinthian manifestation of the body of Christ or church was crippled, for they were not living in harmony with one another, nor were they portraying the proper image of Christ to the world.

Comparing the church and a human body as similar in many ways, Paul developed this analogy along four lines: unity, diversity, sovereignty, and harmony. Regarding **unity** (1 Cor. 12:12-13), all believers share the common life of God, where there are no degrees of importance in terms of greater or less significance. There are to be no spiritual loners, outsiders, drifters, or spectators.

Regarding **diversity** (Eph. 4:7; 1 Cor. 12:14), each believer is uniquely gifted to be very essential to the Body of Christ. All have been given something to share.

Regarding **sovereignty** (1 Cor. 12:18, 24, 28), each believer is exactly where and what God wants each to be by grace, even though they have choices in their place or role. There are no accidents in God's plan, as each believer is designed to be a functioning member by God's design (Eph. 4:16).

Regarding **harmony**, there is to be no rugged individualism or self-sufficiency that appeals to human reason. God wants believers to have a tremendous sense of dependency (though independent), i.e., to be an interdependent family. A believer cannot choose not to be a part somewhere, but only choose to be disobedient. We are neither to under-estimate or over-estimate our importance. Rivalry is not acceptable in the body of Christ, whereas love is the big requirement.

Is this participation and work possible for each member? Yes, because Christ is the Head, and He gives us forgiveness of sins, life, and salvation. He speaks to us through His Word to instruct us and to empower us. Through that Word God equips and prepares us so that we will be mature and be unified in the Christian faith in order to serve Him: "Their purpose is to prepare God's people, to serve, and to build up the body of Christ. This is to continue until all of us are united in our faith and in our knowledge about God's Son, until we become mature, until we measure up to Christ, who is the standard" (Eph. 4:12-13).

The goal is not to discover how many people can be gathered together into a church building or only to keep them in the faith to reach heaven safely, but to bring them to spiritual maturity and to equip them for works of service. They are not spectators, preoccupied with their own interests or entertainment. They are not only to be a gathered people, but also a scattered people. The divine rhythm is gather and scatter, come and go — the rhythmic action of a lively Body.

We are called into a living, loving community of believers. There is nothing like a solitary Christian. Paul shows that no individual Christian can function effectively by himself, and that no member is more or less important than another. Believers can function practically and minister to each other only in close relationships. The only possible way for Christ's body to function dynamically and meaningfully is in the context of local bodies of believers who commit themselves to minister to each other. [11] Disunity is intolerable. When we close our hearts to one another, we close our hearts to God.

Building Up One Another

Paul has given many commands about Christian actions which involve **one to another,** giving both negative and positive ones. The negative ones include that we are not to judge one another, envy one another, lie to one another, speak against one another, complain against one another, or repay another evil for evil.

The Scripture encourages us to love one another, the most essential virtue among Christians, yet the most neglected. Most of the other commands of Jesus flow out of this pre-eminent command to love: be devoted to one another, build up one another, bear with one another, care for one another, be of the same mind toward one another, accept one another, serve one another through love, bear one another's burdens, show forbearance to one another in love, speak the truth to one another, admonish one another, speak to one another in psalms, hymns, and spiritual songs.

We are to comfort and encourage one another, stimulate one another to love and good deeds, seek after good for one another, live in peace with one another, be kind and tenderhearted to one another. We are to be subject to one another, confess our sins to one another, forgive one another, pray for one another, and be hospitable to one another without complaint.

Greet one another with a holy kiss indicates a warm greeting to each other as we meet with handshakes, hugs or whatever is appropriate. We are to live as the family of God which is growing and increasing as it grows. "Christ makes the whole body grow as God wants it to" (Col. 2:19).

Rich Fellowship With One Another

Membership in the family of God begins with the new birth in Christ, but fellowship must be developed and practiced. Such fellowship has many facets, but it is all built upon sharing the love which we have experienced from God.

Acts 2 shows that members in a functioning Body devote themselves to the Apostles' teaching and to fellowship.

The healthy Body is one in which believers keep strong in the Word and function freely and properly. The apostolic objective of all teaching was to create a human fellowship arising from the divine fellowship with Christ as Head. Thus Christian fellowship is not only with God but also with other believers. The question is whether Christians are experiencing the full joy of that relationship. Regarding unity, when each of us is in true fellowship with God, we will be fully in fellowship with one another.

One characteristic that harms or even ruptures this unity and fellowship is an individualism which is expressed by the attitude, "Mind your own business." Those people do not want individual rights curtailed by anyone for any reason. They resent those who dare challenge their personal agendas. These people do not understand the Christian responsibility both for the well-being of the other person and the good of the group, so they do not feel obligated for what others in the Christian community do and become.

It is sinful for us to reject accountability to others and for others. The unwillingness to accept responsibility is expressed in phrases like "Live and let live" or "It's their business how they want to live their lives." Paul was clear that we are accountable to our brothers and sisters in Christ and ultimately to the Lord Himself: "Brothers and sisters, if a person gets trapped by wrongdoing, those of you who are spiritual should help that person turn away from doing wrong. Do it in a gentle way. At the same time watch yourself so that you also are not tempted" (Gal. 6:1); "Let Christ's word with all its wisdom and richness live in you. Use psalms, hymns, and spiritual songs to teach and instruct yourselves about God's kindness. Sing to God in your hearts" (Col. 3:16).

Because of sin, there will be perpetual tension between Christian faith and the human or cultural part of life. Sin breaks the joy of fellowship with other believers in God. One big sin is that few are active in the spiritual battle or are on the battlefront, while the others (some of our wounded members) are shot by all kinds of darts from others within the Body. Another sinful trait is isolation of the family of God from the very world and people whom they are to reach, or they immerse themselves in their surrounding culture to the extent that they fail to maintain the radical identification as Christians and thus become essentially indistinguishable from the world.

Love is the basis. Neighbors are to be loved. Christ's Great Commandment to love stands alongside the Great Commission.

We are not merely called out of the world, but God has called us into the community where He has prepared a place for us to fellowship and work. We are not just individuals responsible for our own growth and maturing in Christ, but we must see ourselves responsible to grow together with others as part of the Body.

The body of Christ is three-dimensional — God, others, and us. The Bible assumes that if we have a personal relationship with God, we will desire to enhance that relationship through people contacts. God gives great spiritual benefits through Christian interaction. God disallows a private faith. Heaven will be a group affair, and fellowship with other Christians is a vital preparation. Being in community with others provides a positive environment for spiritual growth.

B. Living In The Church (Congregations)

Because God required believers as a family to come together to grow and expand, the early Christians carried out the Great Commission by organizing congregations in different areas like Corinth, Ephesus, Galatia, and Thessalonica. Congregations (visible groups) differ from the Holy Christian Church (Invisible Church). The visible church includes both believers and non-believers, for we cannot look into other peoples' hearts. This is the visible church.

The basic foundation on which the visible church rests is a clear understanding of the Christian faith and the mission of the church. The sole objective of the church in its institutional form is the realization of its Biblical purpose. That mission is basically spiritual, not political, ethical or psychological. It does not rely on the force of the Law, but on the Gospel of grace and the power of love. This is the visible church which uses organizational forms and functional approaches to aid the members to grow in their Christian faith.

The nature of God, the Christian Gospel, and the body of Christ have already determined the goals and objectives toward which the institutional church should be moving as it seeks to fulfill its mission. It must be the mouthpiece of God, not of the people. The church is the only institution on earth whose sole mission is to help people find God and eternal life through Jesus Christ.

The important issue in the work of the church as an organization is its functions and tasks, which are often described in the New Testament without a description of forms. When form is named in the Bible, it is incomplete, as form and structure are pictured only partially and vary from one setting to another. Only later through traditions did the institution allow forms to become sacred while functions became perverted.

We need to look behind the facade and traditions to find the real meaning of the church at various times in history. Often, leaders were seeking for a revived traditionalism with emphasis on forms rather than church renewal with a focus on Biblical functions. The church dare never plan its work as though it is merely an extension of the past.

Wherever God's people are, there must be church functions. Wherever we have function, we need form. We cannot have an organism without organization. We cannot communicate a message without a method. We cannot teach truth without developing some kind of tradition. The question is whether the form and tradition are true to the Scriptures or not.

Churches need to commit themselves to a high view of God, a belief in the absolute authority of Scripture, a commitment to teaching of sound doctrine, the spiritual maturity of its people, and the establishment of spiritual leaders. The actual marks of the church in its fundamental nature are pure teaching of the Word and proper administration of the Sacraments.

It is tempting to over-externalize the work of the church by looking at it mainly from a sociological view, defining God's people in external and institutional terms. It is tempting to look at the church historically, over-emphasizing traditions. It is also tempting to look at it pragmatically and think that any new outburst of activity in the church, any cloud of ecclesiastical dust raised by the stamping of excited feet is evidence of strong Christian life.

What is the foundation for a healthy functioning church? It must have these components: an acceptance of truth, an awareness of God's presence, a responsiveness to God's Word, a sensitivity to the reality of sin, a lively and edifying fellowship, fruitfulness in members' lives, and strong evangelistic activity.

Being human, church members easily fall prey to improper institutionalizing of the church. It naturally happens wherever people band together to achieve certain objectives. People plus age plus structure frequently result in institutionalizing the church in a harmful way. What are the symptoms of such institutionalism?

1. The form and organization become more important than people.

2. Individuals function like cogs in a machine.

3. Individuality and creativity are lost.

4. Freedom and openness diminish as they threaten people who are afraid to ask uncomfortable questions.

5. Forms have become rigid and inflexible.

6. People are serving the church as an organization more than the purposes for which God formed it.

7. Red tape breaks down communication.

8. People become prisoners of procedures and policy manuals.

9. People lose their initiative, becoming discouraged and critical.

10. A hierarchy of leadership develops, increasing the problems of communication with the members who feel that they do not count for much in the church.

11. Members feel they must be ministered to, rather than be ministering members.

12. Members are reactive and surrender their initiative for their service and ministry.

13. The church is guided in its spiritual responsibilities by policies and by-laws rather than by God's Word and its principles.

This institutionalizing of the church can be seen in the maintenance or survival approach in its stewardship of people and financial resources. A maintenance approach that drives people to settle for institutional goals will reduce people to nothing more than cogs in the machinery. This is a denial of the total stewardship of Christians, leaving us with only a one-dimensional view of people with institutional responsibilities instead of servants of God. Thus God's Word is suppressed, and man's word controls with a humanistic view of the work of the church.

Then, rules and regulations become supreme. The members become a tool for church leaders to get the church tasks done. Such a situation debases the priesthood of all believers. When any emphasis in the church interferes in any way with the Biblical task to use the resources of Christ better, and to minister more effectively to the needs of people, then the church has lost its way. The church is not programs and buildings, but people.

God's Word For Spiritual Formation

Faithfully teaching the Word will lead to spiritual formation of members that will directly affect the effectiveness of the congregation. A growing number of members should be enlisted in Bible study to gain the knowledge, understanding, and wisdom to conduct His work (Prov. 2:1-6). The Bible is our Master's voice to teach, correct and train us in righteousness to be equipped for every good work (2 Tim. 3:16-17). As we study the Word, we see and hear of God's character, heart, intentions, plans, thoughts and work.

We are not just collecting ideas for our own spirituality or for building congregations, but we are seeking truths and insights from a Personal God for the formation of ourselves and of our congregations. When we hear and follow the Shepherd's voice, we are secure, nourished, built, and edified for all that the future holds. His penetrating Word shines where no human eye can see, where we ourselves are not accustomed to look. In that way, God reveals our true selves, as well as the condition of our congregations.

Searching honestly and deeply into God's Word will penetrate our innermost being. Thus, our deeply ingrained perceptual frameworks will be exposed for the negative effect they sometimes have on our thinking and actions. It will show us when these mental frameworks or filters have become our prisons, and we are in bondage to them.

The congregation is God's "seed-plot" in which the Word is to be planted for bearing abundant fruit. As vital as special programs are, they are no substitute for the process of education by which the Word is planted in minds for character formation. Christian education and character formation should be the main business of the congregation. There should be no place for individualistic or do-it-yourself sowing in side-plots, for the authority of Christ must be allowed to penetrate with full force through the educational program of the congregation.

Everything extraneous to the Gospel should be avoided. The focus must be on the fundamental relationship in which all Christians stand, the relation of disciple to teacher. World-conscious forms of Christian discipleship grounded totally in the Scriptures are to be pursued, so that all members are prepared for their daily encounter with the devil, their own sinful flesh, and the world.

Paul expresses a concern for life related to spiritual formation in the body (Rom. 12:1), in the mind (Rom. 12:2), in the self (Rom. 12:3), in the church and in the body of Christ (Rom. 12:4ff), in the world in general (Rom. 12:14ff), and in the government (Rom. 13:1-7). These are decisive reference points for formational activity.

293

Spiritual stagnation comes when we cling to an intake only of Biblical milk, having no fresh and new Biblical intake of meat to overcome immature attitudes and practices (Heb. 5:12-6:3). Maturing in faith is possible only if the Christian faith is integrated into the whole framework of life personally and communally through Biblical relevance and meaning. When faith is encapsulated only in rituals and religious routine, soon spiritual atrophy and apathy set in with boredom of repetition.

Lack of growth is abnormal or a sign of sickness. Evidences of growth in physical, mental, and emotional areas are well-known by physicians, educators, and counselors. The following summary may stimulate your thinking about your own process of spiritual growth and where you believe yourself to be now:

(Check which sentence, 1 to 5, is closest to a description of your spiritual status)

1) Reborn and regenerated, but no evidence yet of growth.

2) A baby in Christ, having grown very little in understanding, attitude and Christian understanding, attitude and action, dependent upon leaders, and crying for attention.

3) Child in Christ, studying and learning the Bible a bit, and yet independent or able to stand on one's own spiritual feet, emphasizing knowledge but not Christian action.

4) Mature disciple, choosing to identify with Christ as a learner to grow toward maturity, being equipped for service and administering.

5) Discipler of people to train and equip others by teaching them through various Biblical courses, and able to help develop new ministries.

What God Wants The Church To Be

Teaching the Word is central to the life of the church. We learn from the Book of Acts and the Epistles that organization and leadership are vital to the effective functioning of the church. Not only leaders, but also all members must have an understanding and be vitally concerned about the living dynamics of the congregation, and what God wants it to be. This involves a number of things, including the edifying and renewal process, shepherding, support system, fellowship principles, church management, leadership, and the distinctive call of the laymen and of the pastor.

Unless there is submission to the Word of God, the church will have little impact on people, and they will react to the Word as if it were just a pious human opinion. Thus a local congregation can easily become like the Corinthian church with all its problems and divisions.

A godly church needs Biblical objectives and functional goals. Required is a strong emphasis on training the disciples, bringing them to maturity. There will be the goal of an aggressive, active, ministering people, and a plurality of godly leaders. There will be a constant effort to stretch the people's faith. Growing out of a strong Bible-teaching, preaching ministry, there will be a genuine, high-level devotion to the family. Community penetration will be strongly emphasized. With an intense, mutually caring attitude, a spirit of sacrifice will be present. There will be a willingness to change and innovate.

God wants us to see doctrine and justification in relationship to real-life situations. Maturing faith, hope, and love will result from vital learning experiences in the Word of God. Not only did the Jerusalem Christians devote themselves to the apostles' teaching, but also to fellowship, the breaking of bread, prayers, and praising God. They studied together, ate together, and prayed together.

The church is a corporate affair. You yourself are not the church. I am not the church. **We** (all of Christ's disciples) are the church, and we behave as the church by assembling together, studying, worshiping, edifying, exhorting, loving, helping, and giving. Where there is no assembling for various functions, there is no church. There can be no church without fellowship or participation.

The Word of God is the only power and authority which is capable to govern congregations. Let there be no ecclesiastical government which exercises legislative or coercive powers over the congregation's right of self-government. Any group or adjudicatory of congregations remains an advisory body because only God's Word can decide all matters of doctrine and of con-science. Doctrinal matters of the church are not to be settled by majority vote, but by the truth of God's Word.

Any form of church polity which subordinates the con-gregation or Christ's people to human authority through voting on matters of doctrine actually denies the Christians the free-dom which Christ has purchased for them, placing them under the authority of men instead of under Christ alone.

The purpose of church administration is to maintain cor-rect teaching of God's Word, the Gospel, for the peoples' exer-cise of faith. This is spiritual power not mixed with sociological or political actions. Thus church administration should first pro-vide the right feeding, guiding, and direction of the church by means of the Word and the Sacraments. No one has the right in the church to demand obedience to any other authority than the Word, even though church by-laws and rules are important for smooth operation of non-doctrinal matters in the church.

Proper church administration must recognize and express the truth that the Office of the Keys belongs to the whole church, not to any select group or special persons within the church. The Office of the Keys is the right and power given by Christ to the church either to forgive sins or to refuse to forgive sins (Mt. 18:17-18, 20). A Christian congregation with its called pastor uses this power in accordance with Christ's command by forgiving those who repent of their sins and are willing to amend, and by excluding from the con-gregation those who are plainly impenitent, praying that they may be led to repent. This action is as valid and certain in Heaven also, as if Christ dealt with us Himself. Actually, by this action and announce-ment, the congregation carries out on earth what has been already done by Christ in Heaven.

Priesthood Of Believers And The Public Or Pastoral Ministry

There is no authority line or method in the New Testament church other than the Office of the Keys, which is given to the church, the priesthood of all believers. This is publicly admin-istered in a congregation through its called pastor: "Obey your leaders, and accept their authority. They take care of you because they are responsible for you" (Heb. 13:17). Christ gave pastors to the church for this duty (Eph. 4:11). They are to be shepherds of God's flock under their care, serving as overseers (1 Pet. 5:2). The congregation gets its authority from Christ to call a pastor (Mt. 16:19). The church and individual Christians as priests carry out this mission of God by obeying Christ's command and faithfully applying the Word of God and forgiving or refusing to forgive sins.

The pastoral office is sometimes called the public ministry, holy ministry or pastoral ministry. This public ministry is by divine appointment or God's ordinance as we see from the Scriptures in the appointment of pastors at places where local churches had been established (Acts 20:17-18; Titus 1:5), from the description of the personal qualifications (1 Pet. 5:3; 1 Tim. 3:2-7), from the description of their functions and duties (Titus 1:9-11; 1 Tim. 3:5; 1 Pet. 5:1 ff.; Heb. 13:17), from the distinction which the Scriptures make between the elders or bishops, and all other believers (1 Cor. 12:28-29), and from the honor which is ascribed to all who officially teach the Word (Heb. 13:7; 1 Cor. 4:1).

This pastoral ministry does not stand in opposition to the general ministry (spiritual priesthood) of all believers, who as spiritual priests have the duty to proclaim the Gospel everywhere (1 Pet. 2:9). The pastors are first themselves spiritual priests. However, the spiritual priesthood and the pastoral ministry are not identical and are to be carefully distinguished. Though we are all priests, yet only some are called to the public ministry. Those who are given the special calling into the public ministry are to be carefully selected and chosen for that office by the congregation. This office is responsible to the whole congregation. If we tear away or diminish the complete role of either one, we tear away and diminish both positions. It is God who has given pastors and teachers to equip the saints for their ministry (Eph. 4:11-12). The office of the public ministry is ordained by God and is not just a human custom.

Those in the public ministry have no authority other than the authority of the Word of God and of the call given them by God through the congregation. This office is established by God, and the church is commanded to call pastors. The doctrine of the universal priesthood of believers and the doctrine of the holy ministry complement rather than compete with or contradict each other. We ignore or weaken the doctrine of the holy ministry or the doctrine of the universal priesthood of all believers at the peril of the mission of Christ's church.

Caring — Confronting

Proper conduct through interpersonal communication in the church will be seen in a loving attitude of caring-confronting, which is required in the mandate to "lovingly speak the truth" (Eph. 4:15) with the result that members will "grow up completely in our relationship to Christ, who is the head." Truth with love by use of Law and Gospel brings healing, enables people to grow, and produces necessary change. These are the necessary ingredients for any integrity in relationships. No relationship of trust can grow from dishonesty or deceit, and it cannot exist without friendship, respect, and support.

Evangelical confrontation plus caring encourages growth. Judgment blended with grace, confrontation matched with caring, and truth spoken with love will manifest itself among leaders who care enough to want to stay in respectful relationship with the member. They must be faithful to God to confront the member to let him know how deeply they feel about the issue at stake. On the one hand, there will be no pressure or manipulation. On the other hand, there will be an honest viewing of differences. The offending person receives loving, honest respect while the other gives a caring-confronting response. This is what the Bible calls edifying or building each other up in faith by speaking the Word of Law and Gospel to each other.

The first gatherings of Christians usually took place in homes (Acts 12:12; Rom. 16:5), which provided a support system or a care group. Such home or care groups provided teaching

298

of Bible truths under the oversight of the pastors and elders, imitating what we learn in Acts 2. They sought to communicate total doctrine and life with the churches, providing for corporate edification and intercession. They maintained a place where members could share their burdens and give support to family life, and bring single people and families into contact with one another. Care groups today also allow the church to grow while preserving personal support in serving one another in practical ways. They provide for corporate evangelism. They help to get more people involved in leadership of the church.

While care groups give promise for greater vitality, there are also pitfalls to be avoided: the pastor's call and responsibility must not be diminished; leaders should have the ability to lead and have sensitive responsibility in cooperation with the pastor; the leadership group must have a strong sense of purpose and neither be too big nor too small. Care groups must resist the temptation to become a church within a church or a miniature church.

The purpose of small groups or core groups in congregations should be clearly defined by leaders and explained to the members to gain full participation by all. Leaders should be well trained, and they should be provided with effective Bible studies and functional messages for use in their groups. Opportunity should be given in the groups for personal exploration and application for learning and growing. The care groups should be a laboratory to learn how to show love and share fellowship, a place to know and be known in a supportive environment — a place to grow spiritually and be safe, to develop one's gifts. It is to be a setting for meaningful prayer.

Leaders should always maintain a submissive attitude, allowing God to lead others through them. They are to help others fulfill their potential by conveying truth with love. Allowing nothing to hinder Christian relationships, the spirit of forgiveness from God to each of us should be fostered in order to maintain the unity of marriage, the health of the family, a functioning congregation, and of all believers. As we uphold the oneness that God gives us in Christ, we maintain unity with one another. Thus a strong support system will be in place. A creative atmosphere and fellowship is to be built to enable people of varying abilities and interests to find avenues through which they together can serve Christ, the church, and the world.

Evangelical Church Discipline

The preaching of pure doctrine and the proper administering of the Sacraments can soon be lost if there is little or no Biblical and loving exercise of church discipline. Church discipline can be compared to the immune system of the body. Church discipline is the method God instituted to keep spiritual infection from invading the church. Church discipline is God's loving plan for maintaining or restoring the faith of Christians. God does not want disciples to lose their faith because of the invasion of spiritual infections which run rampant in the world.

Through church discipline, congregations minister to those who are in shackles of sin, and present them with the opportunity of being liberated from the power of sin in any and all forms by returning in repentance and faith to the rule of Christ. Such discipline does not bring division and disunity into the church. When Biblical principles are followed, the opposite is true — division and disunity will be overcome and avoided.

In his First letter to the Corinthian congregation, Paul criticized those Christians for their lack of discipline. Their overlooking of one sinful situation led the way to a host of spiritual failures. Insensitivity to one moral issue can easily lead to compromise on others. A church can become an organization without purity, power, or progress. Failing to discipline lovingly, it can lose the wholesome benefits of the congregation's essence and mission.

Problems can be ignored, but they cannot be avoided. Those who avoid confronting the problem will continue to afflict the church with the judgment of God. The result will be the disunity of the church until the problem is dealt with Scripturally. The New Testament contains abundant evidence of the practice of discipline by the Apostolic Church (Acts 5:1-11; 1 Cor. 5:1-5; 2 Cor. 26-8; Gal. 2:11-14; 6:1; 2 Thes. 3:6-15).

The human inclination is to avoid Biblical church discipline, and instead to take the moral sidestep of smoothing feathers and of avoiding rocking the boat. That is why church discipline is an easily neglected teaching of Scripture. Unfortunately, many confine church discipline to what one might call catastrophe discipline, which is discipline that waits until something goes very wrong. However, there are two types of discipline: preventative and corrective. If preventative discipline is practiced, there will be much less need for corrective discipline.

Church discipline is meant to be part of the whole, one component of life under Law and Gospel, a part of the edifying process. Broadly, church discipline is anything which the body of Christ does to train Christians in holiness, encouraging them to follow their Lord more closely. Corrective discipline will be needed when actions do not fully match life under grace.

When the church departs from Christian standards by tolerating sin and does not judge itself, it will never attract the world to Christ because it fails to show visibly the power of Jesus Christ to save us from sin. Church discipline needs Biblical soil in which to take root and a spiritual climate to foster growth. It can flourish only in a fellowship where members make provision for the kind of intimacy where they can share, encourage, exhort and pray for one another lovingly, trustingly. This is the kind of love that will heal the wounded.

A roadblock to discipline is a lack of understanding or sensitivity to the destructive nature of sinful habits. We will resist the idea of dealing with sin in others when our consciences have been dulled. Then we will be selective about sins which Scripture condemns, as we rage against certain ones while ignoring ones like living mostly for money and material possessions, or tolerating pride and gossip. Lack of discipline enslaves us, while the practice of discipline sets us free.

Jesus taught in Matthew 18:5-14 the steps for discipline: private reproof, in which the facts are established and the individual is faced with a necessary rebuke; those who do not respond with repentant action should face one or two more in a private conference so that the facts can be confirmed, the severity established, and the Law and Gospel re-emphasized; if the person repents, the problem is settled, but if he refuses to listen, the matter is to be told to the church, which is the final court of appeal in disciplinary matters; if there is repentance, the matter is concluded; but if there is impenitence, there must be public exclusion for the purpose of showing the individual how serious this matter is in the eyes of God. The purpose is to restore a person to faith and to encourage spiritual healing. It is also to lead the offending member to see the need and availability of the forgiveness of Christ and the loving relationship of our Savior.

Differences can happen between leaders. In the early church, a conflict developed between the two outstanding leaders, Peter and Paul (Gal. 2:11). The church at Antioch was the scene of a major disagreement between Paul and Barnabas (Acts 15:36-41). The acute dissension over the question of faith plus circumcision led to the first Jerusalem Council (Acts 14:26-28; 15:1-4). The important thing is to have the spiritual strength of which Paul speaks in Galatians 6:1, "Brothers and sisters, if a person gets trapped by wrongdoing, those of you who are spiritual should help that person turn away from doing wrong. Do it in a gentle way. At the same time watch yourself so that you also are not tempted."

Proper church administration or polity must recognize and give expression to the truth that the Office of the Keys belongs to the whole church, not to any individuals, nor to any select group. It follows that each congregation owes other congregations in a given church body a brotherly church recognition and cooperation through fellowship. Churches must be willing to admit differences between them when they are occur, and seek reconciliation, rather than pretend that problems do not exist, and simply hope that they will fade away.

The mutual recognition of church fellowship, which might be called pulpit and altar fellowship, rests on the basis of congregations' subscription to the doctrinal or confessional agreement of the churches with the understanding that all pastors and members are under authority of the Word and subordinate themselves voluntarily to keep integrity with their agreement. Groups of congregations bound in a denomination, therefore, do not have selective fellowship or independent action by single congregations or pastors, but preserve the unity of the faith of the group. This is held with integrity through the mutual responsibility and fellowship which such churches have agreed to owe to one another. Such relationship, however, in no way means that there is a divine command which subordinates the individual congregation's rights to a larger group, any more than the individual Christian surrenders some rights and duties as a priest of God by becoming part of a congregation.

Discipline is the process by which the community gathering around Word and Sacrament is kept alive and pure. As no society or state can be preserved without some discipline and mutual agreement in standards of belief and behavior, so the church must have procedures to foster unity. If individuals are allowed to follow their own inclinations, it can easily lead to sickness or the dissolution of the Christian community. It is Christ's community, not any person's.

Discipline and pastoral care do not replace the Word, but the Word is used to enforce it and give it full weight so that members submit themselves to it. The church must be concerned about the confession of its faith founded in the Word. The entire process proceeds from the Word and leads back to the Word.

To preserve the unity of the true faith, and to prevent divisions in the church, supervision of the doctrine and practice of pastors and teachers is not only wholesome, but also necessary. Such supervision is intended to prevent factions created by self-appointed leaders or members who seek to draw people after themselves. This is not imposed upon the congregation by some kind of ecclesiastical authority, but represents a willing and agreed upon subordination of the pastors and congregations to one another under God in the interest of maintaining the unity of the confession and doctrine of the Scriptures. Such supervision of doctrine and practice also requires that pastors who are found guilty of false doctrine or of an ungodly life, and remain impenitent, must be removed from the fellowship. If the congregation is unfaithful, it should be dealt with in the same way.

Every church needs a body of teaching to express its beliefs and to guide its functions, which are designed under the Word to preserve and express what they hold sacred and to keep the church from going astray. This develops community in its structure and tasks, indicating the way in which it is to function. The church, born of the Word of God, will not be unshaped and passive, but very active and maneuverable. This is the way it becomes effective for and through its members. It cannot tolerate members who drop out of a living relationship with Christ or who offend others by their lifestyle. There should be no differences or problems between people that cannot be overcome and eliminated in the fellowship. In dealing with disagreements, the stark facts of earthly existence with human weakness and sin will not be evaded, but tackled and dealt with open-mindedly and fearlessly. This is accomplished by applying the Word and renouncing all human opinions and judgments which contradict the Word.

The institutionalized structures of church bodies (groups of congregations) provide for the ministry of the Word on a broader base to edify those within their fellowship and also to evangelize the entire world. The institutionalized forms of church bodies may be full of hazards, but it is impractical for the church to exist in the world without such communal forms. The cure for bad forms of church groups is not formlessness. The enemy is not institutions, forms, and people, but Satan who sows his seeds of impurity or divisiveness in the church. There must be constant watchfulness so that the forms do not hinder the ministry of the Word or pervert the Gospel by substituting the wisdom and goals of the church organization for that of the Holy Spirit.

God's Kind Of Leaders

A spiritual leader should be concerned infinitely more with the service he renders to God and his fellow men than with holding a position with honors and benefits as a church leader. Leaders must have a clear sense of being chosen by God. A church position is to be seen as a temporary trust from the Lord rather than a permanent assignment without ongoing confirmation for continued service.

Leaders should seek to meet the high standard set by God. They never have the option to be disobedient to the commands of Scripture. They have the responsibility of helping members to know the will of God. They need the strength to correct people who go wrong.

The combined list of qualifications for elders and church leaders is recorded in 1 Timothy 3:1-7, Titus 1:5-10, and 1 Peter 5:2: above reproach with good reputation, husband of one wife, temperate, self-controlled, respectable, hospitable, able to teach, not given to much wine, not violent or quarrelsome, gentle, one who manages well his own family, not a recent convert, having a good reputation with non-believers, not overbearing, loves what is right, upright, devout, holds firmly to the pure message, not quick-tempered, not a lover of money.

Leaders are to be examples in the way in which they talk, love, care, build relationships, and obey God. Godly character and spiritual diligence should be normal qualities of a leader. The church that does not uphold godly standards in choosing their leaders is abandoning godly standards for its membership.

Leaders should have the capacity to learn, communicate, maintain the body-life of the congregation, handle pressure, and be able to do the job.

Leadership that comes from the ascended Christ will be strong to oversee the church, to lead people into God's purpose, to account to God for the people, and to challenge the members to express their faith. They must show themselves to be under the authority of Christ and have a servant's attitude.

Several Ingredients Of Effective Church Life

Building the church must be centered on Jesus Christ and based on Scripture. The best approaches for governing the church are those which allow the Lord to guide His people through faithful and obedient leaders. The purpose of church government is not to see that the will of the people is done, but that the will of God is done through the people.

Every congregation should be challenged to discern the form of mission to which God is calling it. Leaders are to make sure that they and the members keep constantly in touch with the One who sent them and from Whom their mission is derived. The congregation is to be challenged to identify the specific resources needed to carry out the ministries inherent in that mission. Every leader should be an educator, and every educator should be challenged to be a leader.

One of the things that marked Jesus' ministry was His mobility, moving about, coming to a place and quickly going on. Even though we have many modern "miracles" of transportation, most Christians are highly immobile for the Gospel. If Christians as the church are not mobile, there will be great sterility. Jesus left heaven and came to earth to perform His mission. The shepherds left their flocks and went to Bethlehem. The Wise Men came from the East to worship the Heavenly King. Paul and the Apostles went throughout the Mediterranean World to preach the Gospel. Christians went from house to house to study the Word. They were mobile for the Gospel. Immobility is a great problem in the modern church as Christians sit in meetings, or move only from homes to churches. Or they sit in front of television sets, or spend time in social gatherings and spectator sports while the modern inventions of automobiles, airplanes, radios and televisions are highly under-utilized by most Christians for spreading of the Gospel. Only a handful of enthusiasts are involved zealously and are highly mobile in going many places preaching the Word (Acts 8:4).

God has given you your own special ministry. May you be strong, yet flexible — wise, yet always learning — a leader, yet a servant. By God's grace, may you find wisdom for every decision, strength for every responsibility, success in each endeavor, joy in each relationship, and love in everything you do for the Lord Jesus Christ! As you have now completed this study of the many facets of 21st Century Discipleship, may you be strengthened to carry on your task vigorously as a 21st Century disciple of Jesus Christ with a 1st Century faith!

"MAY THE GOD WHO GIVES PEACE MAKE YOU HOLY IN EVERY WAY. MAY HE KEEP YOUR WHOLE BE-ING — SPIRIT, SOUL, AND BODY — BLAMELESS WHEN OUR LORD JESUS CHRIST COMES. THE ONE WHO CALLS YOU IS FAITHFUL, AND HE WILL DO THIS." (1 Thes. 5:23-24).

"GOD CAN GUARD YOU SO THAT YOU DON'T FALL AND SO THAT YOU CAN BE FULL OF JOY AS YOU STAND IN HIS GLORIOUS PRESENCE WITHOUT FAULT. BEFORE TIME BEGAN, NOW, AND FOR ETERNITY GLORY, MAJESTY, POWER, AND AUTHORITY BELONG TO THE ONLY GOD, OUR SAVIOR, THROUGH JESUS CHRIST OUR LORD. AMEN" (Jude 24-25).

APPENDIX

Disciple's Workbook and Discipler's Guide (Teacher's Helps)

This book is the basic resource for the *21st Century Disciples With a 1st Century Faith* discipling course. A *Disciple's (Student's) Workbook* is available to provide 26 weeks of in-depth study for gaining greater spiritual maturity through self-discovery and group-discovery. Discussion questions are provided. A *Discipler's Guide* (Teacher's Helps) which provides help for teachers for the discipling training process provides guidance for those who use this book as a basic resource in the discipling course. Information about its availability may be gained by writing CSS Publishing Company, Lima, Ohio, or ordering from the Discipling/ Stewardship Center, 1914 Wendmere Lane, Fort Wayne IN 46825.

END NOTES

1. *The Origin of Species*, Charles Darwin, 1902 edition, Part 1. page 250.

2. *The Lie Evolution*, Ken Ham, 1987, Creation-Life Publishers, El Cajon, CA 92002, pages 76-78.

3. Reprinted from *Freedom From The Performance Trap*, David A. Seamands, Victor Books (1989), Wheaton IL 60187, pages 13, 17.

4. Ibid., Seamands, page 115.

5. *Let Us Enjoy Forgiveness*, Judson Cornwall, 1978, Fleming H. Revell, a division of Baker Book House, Old Tappan, NJ, p. 159.

6. *Christian Dogmatics*, Franz Pieper, Concordia Publishing House, St. Louis, MO, Vol. III:48.

7. *Freedom For Obedience*, Donald G. Bloesch, 1987, HarperCollins Publishers, pages 238-239.

8. *Kingdoms in Conflict*, Charles Colson, 1987, Judith Markham Books, page 334.

9. The Twelve Steps are reprinted and adapted with permission of Alcoholics Anonymous World Services, Inc. Permission to reprint and adapt this material does not mean that A.A. has reviewed or approved the contents of this publication, nor that A.A. agrees with the views expressed herein. A.A. is a program of recovery from alcoholism *only* — use of the Twelve Steps in connection with programs and activities which are patterned after A.A., but which address other problems, does not imply otherwise.

10. *Ordering Your Private World*, Gordon McDonald, 1984, Thomas Nelson, Inc. Publishers, Nashville, TN, pages 74-78.

11.   The New Testament texts which give us a helpful portrait of the kinds of behavior which characterize the unique fellowship of believers are: Rom. 12:10, 16; 13:8; 14:13, 19; 15:5, 7, 14; 1 Cor. 12:25; Gal. 5:16; 6:2; Eph. 4:1-2, 32; 5:18-21; Col. 3:9, 12-13, 16; 1 Thes. 3:12; 4:18; Heb. 3:13; 10:23-25; James 4:11; 5:9,16; 1 Pet. 1:22; 4:9; 5:5, 14; 1 Jn. 3:11, 23; 4:7, 11-12; 2 Jn 5.